Samuel D. Taylor
Concepts and the Appeal to Cognitive Science

Dissertations in Language and Cognition

Edited by
Hana Filip, Peter Indefrey, Laura Kallmeyer,
Sebastian Löbner, Gerhard Schurz and
Robert D. Van Valin, Jr.

Volume 8

Samuel D. Taylor

Concepts and the Appeal to Cognitive Science

—

düsseldorf university press

D 61 Düsseldorf

ISBN 978-3-11-070803-5
e-ISBN (PDF) 978-3-11-070816-5
e-ISBN (EPUB) 978-3-11-070822-6

Library of Congress Control Number: 2020947456

Bibliographic information published by the Deutsche Nationalbibliothek
The Deutsche Nationalbibliothek lists this publication in the Deutsche Nationalbibliografie;
detailed bibliographic data are available on the Internet at http://dnb.dnb.de.

© 2021 Walter de Gruyter GmbH, Berlin/Boston
d|u|p düsseldorf university press is an imprint of Walter de Gruyter GmbH
Printing and binding: CPI books GmbH, Leck

dup.degruyter.com

"a drift has begun, and it continues [...] there is an increasing readiness to see philosophy as natural science trained upon itself."

Quine, 1981, p. 85

Acknowledgements

This book represents the end result of my PhD at the University of Düsseldorf between 2016-2019. It took shape as I engaged with open problems about the nature of cognitive systems and the way that science can best explain our cognitive capacities. The journey was not always smooth sailing and if this book amounts to anything it is undoubtedly because of the help and guidance of many colleagues, friends, and family.

This book would never have taken shape were it not for my supervisor, Gottfried Vosgerau. The content is influenced throughout by our many discussions and debates, which played a central role in helping me to sharpen and focus my ideas. I also owe a debt of gratitude to my second supervisor, Markus Schrenk, and to Peter Sutton as members of my Advisory Committee. This book improved considerably as a result of their critique, comments, and constructive advice.

I had the great benefit of undertaking my PhD in the interdisciplinary DFG Collaborative Research Centre 991 and I would like to thank everyone at the Centre for their feedback. I would also like to thank all those who took the time to interrogate my work; whether in the Philosophy Department in Düsseldorf, as participants of the Concepts and Explanation workshop, or simply over coffee. In particular, I would like to thank Frances Egan for hosting me during my research stay at Rutgers University and for the many pieces of invaluable advice.

Without my friends this book could not have happened, and I want to thank each of them now, as always, for their help along the way. That I have had the chance to write a PhD thesis is in no small part due my family's continued care and support, and I want to thank them for everything that they have done for me. Finally, I want to thank my fiancée, Maria Coțofan. If this thesis represents any part of the best of me, then it has been brought out by you. There is no measure of the importance of your love or of the depth of my thanks.

https://doi.org/9783110708165-202

Contents

Acknowledgements —— VII

List of Figures —— XI

List of Tables —— XIII

1	**Introduction** —— **1**	
1.1	Concepts: The Standard View —— 1	
1.2	The Appeal to Cognitive Science —— 3	
1.3	Overview of the Book —— 4	

2   **Standard View Theories of CONCEPT —— 7**
2.1   Imagist Theory of CONCEPT —— 9
2.2   Definitionist Theory of CONCEPT —— 14
2.3   Prototype Theory of CONCEPT —— 19
2.4   Exemplar Theory of CONCEPT —— 27
2.5   The Theory Theory of CONCEPT —— 34
2.6   Concluding Remarks —— 40

3   **The Appeal to Cognitive Science —— 41**
3.1   The Explanatory Challenge —— 41
3.2   Responding to the Explanatory Challenge —— 44
3.2.1   Concept Eliminativism —— 44
3.2.2   Concept Pluralism —— 47
3.2.3   Concept Hybridism —— 50
3.3   The Meta-Explanatory Challenge —— 54
3.4   The Meta-Explanatory Challenge Defended —— 59
3.5   Summary —— 64

4   **Problem 1: Explanatory Ambiguity —— 67**
4.1   Kinds of Cognitive Scientific Explanation —— 67
4.1.1   Mechanistic Explanation —— 67
4.1.2   Psychological Explanation —— 79
4.1.3   Dynamicist Explanation —— 93
4.2   Explanatory Pluralism in Cognitive Science —— 100
4.3   Problem 1 and the Meta-Explanatory Challenge —— 107

5 **Problem 2: Explananda Ambiguity** —— 109
5.1 Integrating Mechanistic Explanations: An Example —— 109
5.2 Two Virtues of Integrating Mechanistic Explanations —— 113
5.3 Cross-Explanatory Integration —— 118
5.4 Two Views of Cognitive Scientific Explananda —— 123
5.5 Two Virtues of Cross-Explanatory Integration —— 127
5.6 Problem 2 and the Meta-Explanatory Challenge —— 133

6 **CONCEPT as a Working Hypothesis** —— 135
6.1 Difference and Identity —— 137
6.2 Against the "New Consensus" —— 141
6.3 Putting Cognitive Science First (and Last) —— 145
6.4 Working Hypotheses —— 147
6.5 CONCEPT as a Working Hypothesis —— 149
6.6 Internal and External Theories of CONCEPT —— 153
6.7 Beyond the Meta-Explanatory Challenge —— 157

7 **Why Appeals to Cognitive Science Fail** —— 159

8 **Appendix** —— 163
8.1 Taylor and Sutton's (2020) frame-based model of Bayesian category learning —— 163
8.1.1 The α parameter —— 164
8.1.2 The δ parameter —— 164

Bibliography —— 167

List of Figures

Fig. 2.1 The Duck-Rabbit (Wittgenstein, 1953, Part II, §118). —— **12**
Fig. 2.2 Successive psychological processes during categorisation (inspired by Machery, 2009, p. 97). —— **29**
Fig. 2.3 Transformation of a raccoon into a skunk (Keil, 1989, p. 177). —— **37**

Fig. 3.1 The role of concepts in cognitive tasks according to concept eliminativism (inspired by Machery, 2009, p. 60). —— **45**
Fig. 3.2 The pluralist model of concepts as introduced by (Weiskopf, 2009, p. 156). Arrows indicate retrieval from long-term memory. —— **49**

Fig. 4.1 Biochemical mechanisms at chemical synapses (Shepherd, 1988). —— **70**
Fig. 4.2 Biochemical flow of protein synthesis (Zamecnik, 1953). —— **71**
Fig. 4.3 A partial structural decomposition of the cell (Bechtel and Abrahamsen, 2005, p. 434). —— **75**
Fig. 4.4 Phenomenal level (top) and mechanism level (bottom) (Craver and Bechtel, 2006, p. 475). —— **78**
Fig. 4.5 Lolly frame (Petersen, 2015). —— **85**
Fig. 4.6 A revised model of working memory (Baddeley, Allen, and Hitch, 2011, p. 1399). —— **88**

Fig. 5.1 Levels of spatial memory (left) and integrating levels of mechanisms (right) (Craver, 2007). —— **112**

Fig. 6.1 Rutherford's model of the atom. —— **152**

https://doi.org/9783110708165-204

List of Tables

Tab. 2.1   The prototype of *building* according to Hampton's (1979) model (inspired by Hampton, 1981, p. 459). —— **20**

Tab. 2.2   The Prototype of *banana* according to Smith et al.'s (1988) model (inspired by Smith et al., 1988, p. 490). —— **22**

Tab. 4.1   Some examples of common definitions of the term "dynamical system" from outside cognitive science (Van Gelder, 1998, p. 618). —— **95**

Tab. 4.2   General characteristics of dynamicist explanations (inspired by Van Gelder, 1998, p. 621). —— **99**

Tab. 8.1   Definitions for elements of the frame based Bayesian categorisation model. —— **163**

Tab. 8.2   The effect of α on calculating the prior $p(w|\alpha)$. —— **165**

Tab. 8.3   The effect of δ on calculating the likelihood $p(D|w, \delta)$ for $\delta(n_j) = n_j^0$, $\delta(n_j) = n_j^{-1}$, and $\delta(n_j) = n_j^{-2}$. —— **166**

https://doi.org/9783110708165-205

1 Introduction

1.1 Concepts: The Standard View

Our concepts enable us to entertain thoughts about a rich variety of objects, events, and states of affairs. By employing concepts we are able to ponder the beginnings of the universe, the treatment of disease, the nature of infinity, and the organisation of society. It is through concept use that we are able to rationally deliberate and discuss, and so come to a greater understanding of our surroundings and our place within them. Or so the story goes.

This story, however, is not particularly helpful until we can say what a concept is and what a concept is not. Without an answer in this regard, it is unclear how concepts come to be employed by concept users in the first place. A neutral—one might even say pre-scientific—characterisation of concepts takes them to be the "materials of reason and knowledge" (Locke, 1690). A modern rendering of this view is that concepts are constituents of thought. In this way, it is said that my thought that Eric Cantona played for Manchester United contains or, perhaps, makes use of at least two concepts: *Eric Cantona* and *Manchester United*.[1]

The problem with this view is that it says nothing about what thoughts are or what it takes to be a constituent of thought. As a result, one might think that the question is put back, because in order to characterise concepts as constituents of thought we first require an account of thoughts. Typically, however, the threat of regress is circumvented by arguing that it is concepts that explain what thoughts are and how they behave. So, on this line of reasoning, concepts are taken to be those things that explain thought and thought is that thing we commit ourselves to in order to explain how organisms like us interact with and negotiate our environments. Accordingly, many philosophers have argued that it is our commitment to the kind CONCEPT—as the set of concepts—that helps us to formulate viable explanations of cognitive behaviour (cf. Margolis and Laurence, 1999).[2]

However, in order for concepts to satisfactorily play the explanatory role required of them, a theory of the kind CONCEPT must be developed to explain

---

1 In the remainder of this book, I will denote individual concepts by italics. Although standard practice is to denote concepts by small caps, I will reserve this denotation for kinds (see below).
2 In the remainder of this book, I will denote kinds with small caps. It should also be noted that some philosophers speak of the "concept of concept" instead of the kind CONCEPT. The problem with such a phrase it that it forces us into a mentalistic reading of the kind CONCEPT. This has the potential to cause confusion with regards to the view I eventually defend in chapter 6 , and so I will assume for now that the kind term CONCEPT denotes nothing more or less than a set of objects that are conceptual in kind.

https://doi.org/9783110708165-001

how all concepts—as members of this kind—operate as the constituents of thought. To achieve this end, a theory of CONCEPT would need to satisfy four desiderata—(1) Scope, (2) Intentional/Cognitive Content, (3) Acquisition, and (4) Compositionality—, which I spell-out in detail in chapter two. According to the "standard view," a theory of CONCEPT will be best able to satisfy these desiderata if it takes concepts to be a single kind of "mental representation" storing a single kind of information (see the definition below).[3]

Definition: The Standard View

A theory of CONCEPT that accounts for the properties of concepts will be a theory of a single kind of mental representation storing a single kind of information.

But the standard view is not without its problems. The main problem is that saying that objects of the kind CONCEPT are a single kind of mental representation is not all that informative. The question that naturally follows such a claim is: what *are* mental representations? Mental representations are mental objects that "are said to have "intentionality"—they are *about* or *refer* to things, and may be evaluated with respect to properties like consistency, truth, appropriateness and accuracy" (Pitt, 2018). For example, if I have a mental representation of *Eric Cantona*, then this mental representations will *refer* to Eric Cantona and can be evaluated with respect to how well it consistently, truthfully, accurately etc. represents Eric Cantona (does it represent him as a man, a footballer, etc.).

The idea of the standard view, then, is that mental representations—as concepts—make possible thoughts about, say, Eric Cantona and Manchester United. But even if this is correct, a further question can be asked: what kind of mental representations are concepts? By asking this question, one is forced headways into a debate about the *structure* of concepts. Here one finds a number of competing accounts of conceptual structure that each purport to have one explanatory advantage or another in virtue of better accounting for desiderata (1)–(4). Charting one's way through this debate is deemed necessary if one is to motivate and defend a theory of the representational structure of the members of the kind CONCEPT.

---

3 Some philosophers have taken a different, non-mental representation view of what concepts are (cf. Dummett, 1993; Zalta, 2001, for discussion of concepts as abilities and abstract objects respectively). These views, however, typically deny that concepts can help us to explain cognitive competences such as categorisation and reasoning. I will return to these views in the penultimate chapter of this book, but, for now, I will continue with the assumption that concepts are the kinds of things that can help us to explain cognitive competences. That is, that concepts are mental representations.

Many adhering to the standard view have taken up the task of developing theories of CONCEPT that give an account of the representational structure of concepts as storing one kind of information. For thirty years or more, different theories have been developed and debate has raged about which of these theories is best able to satisfy desiderata (1)–(4). This debate has thrown into relief the difficulties of developing a theory of CONCEPT that satisfies *all* of the desiderata (1)–(4). In fact, some are now coming to realise that although different theories of the representational structure of concepts will better satisfy different desiderata, none are likely to satisfy them all.[4]

1.2 The Appeal to Cognitive Science

In chapter three, I follow recent developments in the literature—e.g. Machery (2009) and Weiskopf (2009)—and argue that the relative satisfaction of the desiderata (1)–(4) cannot help us to decide between different theories of the representational structure of concepts. It follows that a new methodology must be found to decide between available theories of CONCEPT. For many, the solution is an appeal to empirical research. Therefore, many now assume that we can evaluate and compare theories of CONCEPT be considering how consistent each theory is with the explanatory results of *cognitive science*, and that such a process will enable us to determine the "best" theory of CONCEPT (see the definition below).

Definition: The Appeal to Cognitive Science
Deciding on the best theory of CONCEPT by comparing different theories of CONCEPT with respect to how consistent they are with the explanatory results of cognitive science.

Cognitive science is the interdisciplinary study of mind and intelligence, embracing philosophy, psychology, artificial intelligence, neuroscience, linguistics, and anthropology (Thagard, 2014). Although it is widely accepted that these disciplines share unifying theoretical ideas, there are clearly big differences in their outlooks, methods, and results. For example, designing, building, and experimenting with computational models is the central method of artificial intelligence (AI), but does not play a central role in cognitive anthropology. Analogously, (experimental) methods differ both between (e.g. between cognitive psychology and neuroscience) and within disciplines (e.g. between computational linguistics and semantics).

---

4 I consider in detail how well the most prominent theories of CONCEPT satisfy desiderata (1)–(4) in chapter two.

Therefore, one problem presents itself straight away: that it is unclear what counts as the "explanatory results of cognitive science." One could simply view the explanatory results of cognitive science as the sum total all of explanations in cognitive scientific disciplines (e.g. linguistics, neuroscience etc.); where inter-disciplinarity is defined in terms of "theoretical and experimental convergence on conclusions about the nature of mind" (Thagard, 2005). From this perspective, the "explanatory results of cognitive science" would turn out to be the set of all explanations put forward by practitioners of the disciplines mentioned above. This characterisation, as rough and ready as it is, may be the best we can hope for given the diversity of disciplines tasked with explaining the mind.

But even if we endorse such a characterisation a further problem cannot be so easily dismissed; namely, that cognitive science is replete with many different kinds of competing explanations aligning with many different perspectives on the mind as an explanandum. For example, we have mechanistic, psychological, and dynamicist explanations aligning with perspectives of the mind as mechanistic, functional, or dynamic respectively. Advocates of different kinds of explanations often challenge the reality of the explanatory postulates and explanatory force of the other kinds of explanation. For instance, some have argued that "psychological explanations" do not explain at all, but only provide "sketches" of neurally-implemented mechanisms (cf. Piccinini and Craver, 2011).

In chapters four and five, I consider whether or not the tension between these different kinds of explanations can be resolved. If it cannot, then it seems difficult to make sense of how, exactly, we are to bring empirical research to bear on debates about theories of CONCEPT. But even if it can, it remains unclear what effect an appeal to cognitive science will have on long-standing ideas about how we are to theorise about CONCEPT; for instance, the standard view. The appeal to cognitive science, therefore, is an oft promoted, but little understood, methodology in debates about concepts. My central aim in this thesis is to closely examine the commitments and implications of the appeal to cognitive science, and to consider how—if at all—it supports a naturalistic approach to theorisation about CONCEPT.

1.3 Overview of the Book

In order to make progress, I first undertake a negative project, which undermines both the standard view and the appeal to cognitive science as it has been implemented thus far. In chapter two, I argue that the relative satisfaction of desiderata (1)–(4) cannot help us to decide between different theories of CONCEPT adhering to the standard view, because there are a number of different, competing theories of CONCEPT that satisfy different desiderata respectively. More specifically, I consider the imagist, definitionist, prototype, exemplar, and theory theories of CONCEPT, and conclude that none of these theories of CONCEPT adequately satisfy all or even most of the desiderata (1)–(4). The upshot is that none of these theories of CONCEPT is to be preferred to any other.

In chapter three, I argue that an appeal to cognitive science to help us decide between the theories of CONCEPT brings into question the standard view itself, because different theories of CONCEPT, satisfying different desiderata, are required to do the explanatory work in cognitive science. I then consider three "new" theories of CONCEPT, which respond to this "explanatory challenge to the standard view": concept eliminativism, concept pluralism, and concept hybridism. However, I argue that we cannot appeal to cognitive science to decide between these "new" theories of CONCEPT either, because each theory presupposes different specifications of the explananda of cognitive science and so affords the kind CONCEPT a different explanatory roles. I call this the "meta-explanatory challenge to new theories of CONCEPT."

In chapter four, I consider the first of two problems for any attempt to overcome the "meta-explanatory challenge to new theories of CONCEPT": the ambiguity about what counts as a cognitive scientific explanation. I consider three different kinds of explanations in cognitive science: mechanistic explanations, psychological explanations, and dynamicist explanations. Then, I examine long-standing disagreements about whether certain explanations have autonomy (e.g. psychological explanations) or whether we can find a reductive explanatory format that does all the explanatory work required of cognitive science (e.g. mechanistic explanations). This leaves open the question of whether or not "new" theories of CONCEPT agree about the explanatory relevance of different kinds of cognitive scientific explanation.

In chapter five, I consider the second problem for any attempt to respond to the "meta-explanatory challenge to new theories of CONCEPT": the fact that different specifications of the explananda of cognitive science bias one in favour of different cognitive scientific explanations. Connecting to my claims in chapter four, I argue that at least two different kinds of explanatory integration can be identified in cognitive science: integrations of mechanistic explanations and cross-explanatory integrations of mechanistic, dynamicist, and psychological explanation. I go on to argue that one's choice between these two kinds of explanatory integration depends on the attitude one has about the explananda of cognitive science. By then arguing that different "new" theories of CONCEPT will endorse different kinds of explanatory integration in cognitive science, I argue that the meta-explanatory challenge is sealed.

As a result of my arguments in chapter two to five, one may think that theorisation about CONCEPT should be cut off from cognitive science altogether. In chapter six, I resist this conclusion by developing a radically different view on what theorisation about CONCEPT entails. On my account, theorisation about CONCEPT should be thought of a process "internal" to, as opposed to "external" to, cognitive science, which establishes working hypotheses about what concepts are in order to facilitate the investigation and explanation of cognitive competences. From this perspective, it is not necessary or possible to appeal to cognitive science in the traditional sense to decide on the best theory of CONCEPT, because theorisation about CONCEPT is re-conceived as a constitutive part of the diverse explanatory practices of different cognitive sciences. However, it remains possible to appeal to the relative success or failure of many different kinds of cognitive science, each inspired by there own theory of CONCEPT. I conclude, in chapter seven, by briefly considering the implications of my view for theories of other mental states.

2 Standard View Theories of CONCEPT

In the introduction, I set-out the standard view of concepts. On this view, the best theory of CONCEPT will be a theory of a single kind of mental representation storing a single kind of information, because such a theory will be best able to satisfy the desiderata that a theory of CONCEPT is expected to satisfy. Following Prinz (2002), I hereby give a brief introduction of these desiderata.[5]

1. *Scope*: A theory of CONCEPT must explain how we are able to posses and manipulate a large variety of potential concepts; e.g. abstract concepts such a *democracy*; natural kind concepts such as *badger*; social kind concepts such as *liberalism*; artifact concepts such as *iPod*; formal concepts such as *set*; and even concepts pertaining to our own experiences of the world, such as *happiness* or *anxiety*. Another way of putting this is that a theory of CONCEPT must be sufficient to accommodate all putative members of the kind CONCEPT.

2. *Intentional/Cognitive Content*: A theory of CONCEPT must explain how concepts stand in for, refer to, or—more generally—represent things other than themselves (intentional content). What's more, a theory of CONCEPT must explain how concepts that are putatively co-referential—e.g. concepts like *the morning star* and *the evening star* or like *Kurt Gödel* and *the person who proved the incompleteness of arithmetic*—can seem semantically distinct to an agent and so can play different roles in thought (cognitive content) (cf. Frege, 1893, for an account of the importance of "sense"—e.g. cognitive content—for conceptual individuation).

3. *Acquisition*: A theory of CONCEPT must lend itself to an explanation of how concepts are acquired by individuals in ontogenetic development; that is, how concepts that are thought to be learned rather than innate are learnable in principle. Secondly, a theory of CONCEPT must lend itself to an explanation of the phylogenetic origins of innate concepts (if such concepts exist) and of the capacity to learn non-innate concepts; that is, an explanation of how evolution has endowed the human genome with either (or both) an innate conceptual faculty or (and) with the capacity to acquire those concepts that are not innate.[6]

---

5 It should be noted that even if different theories of concepts satisfy different subsets of these desiderata, a conditional thesis is presupposed: that "*if* a theory of concepts can accommodate all of the desiderata, then it has an explanatory advantage over its more modest competitors" (Prinz, 2002, p. 3).

6 A related desideratum might also be *Categorisation*, whereby a theory of CONCEPT must lend itself to an explanation of how we cognitively demarcate those sets of things to which individual concepts refer and how we identify the category—e.g. *dog*—under which a presented object—e.g. a

https://doi.org/9783110708165-002

4. *Compositionality*: A theory of CONCEPT must explain the productivity of thought; that is, the fact that there appears to be no upper bound on the number of beliefs we can entertain, states of affairs we can imagine, uttered sentences we can comprehend, plans we can devise, etc. Moreover, a theory of CONCEPT must account for this boundless capacity for thought in terms of the potentially infinite number of ways that concepts can be combined according to rules of combination (systematicity).[7]

Although there are potentially more desiderata to consider (e.g. categorisation, publicity), focusing on (1)–(4) alone will suffice for me to make my argument in this chapter: that none of the theories of CONCEPT adhering to the standard view come close to satisfying all of these desiderata and so none is clearly preferable to any other.

In order to make this argument, I will consider, in turn, different theories of CONCEPT, which each suppose that the objects that are members of the kind CONCEPT have a different, single kind of representational structure storing a different kind of information. More specifically, I will consider imagist theories of CONCEPT, definitionist theories of CONCEPT, prototype theories of CONCEPT, exemplar theories of CONCEPT, and the theory theory of CONCEPT. It should be noted that my aim is not to give an exhaustive account of each theory of CONCEPT. Rather, my aim is

---

four-legged, barking, mammal—belongs. This desideratum may well be important in its own right, but, for my purposes, enough is said about the individuation conditions of concepts by discussing the desiderata of *Content* and *Acquisition*.

7 There are, of course, intersections between many of these desiderata. For instance, some philosophers attempt to explain compositionality as a function of the contents of the concepts constituting the thought in question together with rules of combination (Fodor, 1987). Thus, some philosophers conflate the desiderata of *Compositionality* and of *Intentional/Cognitive Content*. What's more, there are other desiderata that are controversial and so are not listed above. Consider, for instance, the publicity of concepts, which holds that concepts must be capable of being shared by different individuals at the same time and by one individual at different times (cf. Fodor, 1998; Peacocke, 1992; Rey, 1983). Although it seems obvious that a theory of CONCEPT must satisfy this desideratum, things become more problematic if one considers whether or not children share concepts with adults (cf. Carey, 1985), whether people embedded in different sociocultural or even scientific contexts share concepts (cf. Kuhn, 1962), whether people with mental disorders share concepts with those without such disorders (Stich, 1983), and whether humans share concepts with other animals (Sterelny, 1990). The issues of desiderata-intersections and controversial desiderata complicate matters for those who think that a theory of CONCEPT should satisfy all of the desiderata (1)–(4), because it becomes unclear how to define the desiderata to be satisfied. Fortunately, this problem only strengthens my argument, because I will argue that no theory of CONCEPT has even adequately satisfied desiderata (1)–(4).

simply to show that each theory has as yet failed to satisfy all or most of desiderata (1)–(4), and so none is clearly preferable to any other.[8]

2.1 Imagist Theory of CONCEPT

Imagism has a long history in philosophical discussions of concepts. The basic premise of imagism is that (mental) images should be afforded a central role in our explanations of cognitive competencies. Such an idea can be traced back to Aristotle, who claimed that "The soul never thinks without an image" (Aristotle, 1961, 431a8). But imagism found its most ardent defenders in the British Empiricists, who claimed that the formation of all concepts (or, as they called them, "ideas") is derivative on perception, whether of external objects or of our own metal states (cf. Berkeley, 1710; Hume, 1739/1978). Perhaps the most well-known of these British Empiricists was John Locke, who can naturally be interpreted as holding the view that concepts—or, again, "ideas"—are mental images (Locke, 1690).[9]

A definition of imagism runs as follows: imagism is the view that concepts are representational images derived from conscious perceptual states, storing imagery information (cf. Russell, 1921; Price, 1953). According to imagism, the process of concept formation begins when we perceptually encounter an object and our perception of that object causes the production of a conscious state in our sensory system. This conscious, perceptual state then leaves a trace in the cognitive system—for example, in long-term memory—and it is this trace that is later re-activated and represented, in some way, as an image of the object first perceived. Thus, imagism takes concepts to be representations in the form of images (hereafter "imagery representations") that are

---

8 This is not the first time that such a review of the different theories of CONCEPT has been undertaken. Two of the most comprehensive surveys come from Prinz (2002) and Machery (2009), which I take as my guide and my source of inspiration in this chapter.

9 There is some controversy about how to interpret Locke here (cf. Ayers, 1991). Both Berkeley and Hume, for instance, took issue with Locke's brand of imagism because it permitted that some concepts are not derivative on perception alone, but can abstract away from the information given over by perceptual states (Prinz, 2002, pp. 36–38). For example, the concept—or "single idea"—of dogs could represent dogs without picturing any dog in particular. For Berkeley and Hume, this was unacceptable, because it meant that ideas were in some important way different from images, since images cannot abstract away from the details of what they are images of (Berkeley, 1710; Hume, 1739/1978). Thus, Locke has been charged by some as endorsing an aberrant form of imagism that cannot be made to work on standard imagist terms.

based on—or, at least, are in some sense subservient to—the "impressions" we have formed in cognition as a result of perceptual experience (Hume, 1739/1978).

Scope: At first sight, imagism seems hopelessly ill-equipped to account for the large variety of concepts that a theory of CONCEPT should be able to accommodate. The reason for this is clear: because there are at least some varieties of concepts—e.g. abstract concepts—that do not appear to be imagery representations derived from conscious perceptual states at all. How, for instance, could our concepts of *truth*, *imaginary number*, or *justice* be imagery representations derived from perceptual states? Moreover, if concepts are imagery representations, how could we come to possess concepts that abstract away from individual instances of a category to represent the category as a whole. For example, how could we come to possess the category of *dog* from our perception of different individual dogs when all of those instances have differed in some—potentially subtle—respect; e.g. in size, colour, tail length etc.?

Historical imagists attempted to counter the second of these arguments by insisting that our perception of a particular objects or events could be sufficient for the imagery representation of classes of objects. Both Berkeley (1710) and Hume (1748), for example, claimed that a particular perceptual state—say, the perceptual state that obtains when I perceive a dog—could give rise to imagery representations of a class—say, the class *dog*—, because that perceptual state will contain features or attributes that can be represented as an image and the imagery representation of such features or attributes is sufficient for the representation of the class. In the context of my running example here, the idea is that a particular perceptual state involving a dog can be used to represent a class because that perceptual state can be represented in terms of certain attributes of the perceptual state—e.g. four-legged, barking, has a tail etc.—, but not necessarily all attributes of the perceptual state—e.g. colour, size, etc.

The problem, however, is that it is unclear how our perception of a particular object or event could be sufficient for the imagery representation of abstract objects (Prinz, 2002, pp. 28–29). One may want to say that our imagery representation of *honour* follows from the perception of a many honourable acts in much the same way that our imagery representation of the class dog follows from perception of a many dogs. But this can only be made to work if there is some feature that is shared by—or, at least, similarly perceived—in every honourable act. But what could such a feature be? And how, exactly, would it be represented as an image? In attempting to answer this question, both Berkeley and Hume stumbled upon a *reductio ad absurdum* of imagism (and, perhaps, empiricism in general): the problem of accounting for concepts whose instances lack perceivable similarities and so are not amenable to imagery representation (Descartes, 1637). And given that this class is very large—consider all concepts of emotional states, colours, political systems, and mathematics just as a start—imagism seems not to have the scope required of any theory of CONCEPT.

Content: *Prima facie*, imagism is in a good position with regards to accounting for both the intentional and cognitive content of concepts. To start with, an imagist could explain how concepts stand in for, refer to, or represent things other than themselves by simply noting that concepts are imagery representations of the perceptual states that obtain as a consequence of perception. Therefore, my concept of *red wine* will be about a red, alcoholic liquid in virtue of the fact that it is an imagery representation of red wine. This optimism led Russell (1921) to argue that:

> The 'meaning' of images is the simplest kind of meaning, because images resemble what they mean.

What's more, imagism can explain why putatively co-referential concepts—e.g. *the evening star* and *the morning star*—can seem semantically distinct to a concept user: because the user's concepts of *the evening star* and *the morning star* are two different imagery representations corresponding to the intuitive difference between the perceived instances of either concept.[10]

The difficulty, however, is that images are ambiguous. As has been demonstrated repeatedly by twentieth century philosophers, images can be taken to resemble more than one thing at once. For instance, an image of a duck can be taken to be an image of a rabbit (cf. Wittgenstein, 1953, and Fig. 2.1 below); or an image of a dog could be taken to be an image of a coyote or a wolf (Price, 1953). The point, then, is that the intentional content of images—what they stand in for, refer to, or represent—is not always clear, because it is tied to the notion of resemblance. The central problem with resemblance—as Goodman (1976) convincingly showed—is that resemblance is symmetric and must be understood as a matter of degrees; in other words, if an object *a* resembles an object *b*, then *b* will also resemble *a*, where the resemblance between *a* and *b* may obtain to a greater or lesser extent. Thus, resemblance cannot be sufficient for reference on its own, because any object *a* can be said to resemble another object *b* to some extent (maybe both share the property of being extended objects...), but not all objects can be said to refer to one another.

---

10 The idea here being that the imagery representation of 'the morning star' differs from the imagery representation of 'the evening star' in certain properties such as location in the night sky, location relative to features of the concept users surroundings (e.g. trees, buildings etc.), and even to brightness of the surrounding sky.

Fig. 2.1: The Duck-Rabbit (Wittgenstein, 1953, Part II, §118).

The problem, therefore, is that the even if the imagist can offer a compelling account of cognitive content, she can offer nothing more than a resemblance theory of intentional content. And this will not be adequate to satisfy the *Content* desideratum.

Acquisition: *Prima facie*, imagism seems strongest when it comes to accounting for how concepts are acquired. Consider first the account of the ontogenetic acquisition of concepts that imagism inspires. For imagism, ontogenetic acquisition follows from the imagery representation of perceptual states. Thus, imagism can explain ontogenetic acquisition by appeal to conscious perceptual states alone, since acquiring a concept in ontogenetic development is nothing more than representing perceptual experience in one way or another. Of course, it may be that a concept is a combinatorial representation of two distinct perceptual experiences—e.g. the combinatorial representation that represents the experience of seeing something gold and also seeing a mountain to arrive at the concept *golden mountain* (cf. Hume, 1739/1978)—but, in any case, ontogenetic concept acquisition will always be based on perceptual experience.

Turning now to the account of the phylogenetic acquisition of concepts that imagism inspires, we find once again that imagism seems to be in relatively strong position. This is the case because the phylogenetic acquisition of concepts can be reductively explained purely in terms of how perceptual systems evolved in the human genome to allow for perceptual states to be stored in memory and used in the formation of concepts. Such an approach allows for a reductive explanation of how acquiring concepts is possible, specified as an evolutionary story about the emergence of perceptual systems and the integration of perceptual systems with other aspects of cognition. But this story—of both onto- and phylogenetic acquisition—goes beyond the commitments of imagism and into an account of the evolution and operation of perception. Thus, even if imagism looks promising with regards to satisfying the *Acquisition* desideratum, this satisfaction may depend on an appeal to theoretical commitments—about, say, the development of perceptual system—which go beyond the imagist theory of CONCEPT itself.

Composition: The line adopted by most historical advocates of an imagist theory of CONCEPT is that concepts, even when they are conceived as imagery representations or perceptual states, are combinable. Hume (1748), for example, proposed that we could form combinatorial, imagery representations of perceptual experiences—e.g. the combinatorial, imagery representation *golden mountain* from the perceptual experience of golden and mountain—, and so the composition of concepts could be viewed as derivative on the composition of different perceptual experiences into one imagery representation (cf. Hume, 1739/1978). But the imagist must also accept that two different perceptual experiences—in this case, of gold and of a mountain—could give rise to two different, non-combined, imagery representations; e.g. *gold* and *mountain*. Thus, the imagist must accept that the combinatorial, imagery representation that jointly represents both the perceptual experience of gold and of a mountain can be explained as a combining, in some sense, of two distinct imagery representations of *gold* and *mountain*. And this leads the imagist into trouble.

Images do certainly seem to be combinatorial. If I have an image of a dog and an image of a tree, I can bring them together to form an image of a dog and a tree. In fact, the combined image may appeal to particular features of the distinct images to represent more information; e.g. that the dog is sitting under, next to, or on top of the tree. Such a combination of images is central to certain forms of art and technology; for instance, animation and architecture. However, there are no fixed rules for the combination of images. An animator may combine images in ways that would not be apt for the architect. As a result, we cannot find general laws for image combination. And this brings us to the central problem with the imagist appeal to combinatorial imagery representations: there are many ways to build combinatorial, imagery representations from distinct, imagery representations; but there is no one systematic way to build such combinatorial, imagery representations.

This is problematic, because we can easily think of two distinct, imagery representations—say, the imagery representations of pet and fish—that should be combinable in a systematic way and whose combination we would expect a theory of CONCEPT to be able to explain. But the imagist theory of CONCEPT cannot explain why the combination of an image of a pet and an image of a fish necessarily results in the image of a typical pet fish (e.g. goldfish); it may very well result in fish-shaped dog or a cat-shaped fish. In a similar vein, Prinz (2002, p. 32) argues that:

> Someone who can picture a carnivorous organism and a plant is not necessarily able to form an accurate image of a carnivorous plant.

Examples like this abound and are further compounded by the worry that imagery representations may not be the same in all contexts. For instance, we could have representations of different perceptual experiences of the same kind of object or representations that accentuate different attributes of the same objects. In terms of Prinz's example: "The way carnivorousness or planthood are depicted might vary from one context to the next" Prinz (2002, p. 32). The end result is that even if imagism can explain the productivity of concepts (images can combine in an almost endless number of ways), it offers no convincing account of how it is that concepts can be combined systematically.

2.2 Definitionist Theory of CONCEPT

Like the imagist theory of CONCEPT, the definitionist theory of CONCEPT has a long philosophical history. The idea of the definitionist theory of CONCEPT is straight-forward: concepts are definitions storing definitional information. In practice, this idea holds that concepts are to be identified with sets of individually necessary and jointly sufficient features or conditions. For example, the concept *bachelor* is to be identified with a set of individually necessary and jointly sufficient conditions such as being unmarried, being male, being of legal age to marry, etc. Analogously, the concept *dog* is to be identified with a set of individually necessary and jointly sufficient conditions such as being four-legged, barking, being a mammal, etc. In this way, no superfluous features or conditions are admitted into definitions; e.g. being tall for the concept *bachelor* or being playful for the concept *dog*.

Definitionism was first expounded by Plato, who tried to arrive at definitions of concepts such as *beauty*, *good*, *virtue*, and *love* by identifying the set of individually necessary and jointly sufficient features or conditions that would be satisfied by objects falling under such concepts (cf. Cooper, 1997). And definitionism went on to be adopted—in some form or another—by prominent philosophers such as Descartes (1637), Kant (1985), and Frege (1884). In the era of cognitive science, however, support for definitionism has waned somewhat, but this has not stopped some from defending a broadly definitionist position (cf. Bruner, Goodnow, and Austin, 1956). Katz and Fodor (1963), for example, argued that concepts could be understood as definitions that are stored in a kind of mental lexicon, where each concept is organised as a syntactic tree containing information (read: conditions) at different levels of grain.[11]

A clear example of a modern version of definitionism is the view endorsed by Peacocke (1992). For Peacocke, concepts are to be individuated by their possession conditions, where possession conditions are sets of inferences that a person must master to possess a concept. For instance, the concept *dog* will be possessed by any individual iff that individual masters the inferences associated with that concept; e.g. inferences associates with dogs having four legs, barking, being man's best friend etc. On Peacocke's view, the reference—or intentional content—of concepts is established by a "determination theory," which makes it the case that each concept refers to whatever it is that makes the set of inferences individuating that concept true.[12]

Scope: Definitionism has serious trouble when it comes to satisfying the *Scope* desideratum (Fodor et al., 1980). For while it may be possible to provide definitions of concepts such as *bachelor* and *dog*, there are a host of other concepts that will not be so easily dealt with. Consider, for instance, the difficulty of providing definitions of the aforementioned Platonic concepts such as *love*, *virtue*, or *honour*. What set of individually necessary and jointly sufficient conditions could suffice to define *love*? And how are we to know if every concept of *love* is possessed when the same set of individually necessary and jointly sufficient conditions are met? No answer seems to be forthcoming and serious doubt has been cast onto the project of finding a set of conditions for any that make space for all possible objects that could be said to fall under a given concept (cf. Wittgenstein, 1953, for an account of shortcomings of definitionism with respect to the concept *game*.).[13]

---

11 This approach to developing a definitionist theory of CONCEPT was inspired by Chomsky's ideas about the syntactic structure of the mind, and remains influential in contemporary lexical semantics (cf. Chomsky, 1968; Jackendoff, 1983).

12 A potentially analogous account of concepts has been developed by Brandom, who's "inferentialist" account of concepts holds that "To grasp or understand [...] a concept is to have practical mastery over the inferences it is involved in—to know [...] what follows from the applicability of a concept, and what it follows from' (Brandom, 2009, 48, original italics). Whether or not Brandom should be classified as a definitionist is unclear, however, because of his focus on practical mastery (know-how) as well as theoretical mastery (know-that).

13 In response to Wittgenstein's arguments, definitionists have put forward a disjunctive form of definitionism, where objects fall under concepts iff they satisfy a certain number, but not necessarily all, of a set of conditions (Eifermann and Steinitz, 1971). This view is an aberrant kind of definitionism, because it relinquishes the claim that all conditions in a definition are individually necessary. Whether or not definitionists should be willing to bite this bullet is open to debate (Anisfeld, 1968). However, one thing is clear: if disjunctive definitionism is to be made to

More concerning still, the definitionist approach has not made a great deal of progress despite its long history. In fact, the recent history of the definitionist program is one littered with set-backs. Gettier (1963), for example, showed that the definitionist treatment of the concept *knowledge* as equivalent to justified, true belief could not easily be upheld; a view which is now widely accepted in epistemology (Dancy, 1985). And attempts to find a set of individually necessary and jointly sufficient conditions for the possession of concepts such as *fruit* have been all but abandoned, because such definitions could never accommodate typicality features that have become central to the explanatory work done by such concepts; for instance, the typicality feature of the concept *fruit* that apples are judged to be more representative fruits than, say, apricots or avocados (Murphy, 2002; Smith and Medin, 1981). The conclusion, therefore, is clear: definitionism does not come close to satisfying the *Scope* desideratum.

Content: Things are much better for definitionism when it comes to giving an account of how concepts have both intentional and cognitive contents. To account for intentional contents definitionism can appeal to the notion of satisfaction (Peacocke, 1992). The idea here is that the intentional content of concepts is established whenever there is some object that satisfies the individually necessary and jointly sufficient conditions that constitute a given concept, since the concept in question will then refer to that object (Peacocke, 1992). So, for example, an explanation of the intentional content of the concept *dog* can run as follows: the intentional content of the concept *dog* is determined by the object(s) that *dog* refers to—e.g. four-legged, barking, friends of man—in virtue of that concept having a particular definitional structure—e.g. including the conditions of having four legs, barking, being man's best friend etc. Moreover, this account leaves no room for ambiguity, because definitions are taken to pick out a clearly demarcated group of things and nothing else.

Definitionism also offers a straightforward account of cognitive contents. On the definitionist view, we can have two different concepts, the possession of which depends on two different sets of individually necessary and jointly sufficient conditions, but which still have the same intentional content; that is, still refer to the same thing(s). The classic example is with the concepts *the morning star* and *the evening star*, the possession of which depend on two different sets of

---

work, an account must be given of what percentage or number of conditions need to be satisfied by a given object for it to fall under a concept and if this is the same in every case (Schofield, 1973). This does not seem to be an easy task to achieve and it is made all the more problematic in the case of concepts such as 'love' and 'freedom' where we have no good idea about what kind of conditions—let alone what percentage or number of conditions—might be relevant.

conditions—one being visible in the morning the other being visible in the evening, for example—, even if both have a common referent (Venus) (Frege, 1884). Definitionism, therefore, provides the perfect means to account for cognitive content, because it is possible to have two different definitions of the same thing that play different inferential roles in thought.

One problem here—famously brought out by Kripke (1972)—is that the cognitive content of definitions (here referred to as "descriptions") might not be adequate to determine the correct intentional content (here called "reference"). Kripke (1977) introduces the example of the name 'Feynman,' which Michaelson and Reimer (2017) elaborate as follows:

> Most people, Kripke claims, will at best know that Feynman was a physicist; they will not know anything, aside from the name, that would serve to differentiate Feynman from any other physicist they have heard of. The problem is that an indefinite description like 'a physicist' will not suffice to pick out any particular individual in the world. Even 'a physicist named 'Feynman'' won't do, at least in a world where two physicists bear this name. At best, this sort of description will pick out an arbitrary member of a class of individuals, not a particular one. And yet, as Kripke points out, it seems perfectly coherent for someone who knows nothing about Feynman, who has only overheard someone using the name, to say to herself "I wonder who Feynman is," or to ask her friend "Who is Feynman?" In each of these cases, the natural thing to say is that the speaker is using the name 'Feynman' to wonder or ask about Feynman. How she can manage to do so, however, looks to be something that is going to be very difficult for the descriptivist to explain.

The upshot is that there may be reason to think that even if definitionism can give a satisfactory account of both intentional and cognitive content, in some instances—e.g. with regards to proper names—it may struggle to give an account of the relation between the two. And this difficulty may very well be pernicious, because the definitionist will want to maintain a link between the definition and the information available to the speaker; and s/he will also want to assert that even if different definitions of the same thing are possible—e.g. *morning star* and *evening star*—, still a definition always picks out a determinate intentional content—e.g. Venus. Thus, it remains at least unclear if definitionism gives a satisfactory account of content.

Acquisition: In the case of accounting for the ontogenetic acquisition of concepts, definitionism fails miserably. The problem is that it is unclear how individuals could come to acquire the set of conditions that are individually necessary and jointly sufficient for concept possession. It does not appear that observation will do the trick, because the observation of certain conditions—e.g. 'is unmarried' in the case of the concept *bachelor* or 'is a mammal' in the case of the concept *dog*— does not seem plausible (Rosch et al., 1976; Smith and Medin, 1981). To overcome this issue, definitionists have argued that we do observe such conditions in the form of rules; e.g. if a male person does not have a ring on the third finger of his left hand then he is unmarried (Rey, 1985). But this idea has been shown to be empirically indefensible, because most individuals fail to learn rules without the aid of ostensive definitions, which cannot be said to work independently of factors over and above mere definitions; such as the relative similarity of the ostensively defined stimuli (Allen and Brooks, 1991).

And there are compounding problems for the definitionist account of the phylogenetic acquisition of concepts. The central problem here is that it is unclear how a definitionist could argue that phylogenetic development contributes to the acquiring of concepts (Hampton, 1981; Smith and Medin, 1981). A definitionist could say that phylogenetic development supplies individuals with conditions that function as the basic building blocks for concepts (Rey, 1997). But this idea runs into problems when we consider the fact that many of the conditions for possessing concepts are about as primitive as they can get. The concept *bachelor*, for instance, could be decomposed into a certain set of primitives—e.g. "man," "not," "married" etc.—but it is unclear how these primitive can be further decomposed. And so the definitionist would have to suppose that phylogenetic development equipped us with primitives such as "married," which seems counter-intuitive, because such primitives are often at least as complex and difficult to understand as are the concepts they are supposed to define (Armstrong, Gleitman, and Gleitman, 1983). Taken together, the conclusion is clear: definitionism does not lend itself well to an explanation of how concepts are acquired.

Compositionality: Definitionism seems perfectly able to provide a satisfactory account of the productivity of thought, because composition can be understood as the combining of definitions. In the case of the composition of the concepts *pet* and *dog* into the concept *pet dog*, the definitionist can simply argue that the compound concept is to be identified with a definition that borrows certain conditions from the definitions that are identified with the two distinct, un-composed concepts (Rey, 1997). So, in the example under consideration, the concept *pet dog* would be identified with a definition that includes conditions of having four legs, barking, having an owner, being kept for company, and so on. In short, the view of composition definitionism inspires is based on the inheriting of conditions from the concepts that are composed.

This view, however, is not without its problems. The central concern is once again with ambiguity about the set of conditions that are to be identified with a given concept. For instance, when the concepts of *love* and *honour* are combined into concepts such as *loving dog* or *honourable leader*, what, exactly, are the conditions inherited by the composed concepts? This issue does not only afflict definitionism (imagism is equally as ambiguous with respect to the inherited properties of composed concepts), but it is still in need of an answer. The question, then, is how the right conditions are selected when composition occurs. For instance, with the composition of *pet* and *fish*, we do not want to end up with a composed definition including the conditions of being gill-bearing, aquatic, craniate, lacking limbs with digits, etc. What we want is a definition that is more easily satisfied by certain kind of fish—e.g. small, golden fish—than others—large, carnivorous fish (Osherson and Smith, 1981). It seems again, therefore, that the promise of a definitionist satisfaction of the *Compositionality* desideratum may flounder.

2.3 Prototype Theory of CONCEPT

In response to the failing of so-called traditional views of concepts (e.g. imagism and definitionism), a novel perspective was inaugurated in the 1970's built around the idea that concepts are prototypes (cf. Rosch, 1973; Rosch and Mervis, 1975; Smith, Shoben, and Rips, 1974). According to the prototype theory of CONCEPT, concepts are prototypes, where a prototype of a class or category is defined as a body of statistical knowledge about the properties possessed by the members of this class (Rosch, 1975). Departing from the definitionist claim that concepts store information about individually necessary and jointly sufficient conditions, prototype theories of concepts argue that concepts store information about statistical distributions of properties that are typically or frequently possessed by instances of the concept in question.

For example, the prototype theory holds that the concept *dog* is to be identified with a statistical distribution of properties that are typically possessed by dogs; e.g. the properties of being four-legged, barking, being a pet etc. Unlike the definitionist view, however, prototype theory assumes that the concept *dog* will be identified with the information that is most diagnostic or salient with respect to dogs. So, with the concept *dog*, it might not be the case that information about the property being a mammal is encoded within the concept, because such a property is not (at least in this example) a property that is associated with dogs with a high statistical frequency. It will, however, almost certainly be the case that information about the property having four legs is encoded within the concept, because such a property is associated with dogs with a high statistical frequency.

The central idea of prototype theory is that concepts are representations of statistical knowledge (Smith and Medin, 1981). But two different kinds of prototype theories have been developed, which offer different characterisations of the nature of the statistical knowledge stored in prototypes. To make sense of this difference, note first that prototypes are statistical representations that can encode information

Tab. 2.1: The prototype of *building* according to Hampton's (1979) model (inspired by Hampton, 1981, p. 459).

BUILDING
1. Is a structure with a roof and walls
2. Has rooms
3. Stands (more or less) permanently in one place
4. Human habitat
5. Serves as shelter from weather
6. Place to store belongings
7. Place to live and/or work

about two types of properties: (1) properties that objects either possess or do not possess and (2) properties that objects possess to some greater or lesser degree (Machery, 2009, p. 84). Having a tail is a good example of the first type of property, because an object can either have a tail or not—possession of a tail is binary. But other properties—such as being large or being camouflaged—are of the other type, because they can be possessed to a greater or lesser degree. The distinction between these two types of properties is represented in the difference between approaches to prototype theory employing "featural models" (binary properties) and approaches to prototype theory employing "dimensional models" (discrete value properties) (Smith and Medin, 1981).

Furthermore, some argue that prototypes represent the "typical" properties of categories (e.g. Rosch, 1975), others the "cue-valid" properties of categories (e.g. Hampton, 1995), and other still both "cue-valid" and "typical" properties (e.g. Jones, 1983). The typicality of a property P is defined in terms of the probability that a member of a class C possesses P given that it is a member of C. For instance, the property P of having wings is a typical property for any member of the class *birds*, because any member of the class *birds* is highly probable to have wings. In contrast, the cue-value of a property P is defined in terms of the probability that an object possessing P belongs to a class C. For example, the property of being able to rotate its head up to 270° is a highly cue-valid property for the class *owls*, but having wings is not (since many other birds have wings, but only owls can rotate their heads up to 270°).

According to prototype theories, concepts are prototypes that store some information about which properties are most typical of (or have the highest cue-validity for) objects falling under the concept. Prototype models vary and so it would be too hasty to say that all prototypes store exactly the same type of statistical information. But as a general rule of thumb one can say that prototypes store information that rates potential instances of a class as more or less typical of that class dependent on the number of prototypical properties of the class they possesses.

This leads nicely into a definition of prototype concepts as bodies of statistical information and, hence, to representations of concepts that look something like table 2.1. Following Hampton (1981), table 2.1 is an example representation of the prototype for *building*. It should be noted, however, that this representation is unlikely to correspond exactly to the concept of building possessed by your average person; it is, rather, an example of what an abstraction of different people's concepts may look like (Machery, 2009, p. 87). Working from Hampton's model, then, we would categorise an object *c* as a building when *c* possesses a sufficient number of the typical properties of the concept *building* (cf. Hampton, 1981; Hampton, 1995). Similarly, we would decide that Lassie is a dog because Lassie possesses most of the properties that are typical of dogs.

Although this kind of "list" representation of prototype concepts was successful when first introduced, it has now come under strain. Barsalou (1993), for example, argued that the method is flawed, because it implies that the only bodies of information that we can be sure are represented are those that are retrievable by means of introspection, whether by participants in experiments or by ourselves. This appeal to introspection seems highly suspect, because not all information stored in concepts may be introspectively available and not all information may be linguistically articulable. What's more, it may be that the introspective retrieval of information is biased by pragmatic considerations, which weight certain pieces of information as more or less typical relative to how we use the concept in question (cf. Tversky and Hemenway, 1984). For example, we may not retrieve the property of having a covering or having a head in the case of our concept *dog*, but we are likely to retrieve the property of barking or having four legs. Thus, introspection may be influenced by our use of the *dog* concept to, say, successfully communicate about dogs.

None of these concerns about representing prototypes by means of lists of salient features are fatal. However, they do provide some justification for considering other available models for representing prototype concepts. Perhaps the most well-known of these models was developed by Smith et al. (1988). Their model reflected an attempt to go beyond the model developed by Hampton (1981), which was judged to be too simple and in many ways deficient. According to Smith et al. (1988, p. 487), prototypes store a large amount of information; for example, in the case of the prototype for *apple*, even the information that apples have seeds, are typically red, round, smooth etc. This leads to a representation of prototypes as storing two kinds of information: information about both "attributes"—kinds of properties—and about "values"—properties *simpliciter*. For example, colour is an

Tab. 2.2: The Prototype of *banana* according to Smith et al.'s (1988) model (inspired by Smith et al., 1988, p. 490).

BANANA			
Attributes		Values	
Colour	1	Yellow	26
		Green	4
		Red	0
Shape	0.9	Curved	29
		Straight	1
		Circular	0
Texture	0.2	Smooth	25
		Rough	5
		Spiky	0

attribute in virtue of being a kind of property, but burgundy, violet, and mauve are values in virtue of being properties *simpliciter*.

This distinction allows Smith et al. (1988) to represent prototype concepts as storing information about the subjective frequency—or, put differently, the agent relative typicality—of different properties, even where kinds of properties are still universally diagnostic as "a measure of how useful the attribute is in discriminating instances of the concept from instances of contrasting concepts" (Smith et al., 1988, p. 487). So in the case of the *banana* prototype concept, for example, Smith et al. develop a representation that stores information about both the diagnosticity of kinds of properties such as colour, shape, and texture (attributes) and the idiosyncratic, statistical distribution of properties *simpliciter* (values) among the members of the denoted class (see table 2.2). As a result, the prototype theory of CONCEPT was extended to allow for the representation of more fine-grained statistical information about a variety of attribute-value pairs.[14]

---

14 Note that some philosophers have drawn a distinction between the kind of prototype representations developed by Hampton (1981) and Smith et al. (1988) by labelling the latter, but not the former, "frame" or "schema" representations (cf. Komatsu, 1992). Although there may be something to this distinction—as elucidated in the work of, among others, Barsalou (1992)—I will not have anything to say about it here, because I will assume that any theory of CONCEPT that takes concepts to store statistical information about category members can be classified as a prototype theory of CONCEPT.

Scope: Prototype theory seems to be in a strong position when it comes to accounting for the wide variety of potential concepts we can entertain and put to use. This is the case because, plausibly at least, any concept could be represented as stored statistical information about category members. The kind of typicality effects for which prototypes are responsible can be identified for concepts of everyday things such as *table* and *dog*; for social concepts such as *democracy*; for concepts of events such as *buying* (Barsalou, 1992); for logical operations such as *modus ponens* (Barsalou, 1993); for abstract concepts such as *vacation* or *science* (Hampton, 1981); and even goal-derived concepts such as *things to take from one's home when its burning* (Barsalou, 1983).

In this way, prototypes—unlike images or definitions—are potentially ubiquitous. In fact, we can even use prototypes to represent concepts that seem most amenable to definitions. For example, even concepts such as *irrational number* and *grandmother* exhibit typicality effects; because π is likely to be taken as a better example of an *irrational number* than $\log_2 3$, and an old woman doting on her grandchildren is likely to be taken as a better example of a *grandmother* than is Tina Turner (Armstrong, Gleitman, and Gleitman, 1983).

However, some have argued that this versatility is not necessarily a strength of prototype theory. According to Armstrong, Gleitman, and Gleitman (1983), the fact that individuals can specify more typical instances of concepts such as *irrational number* or *grandmother* does not undercut the idea that such individuals have definitional concepts of *irrational number* and *grandmother*. For instance, it could be argued that individuals are able to discern which objects fall under the concept *irrational number* by applying the definition "irrational numbers are numbers not constructed from ratios (or fractions) of integers," and that they only appeal to typicality effects when making certain kinds of judgements about, say, good or bad examples of irrational numbers. According to this argument, then, prototype theory cannot prove that "concepts are exhausted by or even partially identifiable with prototypes" (Prinz, 2002, p. 59). Thus, an open question remains about what can be inferred from the success of prototype theory in satisfying the *Scope* desideratum, even if it seems on first sight that this success is without doubt.

Content: In order to provide an account of intentional content, prototype theories of CONCEPT suppose that concepts stand in for, refer to, or represent things other than themselves on the basis of the statistical information they store. But there is a problem with this proposal, issuing from the fact that the information stored by prototypes is supposed to be statistical information, which makes it the case that certain objects can be more or less diagnostic for a given category; e.g. that green bananas are less diagnostic for the category *banana* than are yellow bananas

(Fodor and Lepore, 1996). As a result, prototype theories of CONCEPT have had to accept that the intentional content of concepts is "graded"; that is, that the concepts will stand in for, refer to, or represent certain things more or less than they do others. For instance, that the concept of *fruit* stands in for, refers to, or represents apples more than avocados.

As a result, many prototype theories have been forced to bite the bullet by accepting that sentences such as "apples are fruits" are more true—or, at least, true to a greater degree—than sentences such as "avocados are fruits" (Lakoff, 1972; Rosch and Mervis, 1975). And this is strange, because even though avocados may be a less typical fruit than apples, they are fruits nonetheless. Examples like this affect all kinds of prototype concepts—e.g. igloos are atypical buildings, but they are buildings to the same degree as brick houses—and they point to a serious problem with prototype theories: that they inspire a graded account of intentional content based on typicality even where membership of a category has nothing to do with typicality ratings.

A standard reply to this criticism is that prototypes refer equally to all and only those things that pass a certain threshold—perhaps specified in terms of percentages—with regards to the features they must possess (Hampton, 1995). All of the things passing the threshold are then considered to be the intentional content—e.g. members—of a given concept. However, this response cannot be made to work, because even if an object is above such a feature possession threshold this does not guarantee that the object is an instance of a given concept (Barsalou, 1987; Fodor, 1998; Fodor and Lepore, 1996). For example, foxes and wolves are very much like dogs in appearance and likely exceed the feature-possession threshold for the *dog* prototype. But this does not make foxes or wolves dogs, and so being over the feature-possession threshold for the *dog* prototype is not sufficient for being part of the intentional content of the concept *dog*.

Things are better with regards to the account of cognitive content inspired by prototype theories of CONCEPT. Here the story is easy for prototype theories to tell: concepts referring to the same thing can still play different roles in thought because they store bodies of statistical information that are qualitatively different. Returning again to the example concerning our concepts of *the morning star* and *the evening star*, it is obvious how this could be the case: because one concept stores information that its typical instances are observed in the morning and the other that its typical instances are observed in the evening. The point, therefore, is that prototype representations sharing the same intentional content—or set of possible referents—can play different roles in thought, because they store information—e.g. time of visibility—that is diagnostic of the individual concepts but contingent with regards to their intentional content (Prinz, 2002, pp. 56–57).

Still, this is only half of the job required of a theory of CONCEPT satisfying the *Content* desideratum.

Acquisition: Prototype theories of CONCEPT lend themselves to both a plausible and powerful account of ontogenetic concept acquisition. Causal theories of ontogenetic concept acquisition—where concepts are acquired as the result of a causal pathway running through (at least) the visual system between instances of members of concepts and the properties of cognition responsible for concept formation—do not seem to work for definitional or image-based concepts, because individual instances of members of concepts will always differ in some features. However, such a causal story can be made to work if the causal pathway is responsible for establishing statistical frequencies and saliencies of observable features.

A prototype theorist can argue, therefore, that a causal pathway between different instances of, say, dogs establishes, with a high degree of statistical frequency and saliency, that the feature "barking" coincides with the feature "having four legs." And this statistical information—alongside other relevant statistical information—is stored in the acquisition of the concept *dog*, which is nothing more than a grouping of statistical information about the conditional probability of different features co-occurring together in one instance. Such statistical or probabilistic models of concept acquisition—sometimes framed as models of category formation or acquisition—are now well established in the literature (cf. Chater and Oaksford, 2008; Goodman et al., 2008; Kruschke, 2008; Tenenbaum, 1999). What's more, empirical support for such models has already been obtained (cf. Posner and Keele, 1968).

Clearly, then, prototype theories are equipped to account for ontogenetic concept acquisition, but prototype theories do not have a well formulated account of the phylogenetic component of concept acquisition. The first problem in this regard mirrors the problem faced by the definitionist: that prototypes store statistical information about features that are often complex concepts in their own right. Consider, for example, features such as fragile, mischievous, and expensive, which will have a high typicality rating for instances of concepts such as *glass*, *monkey*, and *diamond ring*. The problem is that explaining how we acquire the concept *mischievous* seems more difficult than explaining how we come to have the concept *monkey*, even though the ontogenetic story of how we acquire the concept *monkey* will appeal to statistical information about the feature mischievous (and its relation to other relevant features). Thus, the prototype theory of concept acquisition rests on unstable and unconvincing foundations, because no clear account of the acquisition of certain concepts can be given by appeal to statistical frequency and saliency (Prinz, 2002). And so the prototype theory of CONCEPT cannot yet be said to satisfy the *Acquisition* desideratum.

Compositionality: The account of compositionality inspired by prototype theories can be said to reveal something important about the way that our concepts combine. In a now classic paper, Hampton (1988) spelled-out the prototype account of compositionality and its ramifications. By conducting an experiment about conjunctive concepts—e.g. the concept *tool that is also a weapon*—, Hampton seemed to have shown that compositionality could not be accounted for by a paradigm that takes concepts to be bodies of statistical information. This followed because the judgements of participants in the study were inconsistent with regards to typical features of objects falling under the conjunctive concepts and typical features of objects falling under the un-conjoined concepts. For example, participants would say that screwdrivers are good examples of a *tool that is also a weapon* in virtue of their typical features, but are bad examples of *weapons* given their typical features. Thus, it appeared that prototypes could not explain the compositionality of concepts such as *tool* and *weapon* by appeal to the statistical information stored in either concept.

However, Hampton argues that prototype theory can, in fact, explain the compositionality of concepts (such as *tool* and *weapon*), but only if we mark the difference between the statistical information stored by composed and un-composed concepts. Consider again the example of the concept *tool that is also a weapon*. For Hampton, this concept stores the statistical information related to features in both the concept *tool*—say, statistical information related to features f_1, f_2, f_3, and f_4—and also the statistical information related to features in the concept *weapon*—say, statistical information related to features f_5, f_6, f_7, and f_8. It is then possible to say that an object possessing features f_1, f_3, f_6, and f_8 would fall both under the concept *tool* and under the concept *tool that is also a weapon*, because it will have a reasonably high typicality ranking with respect to the statistical information stored in both concepts. This idea was then further expanded into a fully-fledged account of the compositionality of prototypes, which remains influential today (cf. Osherson and Smith, 1981; Smith et al., 1988).

However, despite this general optimism about the capacity of prototype theories to satisfy the *Compositionality* desideratum, there is one big problem: prototype theories cannot explain features of combined concepts that are not inherited from their constituent concepts. For example, the feature of living in bowls is often taken to be represented in the concept *pet fish*, but is not represented by either the concept *pet* or *fish*. Similarly, the features of being made of wood is often taken to be represented in the concept *large spoon*, but is not represented by either the concept *large* or the concept *spoon*. This problem arises because the typicality rankings of features exemplified by constituent concepts does not necessarily carry over to combined concepts, which may have different typicality rankings altogether.

One response would be to say that combined concepts store their own statistical information about whatever it is they stand in for, refer to, or represent; but this response only makes sense if prototype theory inspires a satisfactory account of intentional content, which it does not. So, ultimately, prototype theories seem unable to account for how it is that the statistical information stored in two distinct concepts causes the emergence of new statistical information when those concepts are combined. And without an account of this process, prototype theories cannot be said to satisfy the *Compositionality* desideratum.

2.4 Exemplar Theory of CONCEPT

Following shortly after the introduction of the prototype theory of CONCEPT, yet another theory of CONCEPT emerged to challenge the traditional imagist and definitionist theories: the exemplar theory of CONCEPT (cf. Brooks, 1978; Medin and Schaffer, 1978). According to the exemplar theory of CONCEPT, concepts are collections of exemplars. Exemplars are bodies of knowledge about the properties possessed by a particular member of a class. In other words, exemplars are representations that store information about previously experienced category instances. For example, we can have an exemplar of my next door neighbour's dog or Lassie, and both of these exemplars are individual instances that come together with other instances to form a collection of representations constituting the concept *dog*. The idea, then, is that concepts store information about sets of exemplars stored in long-term memory (Medin and Schwanenflugel, 1981; Estes, 1994).

The central motivation for the exemplar theory of CONCEPT follows from the identification of a shortcoming with the prototype theory of CONCEPT: that individual instances of a category may not be judged to be typical given the statistical information that they represent. To understand this concern, consider the following example from Prinz (2002, p. 64):

> Imagine a species of tropical fish in which adults have blue scales and juveniles have yellow fins, but very few have both. Because of the prevalence of these two features, a person might abstract a prototype for this species that included both blue scales and yellow fins, even if she had never seen an actual instance with both features. Now suppose, after forming the prototype in this way, that a person finally sees one of the rare instances that actually conforms to the prototype. Prototype theory predicts that she will be able to identify this rare prototypical instance more readily than the nonprototypical instances that she had actually experienced. Ideal cases can outperform less typical familiar cases.

Exemplar theories—like prototype theories—may posit exemplars as featural (Medin and Schaffer, 1978) or dimensional (Nosofsky, 1986) representations. The central difference between exemplar and prototype theories, however, is that the former, unlike the latter, predicts that we form memories of many—if not all—encountered instances of category members. Prototype theory, in contrast, predicts that only information about statistical frequency and salience are stored in long-term memory, which increases the computational costs of, say, categorisation or reasoning (as every episode of categorisation or reasoning must compute various pieces of statistical information), but dramatically reduces the storage and processing costs associated with concept use (since a concept is only one, statistical representation instead of a set of many exemplar representations).

Exemplar theories can respond to the concerns about both storage and processing costs (Prinz, 2002, pp. 68–69). Firstly, they can argue that there is good, empirical evidence that we are capable of storing a large quantity of representations of individual instances (cf. Standing, 1973). This claim is confirmed by studies that show that we can be exposed to a large quantity of individual instances—for example, 1000 images—for a very brief time—e.g. 5 seconds each—, and still be able to identify the majority of those images after exposure. Secondly, they can argue that exemplar theory need not suppose those cognitive competencies involving concepts search through all stored exemplars at the beginning of every task. In the case of categorisation, for instance, an exemplar-based model might presuppose that we only compare perceptual representations with those stored exemplars that are similar enough across a number of dimensions.

Such an exemplar-based model of categorisation would assume that cognitive processes involve the computation of the similarity between exemplars and other representations. For example, when I categorize Bilbo Baggins as a *hobbit*, I begin with a representation of Bilbo—whether perceptual or otherwise—and then match this representation with one or several exemplars of hobbits that are retrieved from long-term memory (together, maybe, with exemplars of other categories, such as *leprechauns*); then the similarity between my representation of Bilbo and these exemplars is computed, and the categorisation of Bilbo as a hobbit follows from the high degree of similarity between the retrieved exemplar(s) of hobbit(s) and the representation of Bilbo. This process was schematised and represented by Machery (2009, p. 97); and I can slightly modify that representation to fit my example as in Fig. 2.2.

Before moving on the consider how well exemplar theories satisfy desiderata (1)–(4), it is worth briefly discussing the most influential of all exemplar-based models of cognitive processes: the Generalised Context Model of Categorisation developed by Nosofsky (1986) and Nosofsky (1992). The Generalised Context Model combines an exemplar theory of CONCEPT, a similarity measure, and a decision

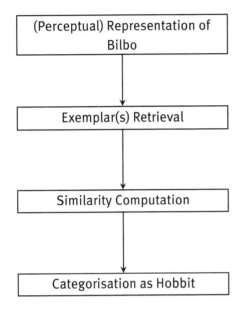

Fig. 2.2: Successive psychological processes during categorisation (inspired by Machery, 2009, p. 97).

rule to account for concept formation. According, again, to Machery's (2009, p. 98) helpful summary of Nosofsky's model, each exemplar represents its referent as a point in a multidimensional space. The similarity measure, then, is a function of the "psychological distance" between a (perceptual) representation and any relevant exemplar retrieved from long-term memory, where psychological distance depends on the extent to which the relevant (perceptual) representation—e.g. a representation of Bilbo—and the retrieved exemplar correspond on the relevant "dimensions" for categorising the representation. The similarity of each relevant dimension is specified in turn and can be formally represented as:

$$| x_{tk} - x_{Ek} | \qquad (2.1)$$

where x_{tk} is the value of the (perceptual) representation—say, the (perceptual) representation of Bilbo—on dimension k and x_{Ek} is the value of the retrieved exemplar on this dimension. The calculation of the "psychological distance" between, say, the representation of Bilbo and some relevant exemplar—e.g. of another hobbit, say, Frodo—depends on whether the relevant dimension is "analyzable"; that is, whether the dimension can be attended to independently of another dimension in the way that we can "attend to the size of an object independently of its weight," but not hue independently of brightness and saturation (Shepard, 1964). Then, the distance between the (perceptual) representation and the exemplar is then calculated for n dimensions as follows:

$$d_{tE} = c \left(\sum_{k=1}^{n} W_k \left(x_{tk} - x_{Ek} \right)^r \right)^{\frac{1}{r}}$$ (2.2)

where r "depends on whether the dimensions are analyzable"; and c is a "sensitivity parameter that measures how much the overall psychological distance between a target and an exemplar affects their similarity" (Machery, 2009). By then supposing that the similarity of a (perceptual) representation and a given exemplar is an exponential function of the psychological distance between them; e.g. is:

$$S_{tE} = e^{-d_{tE}}$$ (2.3)

the overall similarity of a (perceptual) representation—e.g. of Bilbo—and a set of exemplars—e.g. exemplars retrieved from the concept *hobbit*—can be computed as the sum of the similarities that a (perceptual) representation has to each retrieved exemplar of a hobbit by:

$$S_{tc} = \sum_{E \in C} S_{tE}$$ (2.4)

Finally, a decision rule can be applied to resolve ambiguities about categorisation. For example, if both the concepts (e.g. sets of exemplars) *hobbit* and *leprechaun* are retrieved from long-term memory and compared to a (perceptual) representation of Bilbo in terms of their similarity across a number of dimensions, then the probability that the (perceptual) representation of Bilbo will be categorised as a *hobbit* is a function of the overall similarity of the (perceptual) representation of Bilbo to the concept of *hobbit* divided by the sum of the overall similarities to the concepts of *hobbit* and *leprechaun*. Formally:

$$P(t \in A) = \frac{S_{tA}}{S_{tA} + S_{tB}}$$ (2.5)

Scope: The exemplar theory of CONCEPT works from the premise that exemplars are sets of representations that store information about many experienced instances of individual members of a category. But it is clear, therefore, that exemplar theories will struggle to satisfy the *Scope* desideratum. This is the case because a large number of the concepts that we would like to be accounted for by a theory of CONCEPT cannot easily be taken to derive from experience (Rips, 1995). Consider, for example, those concepts—such as the scientific concepts *mass* or *space-time*—that are learned by description rather than acquaintance. Moreover, consider concepts with whose instances we have no experience of; for instance, abstract concepts such as *infinity* or *God* or, perhaps, fictional kind concepts such as *Sherlock Holmes*.

The standard reply to this worry—as we have seen in the case of, e.g., the imagist theory of CONCEPT—is that our concepts of non-experienced things can be explained by conceptual combination or by appeal to operations—e.g. abstraction—over our concepts of experienced things. This line of reasoning, however, cannot easily be exploited by the exemplar theory of CONCEPT, because the exemplar theory holds that concepts are *nothing more than* sets of exemplars, potentially stored in long-term memory. Thus, the exemplar theory of CONCEPT is unlikely to be able to account for concepts of non-experienced things—e.g. *democracy*—by appeal to generalisations or operations over perceptual representations, because concepts of non-experienced things would still have to be accounted for as sets of exemplars constituted by perceptual representations of experienced things. As a result, exemplar theories of CONCEPT cannot easily satisfy the *Scope* desideratum. In the terms of Prinz (2002, p. 70): they can only be "partial theories" of CONCEPT.

Content: Like prototype theories of CONCEPT, exemplar theories also have an issue with accounting for the intentional content of concepts. The problem here is that exemplar theories must contend that concepts stand in for, refer to, or represent things other than themselves in virtue of the fact that the individual exemplars making up a concept are all about one particular thing. For example, that the concept *dog* is about dogs in virtue of the fact that the individual exemplars making up a concept *dog*—e.g. the exemplars for my neighbour's dog, Lassie, etc.—are about different instances of dogs.

The trouble, however, is that since concepts are mere sets of exemplars and not abstractions over exemplars, it seems that the concept *dog* cannot refer to dogs *per se* at all, but rather to a conjunction of the referents of the individual exemplars making up a concept *dog*; that is, to the conjunction my neighbour's dog ∧ Lassie ∧ the dog across the street ∧ etc. And this leads to a further worry, because it then seems that the concept *dog* cannot have the intentional content of being about any dog that has not been experience directly by the concept user; and so my concept *dog* will invariably differ from the concept *dog* possessed by others (Prinz, 2002, pp. 69–70). Whether or not these concerns amount to a knock-down blow for the exemplar theory is unclear, but it does seem to be the case that the exemplar theory inspires an unconventional and potentially problematic account of the aboutness of concepts

Exemplar theories do better at accounting for the cognitive contents of concepts. To see why, consider yet again the concepts of *the morning star* and *the evening star*. On the picture inspired by exemplar theories, both of these concepts are sets of exemplars representing experiences of individual instances of the morning star and the evening star. Thus, even though the concepts of *the morning star* and *the evening star* store different information in virtue of being constituted by exemplars representing a star in the morning sky and a star in the evening sky respectively; still they can both be about the same thing in virtue of the fact that their constituent exemplars are about the same thing; namely, Venus. This is sufficient to show that exemplar theory can explain how two different concepts can refer to the same thing while also playing different roles in thought. However, this explanation only makes sense if exemplar theories have a viable account of intentional content, which remains open to debate. And so too, therefore, does the capacity of the exemplar theory of CONCEPT to satisfy the *Content* desideratum.

Acquisition: When it comes to accounting for ontogenetic and phylogenetic acquisition of concepts, exemplar theories can be evaluated along almost identical lines as prototype theories. As with prototype theories, exemplar theories may offer a convincing account of the ontogenetic acquisition of concepts in terms of causal/perceptual story connecting the properties of cognition responsible for concept formation and category instances via the visual system. In fact, exemplar theories outperform prototype theories in satisfying this desideratum, because the acquisition of concepts does not depend on the integration of statistical information in one representation (Nosofsky, Pothos, and Wills, 2011). Rather, concepts are straightforward groupings of perceptual representations, which each store information about some perceived instance of the concept.

This is beneficial when it comes to explaining how we acquire superordinate concepts such as *furniture* or *vehicle*. The reason for this is because exemplar theory does not have to explain how superordinate concepts organise information in terms of statistical frequency or saliency as do prototype theories. Instead, exemplar theories can simply propose that exemplars of tables, hammocks, cars, and funicular are retrieved in groups based upon certain similar features—e.g. being a movable objects intended to support various human activities or being a machine that transports people or cargo—; and that this is sufficient to explain how we acquire superordinate concepts such as *furniture* or *vehicle*.

Exemplar theories offer no good account of the phylogenetic dimension of concept acquisition, however. And it is clear that the ontogenetic acquisition of exemplars cannot be the whole story of concept acquisition. This follows because exemplars depend on some abstract, featural representations over which to compute the similarity of one perceived instance with stored representations of other instances. Another way of putting this is to say that the computations of similarity between two different exemplars—say, the exemplars of my neighbour's dog and Lassie—must be based on something more basic than those exemplars themselves or else we risk an infinite regress where exemplars are used to explain the acquisition of exemplars (Machery, 2009).

Typically, the more basic component of exemplar acquisition is taken to be some phylogenetically endowed feature recognition mechanism—for recognising, say, the feature of having four legs—that represents features in the form of dimensions in a multidimensional space. But, ultimately, this is just to say that the exemplar theory of CONCEPT can only be made to work if it supplemented with an account of how we came to be able to represent features in the abstract; i.e. without their being bound to an exemplar representation storing information about our experience of some instance. Thus, the potential for the exemplar theory of CONCEPT to satisfy the *Acquisition* desideratum depends on a story of our phylogenetic development of feature representational resources. Unfortunately, no such story has yet been told and, if it were, this would not necessarily favour the exemplar theory of CONCEPT.

Compositionality: Exemplar theories also face difficulties providing an account of the compositionality of concepts. For exemplar theories, conceptually representing some composition of concepts should be a simple case of retrieving exemplars of instances of both concepts and then forming a combined set of exemplars to constitute a combined concept. So, for instance, combining the concepts *elephant* and *balloon* should be as simple as retrieving exemplars of instances of elephants and balloons, and then forming a combined set of elephant and balloon exemplars to constitute a combined concept *elephant balloon*. The problem, however, is that exemplar theory offers no account of the retrieval process when it comes to conceptual combination. And this is an issue, because we need an account of the exemplar-retrieval operations to explain how we come up with concepts of those things we have never and perhaps could never experience; e.g. concepts such as *pet walrus*. As Prinz (2002) explains:

> Without having experienced pet walruses, how can we represent them? Presumably, we perform some kind of combination operation on the exemplar representations of the constituent concepts. But which exemplar representations are chosen? Do we factor in all of the exemplars for pet and walrus, or just some subset? And once the relevant exemplars are chosen, how they are combined? Do we first combine the set of pet exemplars and the set of walrus exemplars separately to form two single representations and then combine those two to form one, or do we combine all these exemplars together at once? If all at once, is the result a single representation or a set of representations? Novel compounds may also generate emergent features. Perhaps pet walruses are presumed to live in swimming pools. How can exemplar knowledge explain this if no familiar pets or walruses live in pools?

The point, therefore, is that exemplar theories have not explained why combined concepts will store the information that we expect them to store. As a result, it is unclear how conceptual composition based on exemplar retrieval could work.

That being said, exemplar theories do have one important advantage over prototype theories when it comes to accounting for the productivity of thought: they can explain how combined concepts can represent features not represented in the un-combined concepts. Consider again the feature of living in a bowl for the combined concept *pet fish* or the feature being made of wood for the combined concept *large spoon*. I noted above that prototype theories cannot explain these features of the combined concepts, because neither are statistically frequent or salient features of their constituent concepts *pet*, *fish*, *large*, or *spoon*.

Exemplar theories, on the other hand, can explain these features by pointing to the fact that most pet fish we experience live in bowls and most large spoons we experience are wooden. Thus, exemplar theories can suggest that the features living in a bowl and being made of wood emerge in conceptual combinations involving the concepts *pet* and *fish* and *large* and *spoon* respectively, because the combination of these two concepts constrains the kinds of exemplars we retrieve; namely, exemplars of fish we have experienced in homes (which typically live in bowls) and spoons over a certain size (which are typically made of wood). Once again the details are not yet clear, but exemplar theories of CONCEPT may, at least, have the potential to spell them out. However, this does not get around the aforementioned problems that prevent exemplar theories from adequately satisfying the the *Compositionality* desideratum.

2.5 The Theory Theory of CONCEPT

The theory theory of CONCEPT departs from the tradition established by the prototype and exemplar theories of CONCEPT in that it does not principally conceive of concepts as storing information on the most salient features of objects or on many experiences of object. In contrast, the theory theory supposes that concepts store information about "beliefs about causal mechanisms, teleological purposes, hidden features, and fundamental divisions in ontology" (Prinz, 2002, pp. 75–76). In this way, the theory theory proposes that concepts are—or, at least, are elements of—theories, because they store information that goes beyond the information given over by experience or by statistical frequencies and typicality ratings (cf. Murphy and Medin, 1985; Carey, 1985; Keil, 1989).

There is some ambiguity about how best to characterise the theory theory. For some psychologists, concepts are literally theories in that they are entirely equivalent to the products of (folk-) science (Rips, 1995; Rehder, 2003a; Rehder, 2003a). For other psychologists, however, concepts are simply elements of theories (Gopnik, Meltzoff, and Bryant, 1997). In any case, the emphasis on concepts being at least "theory-like" representations is at the forefront of the theory theory. As a result, concepts are taken to be equivalent to, or part of, some class of entities that have unique structural, functional, and dynamic properties (cf. Gopnik, Meltzoff, and Bryant, 1997; Prinz, 2002).

Structurally, theories are systems of abstract entities and laws, which posit unobservable objects and relations, and justify such posits only insofar as these posits are supported by the relevant empirical data and help to explain the regularities of experience (Sloman, 2005). Functionally, theories make predictions and retrodictions and support/provide explanations and interpretations of observable (and, in many cases, unobservable) phenomena. Theories, in general, are taken to possess dynamic properties that underlie the accumulation of counter-evidence towards a particular idea, the possibility of theory change over time, and the tendency to reject theory violations.

One problem that arises at the offset for the theory theory is that it is difficult to disambiguate what is meant by the comparison to scientific theories (Machery, 2009, pp. 101–102). For one thing, there is the long debated question of whether theories are syntactic or semantic structures, and hence whether they are comprised of, e.g., sentence-like strings or of (partial) models (cf. Ketland, 2004; Ramsey, 1931; Suppes, 2002; Van Fraassen, 1980, for discussion of this topic). But even putting this debate to one side, there is the problem that scientific theories are far from heterogeneous. In fact, scientific theories are so diverse there are live debates about whether or not they all store the same kinds of knowledge or information.

As an example of this state of affairs, consider the difference between mechanistic scientific theories found in, say, neurobiology, which make explicit the mechanisms responsible for bringing about phenomena (Machamer, Darden, and Craver, 2000); theories in some areas of physics—e.g. Newtonian physics and thermodynamics—, which appeal to (probabilistic) laws to account for the relation between variables; and theories in the formal sciences, which make use of abstract structures to characterise and explain their explananda. Which of these kind of theories does the theory theory take concepts to be equivalent to or part of?

The answer put forward by defenders of the theory theory is deflationary. They claim that concepts are equivalent to, or part of, theories insofar as they play the same functional role as theories in science; namely, to explain—as opposed to merely describe—phenomena (Margolis, 1995). The point of the theory theory, then, is to highlight and place in centre stage certain kinds of information that are omitted from other theories of CONCEPT: information about explanatory relations. Such explanatory relations may be parsed in terms of laws (e.g. all *fruits* have a shape), causal relations (e.g. *glasses* break when dropped from a certain height), functional properties (e.g. *giraffes* have long necks to reach foliage at greater heights), and generic propositions (e.g. that *dogs* have four legs) (Carey, 1985).

It follows for the theory theory that concepts are to be understood as those things that "store some nomological, causal, functional, and/or generic knowledge about the members of its extension" (Machery, 2009, p. 101). So, for instance, the concept *table* will store some nomological, causal, functional, and/or generic information about tables; just as the concept *gene* will store some nomological, causal, functional, and/or generic information about genes.[15]

Perhaps the central motivation for the theory theory is that it provides a way to make sense of the information stored by concepts without appealing to abstractions over statistical information (prototype theories) or over sets of perceptually mediated representations (exemplar theories). Instead of relying on information of this sort, the theory theory points to the role of explanatory information in conceptualisation. This is helpful because we can differentiate between concepts with similar typical features—e.g. being curved in the case of our concepts of *banana* and *boomerang*—by appealing to an explanatory relation; e.g. that the curvature of boomerangs, but not bananas, enables an explanation of why boomerangs return to their throwers (Medin and Shoben, 1988; Prinz, 2002). Thus, the theory theory assumes that the reason why objects fall under a given concept is because their behaviour lends itself to particular explanations.

The upshot is that the theory theory supports the view that concept users have faith in the "hidden essences" of objects, which accounts for the kinds of explanatory relations into which they can enter (Medin and Ortony, 1989; Gelman, Coley, and Gottfried, 1994). This view—called "psychological essentialism"—holds that it is not abstractions over appearances that underlie conceptualisation and concept use, but rather our belief that objects have essences that determine the kinds of explanations in which they can feature. Famously, this view was defended by Keil (1989, p. 177) who argued that certain objects—in his example, raccoons—will continue to be identified as one thing even if their appearance is transformed—in his example, into a skunk (see Fig. 2.3). This follows, according to Keil, because superficial appearances are not sufficient for conceptualisation.

---

15 It has been argued by Machery (2009, p. 102) that:

> Instead of drawing on the accounts of scientific explanation provided by philosophers, psychologists rely on a folk understanding of explanation. It thus seems that [...] the analogy with scientific theories [..] is not the backbone of the psychological notion of theory. Rather, what matters is the folk notion of explanation—the fact that some propositions tell us why things happen.

Machery is certainly right about this point, but since engaging with this topic forces us to enter into deep and difficult questions with regards to the foundations of the theory theory—e.g. about

Fig. 2.3: Transformation of a raccoon into a skunk (Keil, 1989, p. 177).

Scope: The theory theory of CONCEPT has the potential to account for practically any concept we can think of. The reason for this is straightforward: because any concept—whether abstract, formal, or of a fictional kind—can be said to support some explanations of one kind or another.

Consider two examples: the abstract/formal concept *set* and the fictional concept *Sherlock Holmes*. It is clear that the concept *set* can be said to support explanations—or, perhaps, proofs—, because without the concept *set* we could have no understanding of the fact that there are more real numbers than integers or that we should make a distinction between countable and uncountable infinities (cf. Potter, 1993, for further elaboration). Similarly, it is clear that the concept *Sherlock Holmes* can be said to support explanations, because without the concept *Sherlock Holmes* we would have no way to explain why, say, 221B Baker Street is so famous an address or who it was that physician John Watson assisted.

The idea, then, can be summarised neatly as follows: the potential scope of the theory theory is very wide indeed, because practically any concept can be said to store nomological, causal, functional, and/or generic information about the domains, feature relations, and essences of its members. Relevant domains include the (folk) biological domain as with concepts of non-human animal species such as *lion* and *shark* (Medin and Atran, 1999); the (folk) psychological domains as with concepts such as *belief* and *desire* (Carey, 1985); and the domain of artifacts as with concepts such as *sofa* and *hammer* (Bloom, 1996). In general, then, the theory theory separates concepts into domains that distinguish between living things and non-living things, and even between natural and non-natural kinds (Keil, 1979). As such, satisfying the *Scope* desideratum should be no problem at all.

Content: The theory theory is also able to lend itself to a viable account of cognitive content, because it can show how concepts referring to the same set of objects can play different roles in thought. To account for this feature of concepts, the

whether the concepts are the same kinds of theories as the theories of science—I will ignore this problem and focus on evaluating the theory theory against desiderata (1)–(4).

theory theory can argue that two separate theories are able to converge on the same set of objects. Such a possibility is easy to make sense of by paying attention to the history of science. For example, theories of *space* and theories of *time* played different roles in physics and philosophy up until the early twentieth century (and still do so today in a more or less heuristic capacity). However, with the advent of the special relativity theory, our theories of space and time were shown to be about the same thing: *space-time*. It is clear, then, that it is possible for two theories to have the same referent while still playing different explanatory or inferential roles.

But the theory theory does not fare so well when it comes to providing an account of intentional content, because it is unclear how theories can stand in for, refer to, or represent things other than themselves. One proposal could be that the intentional content of these is established on the basis of the descriptions of objects that constitute theories. The problem with this proposal, however, is twofold. Firstly, it is not clear that theories specify necessary and sufficient conditions for concept membership, because theories can be wrong. Examples of this kind are easy to imagine. If I theorise that flowers have colourful petals in order to scare away animals, then this theory is plainly wrong. Thus, theories do not establish necessary conditions for concept membership, otherwise I would be unable to refer to any flower by making use of my mistaken *flowers* theory. Secondly, theories may specify concept membership circularly; for example, if a theory of donkeys explains which animals are and are not donkeys by appealing to the criterion of having donkey parents (Prinz, 2002, p. 86).

In any case, appealing to necessary and sufficient conditions for concept membership does not seem to be a valid move on the part of the theory theorist, because it implies that the theory theory must be supplemented with another theory of CONCEPT—say, the definitionist theory—in order to give a satisfactory account of intentional content. The conclusion, therefore, is that the theory theory cannot account for intentional content on its own. And even if it could there would be another problem; namely, the problem of determining whether or not it is really the case that theories stand in for, refer to, or represent things other than themselves. Resolving this problem would entail resolving the realism vs. anti-realism debate, which does not seem likely (cf. Chakravartty, 2007; French, 2014; Ladyman et al., 2007; Muller, 2011; Psillos, 2005, for an overview of recent—and ongoing—debates about scientific realism). Consequently, for now, the theory theory cannot be said to entirely satisfy the *Content* desideratum.

Acquisition: At first sight it seems that the theory theory can offer a straightforward account of ontogenetic concept acquisition by arguing that we acquire concepts by constructing our own theories of the world in response to incoming sense data

(Keil and Batterman, 1984). On this account, the acquisition of concepts by an individual follows the same template as does our construction of scientific theories: first we form hypotheses that we take to best explain the causal relations and/or functional roles exhibited by objects or groupings of objects, then we test these hypotheses against observed instances, before refining our theories to arrive at the best explanation of the behaviour of objects (Carey, 1985; Soja, Carey, and Spelke, 1991). The problem with this account, however, it that it might be circular: if concepts are the building blocks of theories and we explain theory acquisition as the assembly of concepts, then how does theory construction get started in the first place (Murphy and Medin, 1985)?

One possible response to this problem is to argue that the ontogenetic acquisition of concepts is made possible by some primitive features of our cognitive systems that are not themselves concepts. For example, that ontogenetic concept acquisition involves the construction of theories based upon our identification of putative essences or explanatory relations that are not themselves conceptual in nature. But this response leads us head first into a discussion about how cognitive systems come to acquire and make use of such primitive and nonconceptual information about putative essences or explanatory relations. Thus, in much the same way as with the definitionist and prototype theories of CONCEPT, theory theories are obliged to give some account of the phylogenetic development that makes concept acquisition possible. Unfortunately, however, no such account could be sure to favour the theory theory. And so the theory theory cannot yet be said to adequately satisfy the *Acquisition* desideratum.

Compositionality: In order to satisfy the *Compositionality* desideratum, the theory theory would have to show how theories productively and systematically compose. This is analogous—if not equivalent—to showing how theories are integrated. The problem, however, is that we do not yet have a working account of theoretical integration (cf. Miłkowski, 2016). While it is clear that integration demands that there be some constraints on the combination of two or more theories—for instance, constraints on the representations supported by the either theory—, it is unclear if any given constraint or set of constraints is necessary and sufficient (Craver, 2007; Thagard, 2007). As a result, we simply do not yet know if there is a systematic way of integrating theories and, by proxy for the theory theory, a way of combining concepts.

Furthermore, it is not clear that combined theories are explanatory with regards to the class of objects that they are about. For instance, it is not clear that our combined theories of *pet* and *fish*—e.g. *pet fish*—actually stores explanatory information about, say, small, golden fish kept in bowls in a house. Kunda, Miller, and Claire (1972) make the same point in their example about the combined concept *Harvard carpenter*. They argue that a theory of *Harvard carpenters*—if it is anything like our "naive sociological theory"—should support a non-materialistic explanation of the carpenter's motivations given his/her potential earnings and the average earnings of a carpenter (Werning, Hinzen, and Machery, 2012). The problem, however, is that information about being non-materialistic is stored in neither our concept of *Harvard* nor in our concept of *carpenter*; and so it is unclear how the combined concept *Harvard carpenter* could do the explanatory work we expect of it. The upshot: that the theory theory is not well placed to satisfy the *Compositionality* desideratum.

2.6 Concluding Remarks

In this chapter, I have discussed the most prominent theories of CONCEPT adhering to the standard view. My aim has not been to give an exhaustive account of each theory. Rather, in each case, I have demonstrated that while the theory of CONCEPT in question may be able to satisfy some of desiderata (1)–(4), it is unlikely to be able to satisfy them all.

The imagist theory of CONCEPT may be able to satisfy the *Acquisition* desideratum, but it does not look likely to be able to satisfy the *Scope, Content,* or *Compositionality* desiderata. The definitionist theory of CONCEPT may be able to satisfy the *Content* desideratum, but has as yet failed to satisfy the *Scope, Acquisition,* or *Compositionality* desiderata. The prototype theory of CONCEPT may be able to satisfy the *Scope* desideratum, but is not currently able to satisfy the *Content, Acquisition,* or *Compositionality* desiderata. The exemplar theory of CONCEPT does not seem likely to satisfy any of desiderata (1)–(4) and the theory theory of CONCEPT seems likely to satisfy only the *Scope* desideratum.

Over the past few decades, philosophers have been locked in a controversial debate about what is to be inferred from the failure of these theories of CONCEPT to satisfy desiderata (1)–(4). In this regard, a large number of arguments and counter-arguments have been put forward in defence of one theory or another. However, more recently another idea has emerged: that the reason why we cannot find a theory of CONCEPT able to satisfy desiderata (1)–(4) is because we have been committed to the standard view. The question that follows such a claim is: is our commitment to the standard view justified? As I will explain in the next chapter, one answer that has been given to this question—namely, that the standard view should be abandoned—has given rise to more radical and revisionary theories of CONCEPT. But it remains to be seen whether or not this development has succeeded in moving the debate about the "best" theory of CONCEPT forward.

3 The Appeal to Cognitive Science

3.1 The Explanatory Challenge

In the previous chapter, I considered a number of candidate theories of CONCEPT adhering to the standard view.[16] I found that none of these theories of CONCEPT was better able to satisfy the desiderata of *Scope, Content, Acquisition*, and *Compositionality*—desiderata (1)–(4)—than any other. This causes an obvious problem, because the relative satisfaction of these desiderata was meant to help us decide between competing theories of CONCEPT. As a result of this state of affairs, a novel idea has gained traction in the literature: that the standard view, holding that a theory of CONCEPT should be a theory of a single kind of representation, is wrong. What's more, support for this idea has been reinforced by an appeal to cognitive science, which has led to the development of an argument—which I will call an the "explanatory challenge to the standard view."

The failure of "standard view theories of CONCEPT" to satisfy desiderata (1)–(4) has not inhibited the progress of cognitive science. In fact, cognitive science has moved forward unabated. The problem, however, is that cognitive scientists have simply assumed one or another of the available theories of CONCEPT in their explanations of higher cognitive capacities. For example, some cognitive scientists have developed theories and models of categorisation based on a prototype theory of CONCEPT; whereas others have developed theories and models of categorisation based on exemplar or theory theories of CONCEPT. The same situation obtains in explanations of reasoning, the making of analogies, language comprehension etc. As a result, the failure to find one indisputable theory of CONCEPT has led to a patchwork state of affairs in which different theories of CONCEPT are chosen for their explanatory advantages in different explanatory contexts.

It is easy to see how such a situation could obtain. If one wants to model categorisation computationally, then it is far easier to assume a theory of CONCEPT that takes the information stored in categories to be either statistical information (e.g. prototype theory) or information abstracted from the representation of a set of observed instances (e.g. exemplar theory). And a great deal of progress has been made on the back of such assumptions (cf. Carpenter and Grossberg, 1988; Reed, 1972; Rosch and Mervis, 1975; Rumelhart, Hinton, and Williams, 1986, as examples of such an application of prototype theories). However, if one wants to explain causal reasoning, then it is far easier to assume a theory of CONCEPT that

---

16 This chapter contains some material that is a re-working of Taylor and Vosgerau (2019).

https://doi.org/9783110708165-003

takes the information stored in categories to be nomological, causal, functional, and/or generic knowledge about the members of a categories extension (e.g. theory theory). And, once again, a great deal of progress has been made on the back of this assumption (cf. Carey, 1985; Carey, 2009, as examples of such an application of theory theories).

Moreover, it is not only the case that cognitive scientists assume different theories of CONCEPT to explain different cognitive competences. In fact, cognitive scientists now claim to have identified several distinct types of categorisation judgements, several distinct episodes of inductive/deductive reasoning, several distinct operations of meaning extraction, and so on; and so have been forced to assume a number of different theories of CONCEPT to explain different instances of what are, *prima facie* at least, single cognitive competences. For example, images (Brewer, 1999), definitions (Jackendoff, 1983), prototypes (Lakoff, 1987), bundles of exemplars (Nosofsky, 1988), and theory-like structures (Carey, 1985; Rehder, 2003b) have all been put to use to explain categorisation. In each case, cognitive scientists have either implicitly or explicitly endorsed one particular theory of CONCEPT, satisfying some, but not all, of desiderata (1)–(4), to do the required explanatory work.

Consider explanations of categorisation. In some cases, psychologists have noted that the categorisation of an individual *c* in a category *C* involves the identification of a statistically significant correspondence between the properties of *c* and the typical properties of members of *C*. In cases such as these, psychologists have posited the kind PROTOTYPE to do the required explanatory work and so have (implicitly) endorsed the prototype theory of CONCEPT (e.g. Rosch, 1975). However, in other cases psychologists noted that categorisation of an individual *c* in a category *C* involves a judgement that *c* is sufficiently similar to salient members of *C*. In cases such as these, psychologists posit the kind EXEMPLAR to do the required explanatory work and so have (implicitly) endorsed the exemplar theory of CONCEPT (e.g. Nosofsky, 1986). Thus, we have two different theories of CONCEPT—prototype and exemplar theories—being exploited to explain two different types of categorisation judgement.

The standard view holds that a theory of CONCEPT will be a theory of a single representational kind. However, we have failed to come to an agreement about what kind of representations, with what kind of properties, concepts *are*. As a consequence, we have been left in a situation where different theories of CONCEPT are exploited for heterogeneous explanatory ends. Thus, our failure to decide on a best theory of CONCEPT has left us in an peculiar situation; one where we do not have a definitive theory of CONCEPT and we do not seem to need one. And this situation—where cognitive science proceeds without issue by assuming, at the same time, different theories of CONCEPT for different explanatory ends—has led some to question the standard view entirely. This idea is expressed neatly by Machery (2009, p. 100) as follows:

> If concepts have many properties in common, as the [standard] view would have it, then we would expect our categorization judgments to have many properties in common, and similarly for our episodes of inductive and deductive reasoning, the analogies we make, etc. But suppose that we empirically discover the existence of several types of categorization judgments that have few properties in common, of several types of episodes of inductive reasoning that have few properties in common, and so on. This discovery would be unexpected if the [standard] view were true and would plausibly undermine it.

Philosophers have long supposed that the standard view is correct. That is, that a theory of CONCEPT will be a theory of a single kind of mental representation. But we have not arrived at a single, best theory of this kind and, moreover, cognitive science has not faltered because of this failure. This state of affairs has given rise to an "explanatory challenge to the standard view," which holds that we should give up on the standard view-inspired idea that the best theory of CONCEPT will be a theory of a single kind of representation, because the explanatory work can only be done by a collection of different kinds of representations—e.g. IMAGE, DEFINITION, PROTOTYPE, EXEMPLAR, or THEORY-LIKE STRUCTURE—that do not store the same kinds of information or have the same functional properties (Bloch-Mullins, 2017; Machery, 2006). The argument for this conclusion runs as follows:

A. The explanatory challenge to the standard view:

1. The standard view holds that a theory of CONCEPT should be a theory of a single kind of representation. (Premise)
2. No theory of CONCEPT taking concepts to be a single kind of representation has been successful in accounting for all, or even most, of the phenomena related to the formation and application of concepts. (Premise)

---

3. Indicates: We should reject the standard view claim that a theory of CONCEPT should be a theory of a single kind of representation. (From A1 and A2)

This argument is now accepted by a growing number of philosophers and theorists of CONCEPT (cf. Piccinini and Scott, 2006; Machery, 2009; Weiskopf, 2009).

3.2 Responding to the Explanatory Challenge

In the current literature, one finds three possible responses to the "explanatory challenge to the standard view": concept eliminativism, concept pluralism, and concept hybridism. Not all of these theories of CONCEPT agree with the conclusions of the "explanatory challenge to the standard view," but all take the explanatory challenge seriously. I will now survey each of these theories in turn, using the notation of set theory to elucidate and compare the view of CONCEPT and CONCEPT's explanatory role that each theory defends.

3.2.1 Concept Eliminativism

Concept eliminativism is the position introduced and defended by Machery (2009) (cf. Machery, 2009; Machery, 2010). The theory of CONCEPT inspired by concept eliminativism is highly influenced by the "explanatory challenge to the standard view." So much so, in fact, that concept eliminativism argues that the class of objects that can be grouped under the kind CONCEPT is not of interest for cognitive science, because no theory of a single representational kind will yield scientifically interesting generalisations. Ultimately, then, concept eliminativism denies that we can develop a theory of the kind CONCEPT that adheres to the standard view and satisfies all of the desiderata (1)–(4). The upshot, for the eliminativist, is that we should reject the idea that the kind CONCEPT has an explanatory role in cognitive science.

Underpinning this claim is the "Heterogeneity Hypothesis," which consists of five tenants:
1. The best available evidence suggests that for each category (for each substance, event, and so on), an individual typically has several concepts.
2. Coreferential concepts have very few properties in common. Thus, coreferential concepts belong to very heterogeneous kinds of concept.
3. Evidence strongly suggests that prototypes, exemplars, and theories are among these heterogeneous kinds of concept.
4. Prototypes, exemplars, and theories are used in distinct cognitive processes.
5. The notion of concept ought to be eliminated from the theoretical vocabulary of psychology (Machery, 2009, p. 75).

For the eliminativist, therefore, there are potentially many different representations of one and the same thing. For example, for cats there could potentially be a cat-prototype representation, a cat-exemplar representation, and a cat-theory-like-structure representation. Thus, there could be at least three different tokens of mental representations standing for cats; namely p_{CAT} (the cat-prototype), e_{CAT} (the cat-exemplar), and t_{CAT} (the cat-theory-like-structure). And each and any of these representations can play a role in any cognitive task; e.g. categorisation, reasoning, meaning extraction etc. This idea was set out diagrammatically by Machery (2009, p. 60) and I have followed his lead in Fig. 3.1 below.

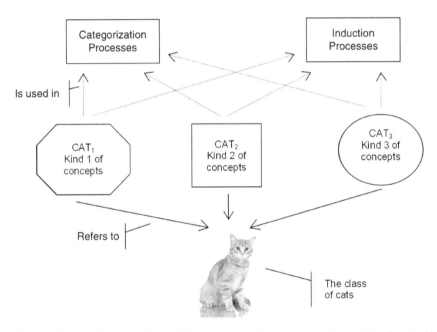

Fig. 3.1: The role of concepts in cognitive tasks according to concept eliminativism (inspired by Machery, 2009, p. 60).

The kind PROTOTYPE, for instance, can then be described as the set of all prototype tokens, where the defining property of this set is the (complex) property P of being a prototype, whatever that might be in detail:

$$PROTOTYPE = \{x \mid P(x)\} = \{p_{CAT}, p_{DOG}, \ldots\} \tag{3.1}$$

And the eliminativist interpretation of the kind CONCEPT can then be construed in one of two ways: either as the set of all representational kinds with the defining property, x, of figuring in scientific explanations of higher order cognitive capacities; or as the set of all representations with the complex property, C_E, where C_E is no more than the exclusive disjunction of the different defining properties of the explanatorily valuable kinds.

$$CONCEPT_{E_1} = \{x \mid x \text{ figuring in scientific explanations}\} =$$

$$= \{\{x_1 \mid P(x_1)\}, \{x_2 \mid E(x_2)\}, \{x_3 \mid T(x_3)\}\}$$

or

$$CONCEPT_{E_2} = \{x \mid C_E(x), \text{ where } \forall y \, (C_E(y) \leftrightarrow (P(y) \vee E(y) \vee T(y)))\} =$$

$$= \{p_{CAT}, e_{CAT}, t_{CAT}, p_{DOG}, e_{DOG}, t_{DOG}, \dots\} \tag{3.2}$$

The first set $CONCEPT_{E_1}$ is simply the set that contains all the different representational kinds as sets, which are in my example the set of all prototypes, the set of all exemplars, and the set of all theory-like structures; but could also include the set of all images, the set of all definitions etc. The second set $CONCEPT_{E_2}$ is the set that contains all tokens of the different representational kinds; so, it contains all prototypes (but not the set of all prototypes), all exemplars (but not the set of all exemplars), and all theory-like structures (but not the set of all theory-like structures). P_{CAT} is meant to stand for the cat-prototype, and the idea is that all such token prototypes are in $CONCEPT_{E_2}$ as well as all token exemplars and all token theory-like structures.

In both cases, however, $CONCEPT_{E_x}$ does not play an explanatory role in cognitive science: in the first case, because the defining property x is nothing more than a property of all the sets that play an explanatory role in cognitive science, and so does not play an explanatory role additional to the roles already played by its members. In the second case, because the complex property C_E is no more than the exclusive disjunction of the different defining properties of the explanatorily valuable kinds and so does nothing to further explain cognitive capacities. It follows that eliminativism affords CONCEPT no explanatory role, because all of the explanatory work is done on the level of representational kinds like PROTOTYPE, EXEMPLAR, and THEORY-LIKE STRUCTURE (Machery, 2009; Machery, 2010).

To illustrate why this is the case, consider the weird set that contains ELECTRON, GENE, and ANIMAL POPULATION as members. This set thus contains only kinds posited in scientific explanations:

{ELECTRON, GENE, ANIMAL POPULATION}

In this toy-example, whilst it may be the case that all of the members of the set either have the property of figuring in scientific explanation or have some defining properties of their own, it does not follow that the set {ELECTRON, GENE, ANIMAL POPULATION} is itself explanatory. Analogously for concept eliminativism, whilst it may be the case that PROTOTYPE, EXEMPLAR, THEORY-LIKE STRUCTURE all either have the property of figuring in scientific explanations or have some defining properties of their own, it does not follow that the defining properties C_E of the set of these representations—e.g. the set $CONCEPT_{E_x}$—is itself explanatory. This holds because PROTOTYPE, EXEMPLAR, and THEORY-LIKE STRUCTURE are all taken to figure in incommensurable scientific explanations of different cognitive processes, because their defining properties afford them different explanatory roles (cf. Machery, 2009, p. 251).[17]

The eliminativist, therefore, argues that the kind $CONCEPT_{E_x}$ does not yield to scientific generalisations and so is redundant in cognitive science (cf. Machery, 2009, Ch. 8). It follows that we should give up on the task of developing a theory of $CONCEPT_{E_x}$ that satisfies all of the desiderata (1)–(4).

3.2.2 Concept Pluralism

Another response to the "explanatory challenge to the standard view" comes from a view developed and endorsed by Weiskopf (2009): concept pluralism. Concept pluralism argues that we can develop a theory that satisfies all of the desiderata (1)–(4) and accounts for the explanatory role of CONCEPT as a single, unifying kind. However, in order to be able develop such a theory, concept pluralism offers a novel perspective on the kind CONCEPT itself. Like concept eliminativism, concept pluralism also assumes that there can be different kinds of representation for one thing, but it also holds that all explanatory representations have certain properties in common:

$$CONCEPT_P = \{x \mid C_P(x) : \text{where } \forall y \, ((P(y) \rightarrow C_P(y))$$

$$\wedge (E(y) \rightarrow C_P(y)) \wedge (T(y) \rightarrow C_P(y)))\} =$$

$$= \{p_{CAT}, e_{CAT}, t_{CAT}, p_{DOG}, e_{DOG}, t_{DOG}, \dots\} \tag{3.3}$$

---

17 This view is consistent with the claim that PROTOTYPE, EXEMPLAR, and THEORY-LIKE STRUCTURE are domain-specific representational kinds that are suited to explain only particular domains of higher cognition. And, if this is the right way of thinking, then eliminativism is right to argue that focusing on the explanatory role of CONCEPT only distracts us from developing more accurate and empirical verified explanations of the modular—that is, the encapsulated, dissociable, automatic, neurally localized, and centrally inaccessible—operation of components of cognitive systems (Carruthers, 2006, p. 62).

So, on the concept pluralist view, the "explanatory challenge to the standard view" is to accepted, because we cannot have a theory of CONCEPT that is a theory of objects with the same representational structure. However, concept pluralism submits that all concepts—whether they have different representational structures or not—will share some of the same properties; namely, C_P. These properties group different representational kinds into the single, unifying kind CONCEPT as "a functionally specified category, at the level of role or realizer" (Weiskopf, 2009, p. 147). As Weiskopf (2009, p. 147) explains, the idea here is that:

> Once we specify their explanatory or functional role, concepts *just are* whatever entities perform the relevant cognitive tasks. I suggest that concepts should be thought of as (1) mental representations that (2) are employed in categorization and (3) are capable of combining productively and systematically into larger and more complex structures.

Concept pluralism holds that the defining properties C_P of $CONCEPT_P$ are taken to be the functional properties of having (i) a logical form that allows for inferential processing; (ii) an ability to be combined; (iii) an ability to be acquired; and, finally, (iv) an ability to be stored, linked together, and retrieved by a set of memory processes (Weiskopf, 2009, pp. 163–167). All of the representational kinds that are members of the set $CONCEPT_P$ are taken to possess these functional properties; i.e. the "superordinate functional roles" that all members of $CONCEPT_P$ share and that are the defining properties of $CONCEPT_P$ as a set.[18]

So, for concept pluralism, the conceptual system is organised in such a way so as to be able to employ a variety of different representational structures all falling under the kind $CONCEPT_P$ in virtue of shared functional properties. And so although these representations may differ in the "kind of information they encode, some of the ways they are acquired and processed, the domains they favor, and the tasks that promote their use"; they all fall under the kind CONCEPT in virtue of their shared functional roles Weiskopf (2009, p. 155). The end result is that the pluralist accepts that many different kinds of concepts are stored in long term memory, as was illustrated schematically by Weiskopf (2009, p. 156) in Fig. 3.2 below. And so it is possible to develop a definitive theory of the kind CONCEPT: one that unifies all representations employed in higher cognitive tasks based upon their shared functional properties.

In contrast to concept eliminativism, concept pluralism reacts to the "explanatory challenge to the standard view" by arguing that the kind

---

18 As I have shown in chapter two, it is not necessarily clear how the all representational kinds are, say, be combined or acquired. Concept pluralism does not concern itself with this problem, but simply supposes that any representational kinds used in cognitive competences will have the functional properties (i)-(iv).

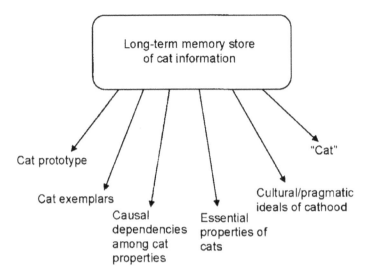

Fig. 3.2: The pluralist model of concepts as introduced by (Weiskopf, 2009, p. 156). Arrows indicate retrieval from long-term memory.

CONCEPT$_P$ does have an explanatory role in cognitive science, because the defining properties C_P of *CONCEPT*$_P$ have an explanatory role that cannot be reduced to the explanatory role of the properties P, E, T etc. of the kinds PROTOTYPE, EXEMPLAR, THEORY-LIKE STRUCTURE etc. Thus, from the perspective of concept pluralism, *CONCEPT*$_P$ has an explanatory role to play in cognitive science, albeit to answer to "top-level [explanatory] demands" that "tend to favor unification" (Weiskopf, 2009, p. 167).[19]

To make perspicuous the explanatory role of *CONCEPT*$_P$, consider the explanatory role that *CONCEPT*$_P$ is afforded in virtue of possessing the defining, functional property (i): having a logical form that allows for inferential processing. According to concept pluralism, if it can be shown that all representational kinds that are member of *CONCEPT*$_P$ have an internal, logical structure, "then it is reasonable to suppose that there are mental processes that are sensitive to that structure, rather than to the particular concepts that are being combined in that structure" (Weiskopf, 2009, p. 163). By then identifying formal inference processes that generalise over different representational kinds—e.g. the inference process that runs from 'dogs are mammals and canines' to 'dogs are mammals' and 'dogs

---

19 Consider the explanatory value of the kind MAMMAL, which answers to top-level explanatory demands in the same way that, e.g., RODENTS, UNGULATES, and PRIMATES answer to bottom-level explanatory demands.

are canines'—concept pluralists argue that the different representational kinds do, in fact, share the functional property of playing the same syntactic role in inferential thought.

Therefore, the explanatory import of $CONCEPT_P$ is justified because it is only by formulating propositions featuring $CONCEPT_P$—e.g. "all representations have the same inferential role in thought in virtue of being members of $CONCEPT_P$"— that we can explain the inferential nature of thought *in general*, instead of having to formulate as many different explanations of inferential processing as there are representational kinds in the set $CONCEPT_P$. The same reasoning applies to concept pluralism's discussion of the functional properties (ii), (iii), and (iv) above. For example, in the case of (iii), concept pluralism argues that modes of acquisition are not sensitive to representational subkinds, because all representational kinds are acquired in the same way.

For concept pluralism, then, the explanatory import of $CONCEPT_P$ is that it makes possible the formulation of propositions—e.g. 'all representation are acquired in processes involving x, y, z in virtue of being members of $CONCEPT_P$'— that explain the acquisition of mental states in general, instead of having to formulate as many different explanations of the acquisition of mental states as there are representational kinds in the set $CONCEPT_P$. It follows that the kind $CONCEPT_P$ has a higher-order explanatory role in cognitive science. And it is by developing a theory of $CONCEPT_P$ in these terms that we can have a theory of CONCEPT that satisfies all of the desiderata (1)–(4) and accounts for the explanatory role of CONCEPT as a single, unifying kind.

3.2.3 Concept Hybridism

Concept hybridism concurs with concept pluralism that a theory of CONCEPT can be developed that satisfies all of the desiderata (1)–(4) and accounts for the explanatory role of CONCEPT as a single, unifying kind. However, concept hybridism rejects the "explanatory challenge to the standard view." This is the case because concept hybridism doubts that PROTOTYPE, EXEMPLAR, and THEORY-LIKE STRUCTURE constitute disjunctive kinds. Whereas eliminativism and pluralism assume that every mental representation falls into exactly one of the representational kinds PROTOTYPE, EXEMPLAR, THEORY-LIKE STRUCTURE etc., hybridism assumes that a single mental representation can fall into two or even three of these kinds at the same time. In this way, concept hybridism asserts that the best theory of CONCEPT will be a theory of objects with the same representational structure. In the case of hybridism, therefore, my example reads:

$$CONCEPT_H = \{x \mid C_H(x)\} = \{x_{CAT}, x_{DOG}, \dots\}$$

$$\{x \mid P(x)\}, \{x \mid E(x)\}, \{x \mid T(x)\} \subseteq CONCEPT_H{}^{20} \tag{3.4}$$

Thus, the elements of $CONCEPT_H$ do not necessarily possess only one of the properties P, E T etc.; they may possess all of these properties at the same time. Accordingly, $CONCEPT_H$ is a set of "integrated representations" that have PROTO-TYPE-like, EXEMPLAR-like, and THEORY-LIKE STRUCTURE-like pieces of information as their parts. The elements of the set denoted by $CONCEPT_H$ are not, therefore, taken to be the finer-grained representational kinds PROTOTYPE, EXEMPLAR, and THEORY-LIKE STRUCTURE etc., but, rather, are taken to be "richly structured representations" that have the potential to encode all of the pieces of information ordinarily taken to be encoded by the disjoint set of representational kinds. As Vicente and Martinez Manrique (2014) put it:

> In a nutshell, the idea [of concept hybridism] is that different structures can be regarded as constituting a common representation when they are activated concurrently, in a way that is functionally significant for the task at hand, and in patterns that remain substantially stable along different tasks related to the same category.

From the perspective of concept hybridism, therefore, the explanatory relevance of the kind CONCEPT cannot lie in an additional property that mental representations share. Indeed, the defining property C_H of $CONCEPT_H$ might be nothing but the disjunctive property of the properties of PROTOTYPE, EXEMPLAR and THEORY-LIKE-STRUCTURE etc., such that $\forall x(C_H(x) \leftrightarrow (P(x) \lor E(x) \lor T(x)))$. As such, the decisive difference between $CONCEPT_H$ and $CONCEPT_E$ is that the $\lor$ is to be understood as exclusive in the case of eliminativism, but as inclusive in the case of hybridism.

Therefore, the two sets $CONCEPT_H$ and $CONCEPT_E$ contain very different elements. The first ($CONCEPT_H$) contains mental representations that have different functionally integrated aspects; namely, prototype-aspects, exemplar-aspects, theory-like structural aspects, and so on. The second ($CONCEPT_P$) contains prototypes, exemplars, theory-like structures, and so on, that have no common aspects. Moreover, the inclusive disjunction endorsed by concept hybridism makes it the case that while two elements of $CONCEPT_H$ need not share a single property, some may share two and some may share all three. For example, the concept ELECTRON might have only a theory-like structural aspect, while the concept DWARF might have only a prototype-aspect. However, it is likely

---

20 Since some concepts might not have all different kinds of aspects, the set of, say, prototypes might be only a subset of the set of concepts.

that most representations that are the elements of $CONCEPT_H$ will have multiple aspects in common.

Concept hybridism supposes that $CONCEPT_H$ is relevant to explanation because it makes transparent the interplay of different aspects of individual mental representations in cognitive tasks according to patterns of functional integration. Thus, for the hybridist, it does not make sense to assume that PROTOTYPE, EXEMPLAR, THEORY-LIKE-STRUCTURE etc. are mutually exclusive kinds with no overlap. Instead, a single representational token is posited—a member of $CONCEPT_H$— that possesses all of the different properties of the kinds PROTOTYPE, EXEMPLAR, THEORY-LIKE-STRUCTURE etc. at once without enforcing an internal hierarchy. It follows as a matter of course that explanations in cognitive science need not be confined to one specific aspect, but can appeal to the different aspects are functionally integrated in members of $CONCEPT_H$ concepts. The explanatory role of $CONCEPT_H$ is to make this distinction clear.

Concept hybridists argue that their theory supports better—that is, more powerful—explanations of cognition, because we can explain efficiency and variability in cognitive tasks in terms of a switching between the different kinds of information encoded by members of the set $CONCEPT_H$. This follows because the members of the set $CONCEPT_H$ are thought of as being "integrated concepts" instead of as representations belonging to only one representational kind; e.g. PROTOTYPE, EXEMPLAR, THEORY-LIKE STRUCTURE etc. To make this idea explicit, consider the claim by concept hybridists that we fare better in explaining categorisation if we presuppose $CONCEPT_H$ and so posit integrated representation that have PROTOTYPE-like, EXEMPLAR-like, THEORY-LIKE STRUCTURE-like etc. parts.

According to the hybridist, we fare better in explaining categorisation if we assume concept hybridism because we can appeal to the interrelated and complementary functional roles played by the integrated parts of representations in $CONCEPT_H$, depending on background factors and the task at hand (Vicente and Martínez Manrique, 2014, p. 73). For instance, we can appeal to typicality effects associated with the PROTOTYPE-like part to explain why a four-legged, barking object is categorised as a dog; but, equally, we can appeal to essences associated with the THEORY-LIKE STRUCTURE-like part to explain why we categorise 'Bobby' as a dog after hearing the sentence, 'we left Bobby in the garden to play with his chew-toy.'[21] The point, then, is that $CONCEPT_H$ will have an explanatory role in cognitive science, because without $CONCEPT_H$ we could not formulate

---

21 In cognitive science, a number of models of categorisation have already been developed that account for categorisation effects by appealing to the interplay of more than one kind of representational structure (cf. Erickson and Kruschke, 1998; Anderson and Betz, 2001).

explanatory propositions—e.g. 'categorisation involves comparing input with a dog concept, DOG_H, across various pieces of information'—that best explain the explananda of cognitive science.

In a similar vein, concept hybridists argue that their theory supports better explanations of meaning extraction. In this case, concept hybridists hold that we fare better if we posit integrated representations, because we can then provide explanations of the linguistic comprehension of lexical items in terms of our switching between different pieces of encoded information depending on the context (Vicente and Martínez Manrique, 2014, p. 77). For instance, we can formulate explanations that account for the processing of the lexical item 'dog' in terms of accessing the single rich concept DOG_H, even if only some parts of this concept come to be selected. In this way, the explanation can appeal to the survey and selection of the best suited information for a given task in a given context, because all information is "active and functional in meaning extraction," even if only some pieces are selected for processing to a greater or lesser extent (Vicente and Martínez Manrique, 2014, p. 81). And, again, the fact that such better explanations of meaning extraction are possible only if we endorse $CONCEPT_H$ is enough for the hybridist to assert that $CONCEPT_H$ must have an explanatory role in cognitive science.

Vicente and Martínez Manrique (2014) do not spell out what they mean by functional coactivation in operational terms; i.e. in terms that account for how functional integration would be manifested in the data to be explained. Therefore, one could argue that it remains unclear what exactly the explanatory advantage of their conception is. To illustrate, consider that the effects described above can be just as well explained by a concept pluralist, if the pluralist introduces an additional premise that there are context-specific processes that activate other concepts if needed.

One could assume that the best data speaking against such a pluralist plus cross-activation account would be data showing that the switching between different kinds of concepts is too fast and too easy—i.e. too reliable—to involve another cognitive mechanism. For example, if two kinds of concepts are needed for the comprehension of a single sentence, such as in "Linda can afford to keep Bobby the dog, because chew-toys and dog licence fees are not too expensive," it could be measured whether hearers need additional time to activate T_{DOG} related to the dog licence fee after having already activated P_{DOG} related to the chew-toy. If not, we have good reasons to think that theory-like structural and the prototypical pieces of information are "functionally integrated" within a single dog-representation. If this were the case, then timing would be the relevant explanandum that could be explained by the hybridist but not by the pluralist.[22]

In any case, this discussion of how best to compare concept hybridism and concept pluralism can be bracketed when it comes to evaluating concept hybridism's response to the "explanatory challenge to the standard view." In this regard, things are perfectly clear: concept hybridism holds that the "explanatory challenge to the standard view" is wrong; by developing a theory of $CONCEPT_H$ we can have a theory of CONCEPT that satisfies all of the desiderata (1)–(4) and is a theory of a single representational kind.

3.3 The Meta-Explanatory Challenge

I have shown in this chapter that eliminativist, pluralist, and hybrid theories of CONCEPT disagree about the explanatory role of CONCEPT in virtue of endorsing three different interpretations of the kind CONCEPT; that is, in virtue of endorsing $CONCEPT_E$, $CONCEPT_P$, and $CONCEPT_H$ respectively. In this way, eliminativist, pluralist, and hybrid theories of CONCEPT respond differently to the "explanatory challenge to the standard view," because they disagree about whether or not CONCEPT should have an explanatory role in cognitive science in virtue of disagreeing about whether CONCEPT is a heuristic grouping of different representational kinds, a grouping of different representational kinds in terms of their shared functional properties, or, in fact, a grouping a kinds with the same representational structure.

---

22 At this stage, it is also worth mentioning a relatively recent theory of CONCEPT as set out by Bloch-Mullins (2017): concept integrationism. Concept integrationists argue that the kind CONCEPT is a grouping of representations that are integrated with respect to the kinds of statistical and causal information they store. In essence, therefore, concept integrationism cannot be distinguished from concept hybridism, because both reject the idea that the information stored by concepts is compartmentalised. Thus, I think we can classify concept hybridism and concept integrationism together. With this in mind, we can view the integrated model for classification and categorisation developed by Bloch-Mullins (2017, pp. 18–21) as complimentary to the concept hybridist perspective discussed here. This follows because the "integrated theory" of CONCEPT she develops agrees that "the various elements of the concept are activated concurrently and have some functional significance for the task at hand" (Bloch-Mullins, 2017, p. 23). Although there is room for confusion—especially given that Bloch Mullins argues that concepts are not "constituted by several 'parts', which store distinct types of knowledge and which functionally interact—it is clear that the differences between the two views are negligible, because both deny that the elements of concepts are "semi-separable in the quasi-modular sense" (Bloch-Mullins, 2017; Vicente and Martínez Manrique, 2014, cf.).

The dispute between eliminativist, pluralist, and hybrid theories of CONCEPT illustrates that the debate about how best to theorise about CONCEPT has not yet been settled. We still do not yet know whether or not to accept or reject the standard view idea that a theory of CONCEPT will be a theory of a single kind of representation; just as we do not yet know whether it is worthwhile to theorise about CONCEPT at all. One response to this uncertainty would be to once again appeal to the explanatory results of cognitive science and to endorse the theory of CONCEPT that is most consistent with these results. Thus, we find ourselves at a kind of meta-appeal to cognitive science, whereby we appeal to cognitive science to decide between those theories of CONCEPT—e.g. eliminativist, pluralist, and hybrid theories of CONCEPT—that were inaugurated as a result of a first appeal to cognitive science.

The meta-appeal to cognitive science differs from the appeal to cognitive science discussed in section 3.1 above, because it concerns the competition between different "new" theories of CONCEPT that take for granted that we store different bodies of information—e.g. at least prototype-like, exemplar-like bodies of information—in long term memory. In other words, the meta-appeal to cognitive science differs from the appeal to cognitive science, because it is not about choosing between imagist, definitionist, prototype, exemplar, or theory theories of CONCEPT; but, instead, is about choosing between higher-order theories of CONCEPT, which accept that none of the aforementioned theories of CONCEPT are adequate on their own. Still the dialectic is the same: appealing to empirical research to determine which theory of CONCEPT is to be favoured.

The working assumption of the meta-appeal to cognitive science is that the dispute between "new" theories of CONCEPT will be settled by considering cognitive scientific explanations of cognitive competencies. On this argument, the tension between eliminativist, pluralist, and hybrid theories of CONCEPT will be dissolved when we empirically uncover the workings of cognition, because we will then be able to decide whether or not the representations stored in long term memory belong to disconnected kinds (eliminativism), can be unified by shared functional roles (pluralism), or are a single kind of integrated representations storing prototype-like, exemplar-like, theory-like structure-like etc. information (hybridism). It would then be a simple task to decide whether or not we expect theories of CONCEPT to be theories of a single representational kind, which satisfies desiderata (1)–(4). There is a problem here, however, concerning an incompatibility in eliminativist, pluralist, and hybrid specifications of the explananda of cognitive science.

At a superficial level, eliminativist, pluralist, and hybrid theories of CONCEPT all take cognitive science to have the same explananda: (the operations of) cognition. As a result, all three theories seem to accept that the relevant explananda associated with the positing of CONCEPT are, for instance, the kinds of category judgements and inferential processing taking place in the mind. One may suppose, therefore, that there is significant overlap between eliminativist, pluralist, and hybrid theories of CONCEPT with regards to their specifications of the explananda of cognitive science. If we dig a little deeper, however, fissures begin to appear in the descriptions of the explananda favoured by eliminativist, pluralist, and hybrid theories of CONCEPT.

Consider the explanandum of category judgements as an illustration of this idea. All theories of CONCEPT will begin from the same patterns in data; typically, data that evidences particular behaviours including, but not limited to, the identification and discrimination of objects according to diagnostic features and/or properties. For the eliminativist, however, category judgements must come in a diverse number of kinds. There will be category judgements involving at least the kinds PROTOTYPE, EXEMPLAR, and THEORY-LIKE STRUCTURE; each different with respect to the salient properties identified and processed in any instance of categorising an individual c in a category C. It follows, for the eliminativist, that category judgements is not one explanandum, but several.

Like the eliminativist, the pluralist will accept that category judgements come in a diverse number of kinds. For the pluralist, however, category judgements will only constitute one explanandum, because any given kind of category judgement involving any given kind of representation can be explained by the shared functional properties of all representational kinds. Thus, the pluralist recognises a general ability to categorise. The hybridist concurs with the pluralist that there is only one explanandum of category judgements, but for different reasons. For the hybridist, the explanandum of category judgements does not even divide into a diverse number of different kinds of category judgements involving different representational kinds. This is the case because the hybridist takes all category judgements to involve only one representational kind: integrated and richly structured representations. Thus, the explanandum of category judgements is specified in three different ways by eliminativist, pluralist, and hybrid theories of CONCEPT even where the data to be explained—the evidence of people undertaking categorisation tasks—is the same.

The same pattern can be observed in the way eliminativist, pluralist, and hybrid theories of CONCEPT specify the explanandum of inferential processing. In this case, eliminativists specify that there are as many different explananda of inferential processing as there are representational kinds; pluralist specify that even if there are many different kinds of inferential processing, all can be subsumed under the single explanandum of our general (and conceptual) ability to inferentially process; and hybridists specify that there is only one kind of inferential processing (involving integrated representations) and so there is only one explanandum of inferential processing for cognitive science to explain. The same will be true of their respective specifications of other explananda; for instance, the combination of mental representations. Thus, we find that eliminativist, pluralist, and hybrid theories of CONCEPT specify the explananda of cognitive science differently even when they agree on the data to be explained.

Moreover, it is not always the case that these theories agree about how to interpret the data to be explained. An example of this state of affairs is the relevance of chronometric data for cognitive science. The eliminativist, for example, will likely deny that timing in task switching scenarios is an explanandum of cognitive science and so will eschew the relevance of chronometric data.[23] The reason for this is because chronometric data could never support the eliminativist position, because even if it could be shown that the diachronic switching between different kinds of concepts is fast and easy—i.e. reliable—, still the eliminativist would deny that the two different kinds of concepts share any properties. More concretely: even if two kinds of concepts were needed for the comprehension of a single sentence, such as in "Linda can afford to keep Bobby the dog, because chew-toys and dog licence fees are not too expensive," the eliminativist would have no interest in measuring whether hearers need additional time to activate T_{DOG} related to the dog licence fee after having already activated P_{DOG} related to the chew-toy.

Of course, another possibility is that the eliminativist just overlooks such chronometric data, but is ready to concede their relevance. In this case, the data could turn into empirical counter-evidence to eliminativism. Still another possibility is to find an explanation of such chronometric data consistent with eliminativism. My purpose in discussing chronometric data is not to deny these possibilities, but rather to provide an example of how the interaction between a theory and its explananda could influence the interpretation of the data favoured.

To make this point concrete, consider first the explananda of working memory. *Prima facie*, the data regarding working memory limitation seems to be shared by all cognitive scientists. However, we find competing explanations of working memory limitations. Miller (1956), for instance, argued that the capacity of working memory is 7 ± 2 objects (or chunks of information). Later, however, Baddeley (1992) proposed a more detailed account of working memory with different sub-

---

23 One will certainly not find any explicit rejection of the relevance of chronometric data in the writings of eliminativists such as Machery, but this is unsurprising. To mention such data would be to concede that such data is relevant for cognitive science, which serves only to undermine the eliminativist's position with respect to competing theories of CONCEPT. So even though the existence of chronometric data does not depend on the theory of CONCEPT one adopts, one's conception of what cognitive science aims to explain can cause such data to be irrelevant. In this sense, the data in question become "invisible" as explananda.

systems; among them the "phonological loop" of about two seconds, the average time needed to speak about seven words in English (see also Baddeley, 1996).

This difference in the explanation/explananda of working memory corresponds to a difference in interpretations of the data evidencing working memory: while an information-theoretic approach measuring amounts of information is the obvious choice for Miller, such accounts could not explain the data when interpreted in accordance with Baddeley's specification of the explananda. Within Baddeley's model, therefore, explanations based on the articulatory apparatus are much more promising.[24] The upshot is that the data to be explained—e.g. data regarding learned responses to stimuli—are interpreted differently by the two theories: one takes it as evidence for limitations on the storage of chunks of information; the other as evidence for limitation on the storage of auditory memory traces.

Another example concerns our capacity to reason with conditionals as tested in the famous Wason Selection Task (Wason, 1968; Wason and Shapiro, 1971). If the conditional rule that is to be tested is formulated in an abstract way (e.g. "if there is a vowel on the one side of a card, there is an even number on the other side"), subjects perform poorly when compared to the solution that is correct according to standard sentential logic of the if-then-operator interpreted as material implication. However, if the rule is more concrete (e.g. "if a person is drinking alcohol, he must be older than 21 years"), the accuracy of subjects' reasoning improves dramatically. This is sometimes referred to as the "content effect."

Given this data, one possibility is to specify the explanandum of cognitive science as the capacity of conditional reasoning, which is modulated by another factor; namely, the content of the rule. Another possibility—taken by, e.g., Cosmides and Tooby (1992)—is to deny that there is such a thing as the capacity of conditional reasoning at all, but only a capacity to deal with social rules. Thus, even though both would agree that data about the "content effect" is something that has to be taken into account in the explanation of the phenomena, they still interpret that same data in different ways: one takes it as evidence for the interaction of the capacity of conditional reasoning with some other aspect of cognition; that other takes it as evidence that the capacity of conditional reasoning should be eschewed altogether as an explanandum of cognitive science.

The problem, therefore, is that cross-theoretical agreement about the data (or the interpretation of the data) to be explained is not always apparent. In the context of our discussion about theories of CONCEPT, the eliminativist will likely reject the idea that chronometric data is relevant for cognitive science. This can

---

24 Since this is only an illustrative example, I am not trying to evaluate the two approaches at all. Of course, there has been further research concerning working memory than presented here.

be seen as analogous to Baddeley's (1992) refusal to interpret the data as show-ing that people remember a certain amount of information; and Cosmides and Tooby's (1992) refusal to interpret that data as evidence for a general capacity of conditional reasoning that is modulated by other factors. And where there is no cross-theoretical agreement about how to interpret the data to be explained, we find ourselves at a loss when it comes to evaluating competing theories by appeal to cognitive science.

Thus, if one thinks that the explanandum of category judgements ought to involve only one representational kind, then one has good reason for endorsing $CONCEPT_H$. But if one thinks that the explanandum of category judgements ought to involve many representational kinds, then one has good reason for endorsing either $CONCEPT_E$ or $CONCEPT_P$; depending, that is, on one's views about the superordinate unity of those kinds. Thus, we find that one's view on the explananda of cognitive science—and, hence, on the interpretation and (ir)relevance of certain bodies of data—bias one towards a certain theory of CONCEPT; just as one's theory of CONCEPT biases one towards a certain view on the explananda of cognitive science. As a result, any appeal to cognitive science will be futile. Thus, we can formulate a "meta-explanatory challenge" to deciding between eliminativist, pluralist, and hybrid theories of CONCEPT as follows:

B. The meta-explanatory challenge to new theories of CONCEPT:

1. "New" theories of CONCEPT disagree about explananda of cog-nitive science and how to interpret relevant bodies of data. (Premise)

---

2. Indicates: Cognitive science cannot help us to decide which new theory of CONCEPT to favour. (From B1)

---

3. Indicates: Even after rejecting the standard view, appealing to cognitive science does not help us to decide on the "best" theory of CONCEPT. (From B2)

3.4 The Meta-Explanatory Challenge Defended

Now, one may think that the "meta-explanatory challenge" goes too quick, because it simply assumes that there will be a disagreement between the "new" theories of CONCEPT about how to specify of the explananda of cognitive science. Plausibly, then, one may think that it is at least possible for eliminativist, pluralist, and hybrid theories of CONCEPT to have a shared specification of the explananda of cognitive science in such a way that would undermine the apparent disagreements between them. For example, one may think it is possible to follow Cummins (2000, p. 120) and argue that the explananda of cognitive science should be divided into primary and undiscovered *capacities*—e.g. "to see depth, to learn and speak a language, to plan, to predict the future, to empathize, to fathom the mental states of others" (Cummins, 2000, pp. 124–125) —and secondary and discovered *effects*— e.g. well confirmed regularities that can be specified as laws *in situ* that "restate the phenomenon in more general terms" (Cummins, 2000, p. 120).[25] Working from this premise, one could argue that:

> the explanation of incidental effects [...] have little interest in their own right: no one would construct a theory just to explain them. But their successful explanation can often be crucial to the assessment of theories or models designed to explain the core capacities that are the primary targets of psychological inquiry (Cummins, 2000, p. 128).

Accordingly, one could submit the following counter-argument to the "meta-explanatory challenge": the disagreement between eliminativist, pluralist, and hybrid theories of CONCEPT is about the effects identified by cognitive science and not about the capacities that cognitive science aims to explain. If this counter-argument were right, then the dispute between these theories would not be about the explananda of cognitive science *tout court*, but would be about fine-grained explanatory issues found at the level of effects; for instance, the speed of categorisation and shifts in categorisation when different aspects of the stimuli are emphasised (Ahn and Kim, 2000; Ahn and Dennis, 2001). In Cummins' terms, the dispute would be about "what happens" and not "why or how."

This counter-argument, however, fails to appreciate the difficulty in differentiating between capacities and effects when we factor in the contradictory viewpoints endorsed by the different theories of CONCEPT. For it is clear that specifying the explananda of cognitive science in terms of both capacities and effects is highly non-trivial. Cummins (2000, 127) himself states that "it can be a matter of substantive controversy whether we are looking at an exercise of a capacity or an incidental effect." This controversy is heightened in the case of the debate between different theories of CONCEPT, because the question of how to draw the line between capacities and effects cannot be conveniently segregated from a deeper question about what the capacities are in the first place.

---

25 A good example of an effect would be the McGurk effect, which can be paraphrased as a law that states that one will have the illusion of hearing a particular sound when the auditory component of another sound is paired with the visual component of yet another sound.

For example, one could argue—in accord with the pluralist—that differences in categorisation judgements involving different kinds of representations are merely effects incidental to the exercise of a superordinate capacity to categorise. But, equally, one could take the eliminativist view that there are as many different capacities to categorise as there are representational kinds operative in cognition. And this highlights an important point; namely, that there will be no agreement between eliminativists, pluralists, and hybridists about how to enact a functional analysis that delivers a demarcation between capacities and effects. Thus there will be no agreement about which explanations best explain either capacities or effects, or about the structure of the system giving rise to both capacities and effects.[26]

The same point can be made against those who would argue that the "meta-explanatory challenge" does not consider in enough detail the explanatory targets of working cognitive scientists. For example, those who insist that working cognitive scientists could never get on board with CONCEPT eliminativism, because the kind CONCEPT is to them an indispensable explanatory tool. Keil (2010, p. 216), for instance, argues that there will be "a strong tendency to resist" the claim that there are "an indefinitely large number" of representations operative in cognition (e.g. p_{DOG}, e_{DOG}, t_{DOG}, p_{CAT}, e_{CAT}, t_{CAT}...). Underlying this claim is the worry articulated by Hampton (2010, p. 212) that:

> the term "concept" is needed as part of an account of the many situations in which PET systems [(e.g. PROTOTYPES, EXEMPLARS, and THEORY-LIKE STRUCTURES representations)] interact. How does one discuss concept combination, including the formation of composite prototypes, the importing of exemplar knowledge, and the coherence checking of the result through background theory, if one cannot have the integrative term "concept" to specify just what it is that is being combined. The combination occurs at the concept level, and the description of the processes involved then requires elaboration in terms of the PET systems.

The counter-argument, therefore, is that given the state of cognitive scientific research there are some explananda—e.g. explananda that require cross-representational processing such as "concept combination"—that demand that CONCEPT be afforded an explanatory role in cognitive science. The problem, however, is that one need not endorse the claim that putative explananda involving cross-representational processing are part of the explanatory remit of cognitive science. Instead, one may think that the composition of PROTOTYPES is distinct from the composition of EXEMPLARS and THEORY-LIKE STRUCTURES; the use of EXEMPLAR

---

26 Note that I do not want to take a stand on how we should specify the explananda of cognition. Rather, I only want to show that different specifications are possible but will be mutually contradictory.

knowledge is distinct from the use of PROTOTYPE and THEORY-LIKE STRUCTURE knowledge; and that coherence checking is limited to one representation kind at a time.

Thus, in terms of Cummins' distinction, one may hold that the capacities associated with each kind of representation are distinct and that the specification of an effect of cross-representational processing fails to pick out a regular behavioural pattern characteristic of the structure of cognition. This strictly modular view of cognitive structure may strike some as unappealing, but it will dovetail with the specification of the explananda favoured by the eliminativist and with the eliminativist's view on CONCEPT's explanatory role.[27]

The upshot is that the appeal to the working of explanatory interests of cognitive scientists underdetermines the specification of the explananda. For while it is true that many cognitive scientists have been willing to characterise behavioural patterns as characteristic of a particular kind of structure responsible for cross-representational processing, it is also true that all cognitive scientists need not characterise the same behavioural patterns in the same way. For instance, one may characterise an infant's switch from PROTOTYPE-based categorisation judgements to THEORY-LIKE STRUCTURE-based categorisation judgements in terms of a structure responsible for cross-representational processing (Keil, 1989). But, equally, one may characterise the same switch as a binary change in the operation of two, distinct capacities: the capacity to categorise using PROTOTYPES and the capacity to categorise using THEORY-LIKE STRUCTURES. The point, then, is that one cannot assume *ex ante* what the capacity or capacities for conceptual change consists in, because it is possible that the switch in development from categorising with PROTOTYPES to categorising with THEORY-LIKE STRUCTURES is a mere incidental effect. According to the "meta-explanatory challenge," the view one takes on these matters will cohere with the theory of CONCEPT and of CONCEPT's explanatory role one favours.

Note, that the "meta-explanatory challenge" should not be taken as an argument for the claim that a unification of cognitive science is, in principle, impossible. Rather, the "meta-explanatory challenge" should be taken as argument for the

---

27 It is worth making explicit at this point that the claim of the "meta-explanatory challenge" is not that there are *no* reasons to accept one or another theory of CONCEPT. Of course, one could find any number of reasons; for example, reasons concerned with putative theoretical virtues such as *beauty*, *simplicity*, and *coherency* (cf. Keas, 2018, for a good summary of such virtues); or sociological reasons concerned with one's experience with and preference for distinct explanatory tools or one's institutional embedding. The only argument, then, is that the explanatory success of theoretical terms like CONCEPT cannot be determined independent of a theory, and thus there is no out-of-theory reason to accept this or that ontological claim about the existence of such things as concepts.

claim that we do not currently have an agreement about what cognitive science aims to explain; as evidenced by the fact that different theories of CONCEPT take cognitive science to be targeting different explananda. Although it is clear that are overlaps in what different theories of CONCEPT take cognitive science to be in the business of explaining, there is also enough disagreement to undermine the search for a definitive account of CONCEPT's explanatory role. Thus, to make progress in this regard we would first have to arrive at a *consensus* specification of the explananda of cognitive science.

To decide between theories of CONCEPT, it seems therefore that we would first have to find a way to settle the explananda of cognitive science. But this cannot be easily achieved. To illustrate this point, consider the following two explananda: (a) a stick half under water that looks bent even though it is not; and (b) two lines of the same length, one with inward pointing arrow heads, the other with outward pointing arrow heads, which look like they are of different length even though they are not (the "Müller-Lyer-Illusion"). The first explanandum is one of optics, the second is one of psychology of perception. Accordingly, the first is easily explained by the laws of optics, whereas the second is not; to explain the second phenomenon, we need to appeal to basic psychological principles of perception that are not related to the laws of optics.

However, why (a) and (b) belong to the subject matter of different disciplines is not *prima facie* obvious, and I doubt that there could be a specification of the explananda that would make the difference clear, unless that specification already presupposes the difference between optics and psychology. For example, one could try to specify that (a) is an explanandum belonging to the subject matter of optics and (b) an explanandum belonging to psychology by arguing that everything in front of the retina is optics; and since (the image of) the stick is bent on the retina but (the images of) the two lines are not of different sizes on the retina, the first would be specified as an optical phenomenon and the second not. However, this specification already presupposes that optics is confined to certain visual phenomena and psychology to the processing of visual phenomena, which presupposes a certain understanding of the disciplines and their subject matter, which then biases our specifications of the explanandum itself.[28]

---

28 One can see clearly here how finding better specifications of the explananda is part of the remit of science. For example, as soon as the "Müller-Lyer-Illusion" is identified as a psychological explanandum, psychology will find better specifications of the phenomenon giving rise to the explanandum; that is, that it is a phenomenon made manifest by a default heuristic in the visual system that processes the configuration of angled lines so as to optimise judgements about depth and distance (Gregory, 1966).

As with my example of the specification of explananda (a) and (b), eliminativist, pluralist, and hybrid theories of CONCEPT endorse specifications of the explananda of cognitive science that dovetail with their understanding of the discipline and its subject matter. The overall conclusion, therefore, is that the "meta-explanatory challenge to new theories of CONCEPT" can only be overcome when we reach an agreement on the explananda of cognitive science. We cannot hope to appeal to cognitive science to help us decide between competing theories of CONCEPT until this happens. This follows because in our evaluation of different theories of CONCEPT by appeal to cognitive science can only succeed where we have a theory-neutral standard of epistemic justification by which to compare the explanations and explananda-specifications favoured by eliminativist, pluralist, and hybrid theories of CONCEPT (Appley and Stoutenburg, 2017; Poston, 2016; Stoutenburg, 2015).

3.5 Summary

The long-standing assumption in the philosophy of concepts is that we can arrive at a best theory of CONCEPT. Traditionally, it was thought that the best theory of CONCEPT would adhere to the standard view, which holds that a theory of CONCEPT should be a theory of a single representational kind. As a result, a great variety of theories of CONCEPT were developed, which each gave an account of the unique representational structure of all objects falling under the kind CONCEPT (e.g. imagist, definitionist, prototype, exemplar, theory theory, hybrid, and integrationist). However, we have been unable to decide between these theories of CONCEPT, because different theories of CONCEPT better satisfy different desiderata (chapter two).

One potential way of making progress is to endorse the theory of CONCEPT most consistent with the explanatory results of cognitive science. However, appealing to cognitive science fails to decide between theories of CONCEPT adhering to the standard view, because many different theories of CONCEPT have been exploited by cognitive scientists in their explanations of higher cognitive competences. Therefore, some philosophers have come to a radical conclusion: that we should abandon the standard view altogether. Following this "explanatory challenge to the standard view," "new" theories of CONCEPT have been developed, which conceive of the kind CONCEPT in new and highly revisionary ways.

For example, an eliminativist theory CONCEPT has been developed, which asserts that the grouping of objects falling under the kind CONCEPT does not possess scientifically relevant properties, such that the kind CONCEPT is a mere heuristic grouping of differently structured objects (e.g. CONCEPT eliminativism). So has a pluralist theory of CONCEPT, which asserts that that the objects falling under the kind CONCEPT are, in fact, higher-order functional properties shared by representational structures (e.g. CONCEPT pluralism). And, finally, so has a hybrid theory of CONCEPT, which asserts that all objects falling under the kind CONCEPT do have the same representational structure, but only because the posited representational structures integrate many different bodies of information.

We have found, therefore, that even after appealing to cognitive science and rejecting the standard view a number of viable theories of CONCEPT are left open. The question, then, is how to decide between these "new" theories of CONCEPT. The hope might be that a further—and, perhaps, closer—examination of the results of cognitive science will be sufficient for deciding between these theories of CONCEPT. But I have argued that we face a problem here: the fact that eliminativist, pluralist, and hybrid theories of CONCEPT disagree about what cognitive science explains. This disagreement forms the basis on the "meta-explanatory challenge to new theories of CONCEPT," which undermines our ability to decide between "new" theories of CONCEPT.

The pertinent question, then, is whether or not one interpretation of the explananda of cognitive science—as made manifest in a given theory of CONCEPT—can be shown to be preferable to any other. If an appeal to cognitive science is to be able to adjudicate between the "new" theories of CONCEPT, then this question must be answered. In the next two chapters, however, I will argue that giving a satisfactory answer to this question is highly unlikely.

4 Problem 1: Explanatory Ambiguity

4.1 Kinds of Cognitive Scientific Explanation

In chapter three, I argued that the meta-appeal to cognitive science risks failing as a methodology for deciding between "new" theories of CONCEPT, because different new theories of CONCEPT endorse different specifications of the explananda of cognitive science. I called this the "meta-explanatory challenge to new theories of CONCEPT." Thus, I said that we can only appeal to cognitive science to decide between the "new" theories of CONCEPT if we can reach an agreement about what cognitive science explains in the first place. In this chapter, however, I will introduce and elucidate one problem for reaching such a consensus about the explananda of cognitive science: the plurality of kinds of explanations formulated in cognitive science.

Cognitive science is now replete with a number of different kinds of explanation. For instance, we find explanations of cognitive competencies that are *mechanistic*, *psychologistic*, and *dynamicist*. Each of different kind of explanation accounts for the organisation and operation of cognition in a different way. In this chapter, I will introduce each kind of explanation in turn, before considering the disagreements and discontinuities between them. This will lead me to a the following conclusion: that we simply do not yet know which kinds of explanations in cognitive science are genuinely explanatory. The consequence is that the "meta-explanatory challenge to new theories of CONCEPT" is potentially strengthened, because different "new" theories of CONCEPT may take different views about what counts as a viable explanation in cognitive science.

4.1.1 Mechanistic Explanation

The term 'mechanism' has a long history in philosophy and science, stretching back at least as far as Descartes (Dijksterhuis, 1969). Modern usage of the term refers to a system or process that produces a phenomenon or collection of phenomena in virtue of the arrangement and interaction of its parts. Intuitively, the term refers to technological products of human creation. For example, one might say that my bicycle has a mechanisms that allows for forward momentum given the peddling of my legs. However, the term has been used to describe natural systems—like cells—or processes—like the processes that produce sunspots—since at least the seventeenth century (Dijksterhuis, 1969). In this sense, the term 'mechanism' has

https://doi.org/9783110708165-004

been employed for some time to explain the structure and operation of the natural world.

Standard definitions and philosophical analyses of the concept *mechanism* explicate the concept in terms of other causal concepts such as *production* and *interaction* (Glennan, 2008). As a result, philosophical treatment of the concept *mechanism* is often taken to be helpful when it comes to making sense of what causal explanations amount to, because mechanisms are most straightforwardly understood as having a "causal aspect" in virtue of the fact that causal relations obtain between their components (Craver and Bechtel, 2006, p. 469). While it is not the case that an analysis of *mechanism* will tell us what causal relations *are*; it is the case that an analysis of *mechanism* will help us to understand how causal relations are manifested. Thus, mechanisms are typically understood as systems that are governed by—or, perhaps, organised or structured according to—causal relations.[29]

In the past, some have argued that mechanisms are a nexus of continuous physical processes. For example, Salmon (1984) and Dowe (2000). However, it is now commonplace to conceive of mechanisms as systems of parts and interactions, which are organised spatio-temporally in the production of a phenomenon (Craver and Bechtel, 2006). This view is upheld by, amongst others, Bechtel and Richardson (1993), Glennan (1996), and Machamer, Darden, and Craver (2000). It is clear, therefore, that even giving a working definition of mechanism is not without controversy. This state of affairs has led some in the mechanistic literature to eschew attempts to spell out necessary and sufficient conditions for something being a mechanism altogether; preferring instead to "offer qualitative descriptions designed to capture the way scientists use the term and deploy the concept in their experimental and inferential practices" (Craver and Tabery, 2017).

Others, however, have attempted to get clear on what mechanisms are. Glennan (1996, p. 52), for instance, defines mechanisms as follows:

> A mechanism underlying a behavior is a complex system which produces that behavior by the interaction of a number of parts according to direct causal laws.

But even if mechanisms can be thought to operate according to causal laws, it is important to recognise that mechanisms need not be conceived of as exclusively mechanical (e.g. push-pull) systems. As Machamer, Darden, and Craver (2000, p. 2) note, "What counts as a mechanism in science has developed over time and presumably will continue to do so." At one time, a mechanism may just have been

---

29 This is not necessarily always the case, as we will see below.

a physical system—e.g. a heart—, but now it may also be possible to conceive of mechanisms of, say, social interaction as well (e.g. Conley et al., 2015).

Machamer, Darden, and Craver (2000, p. 4) defend an alternative conception of mechanisms as "activities." On this view, mechanisms are "producers of change" that "are constitutive of the transformations that yield new states of affairs or new products." This contrasts with Glennan's view, because Machamer, Darden, and Craver (2000, 22) reject the focus on causal laws, because, in their terms, "there may not always be direct causal laws that characterise how activities unfold." Instead, they hold that "It is not the regularities that explain but the activities that sustain the regularities."

To defend their interpretation of mechanisms, Machamer, Darden, and Craver (2000) refer to the mechanistic explanation of chemical transmission at synapses presented by Shepherd (1988). On this explanation, "Chemical transmission can be understood abstractly as the activity of converting an electrical signal in one neuron, the relevant entity, into a chemical signal in the synapse" (Machamer, Darden, and Craver, 2000, p. 8). For Shepherd, then, the mechanism of chemical transmission at synapses involves parts—such as cell membranes, vesicles, microtubules, molecules, and ions—; as well as the activities—such as biosynthesis, transport, depolarization, insertion, storage, recycling, priming, diffusion, and modulation.[30] Each of these parts and activities play a role in the complex mechanism (diagrammatically represented in Fig. 4.1), which produces the change we observe as the phenomenon of chemical transmission.

Machamer, Darden, and Craver (2000) also refer to Zamecnik's (1953) mechanistic explanation of protein synthesis as the product of a process involving energy production (formation of ATP) and the incorporation of amino acids into the protein's polypeptide chain (diagrammatically represented in Fig. 4.2). Zamecnik's mechanistic explanation once again highlights the productive aspects of mechanisms by supposing that the phenomenon we observe as protein synthesis is produced by component parts—e.g. the activities of amino acids, ATP, etc.—(inter)acting in some way.

Interestingly, the mechanistic explanation formulated by Zamecnik (1953) was later recognised to be flawed, because it was theorised prior to the discovery of messenger RNA (mRNA) (Machamer, Darden, and Craver, 2000, p. 18). As a result, it did not reveal the correct productive relations giving rise to protein synthesis, because no active entity was posited that would produce the necessary ordering of amino acids. However, by correlating Zamecnik's biochemical mechanism with

---

30 For my purposes, it does not matter what each of these parts or activities *are*, but only that they are conceived of as parts and activities.

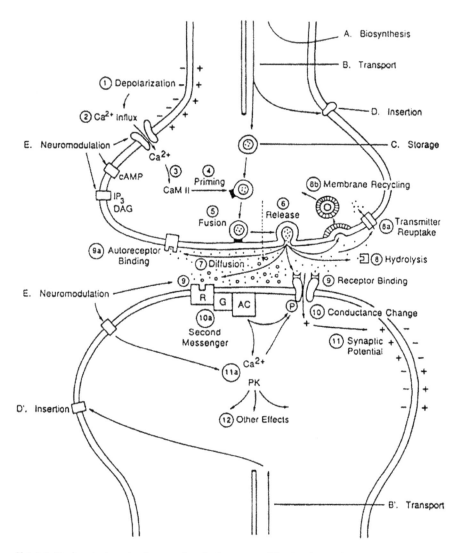

Fig. 4.1: Biochemical mechanisms at chemical synapses (Shepherd, 1988).

According to Shepard's own caption, Fig. 4.1 provides "A summary of some of the main bio-chemical mechanisms that have been identified at chemical synapses. A-E. Long-term steps in synthesis, transport, and storage of neurotransmitters and neuromodulators; insertion of membrane channel proteins and receptors; and neuromodulatory effects. ①-⑫ These summarize the more rapid steps involved in immediate signalling at the synapse. These steps are described in the text, and are further discussed for different types of synapses in Chapter B. Abbreviations: IPJ, inositol triphosphate; CAM II, Ca/calmodulin-dependent proteinkinase II; DAG, diacylglycerol; PK, protein kinase; R, receptor; G, G protein; AC, adenylate cyclase."

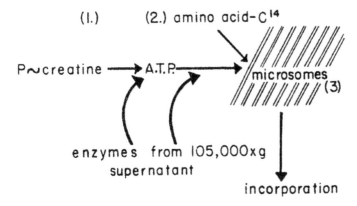

Fig. 4.2: Biochemical flow of protein synthesis (Zamecnik, 1953).

another mechanism—in this case, Watson's mechanism of the flow of information (Watson, 1963)—theorists were able to "correct and elaborate hypotheses about the RNA stage of the mechanism and to find the appropriate activity, hydrogen bonding, for ordering amino acids during protein synthesis" (Machamer, Darden, and Craver, 2000, p. 20). This lends further support to Machamer, Darden, and Craver's conception of mechanisms, because it demonstrates that the search for a correct mechanistic explanation of protein synthesis involved the postulation of more accurate and well-defined productive activities.

For Machamer, Darden, and Craver (2000), the activities of the parts of mechanisms are causally efficacious. However, they argue that we do need not suppose that there is any law according to which these parts (inter)act. In fact, they suggest that the direction of explanation might go the other way, such that our formulation of causal laws depends on our apprehension of productive relations in natural mechanisms. This conception of mechanisms leads Machamer, Darden, and Craver (2000, p. 3) to the definition of mechanisms as "entities and activities organized such that they are productive of regular changes from start or set-up to finish or termination conditions."[31] In this way, they hold that both the entities and activities that compose mechanisms have an irreducible ontological status.

Notably, however, one need not endorse this "dualist" view, because one can reject the claim that both entities and activities are ontologically irreducible categories. Instead, one may take a "substantivalist" view, whereby one "confine[s] their attention to entities and properties, believing it is possible to reduce talk of activities to talk of properties and their transitions" (Machamer, Darden, and Craver, 2000, p. 4). Alternatively, one may endorse a view informed by process

---

31 I will discuss set-up and termination conditions in greater detail below.

ontology—for instance, Rescher (1996, p. 18)—which "reif[ies] activities and attempt to reduce entities to processes" (Machamer, Darden, and Craver, 2000, p. 4). These three views—substantivalist, process ontology, and dualist—represent the three possible ways of conceiving of mechanisms.

Machamer, Darden, and Craver are critical of any view of mechanism that confines itself to talking about the entities and their properties alone, because they think that we also need an account of what happens or what is done by mechanism. In this vein, they claim that:

> [I]t is artificial and impoverished to describe mechanisms solely in terms of entities, properties, interactions, inputs-outputs, and state changes over time. Mechanisms do things. They are active and so ought to be described in terms of the activities of their entities, not merely in terms of changes in their properties (Machamer, Darden, and Craver, 2000, p. 5).

However, Glennan (2008, p. 10) argues that Machamer, Darden, and Craver's concerns do not necessarily count against the conception of mechanism advocated by so-called substantivalists. This is the case because those who Machamer, Darden, and Craver characterise as substantivalists—e.g. Bechtel and Richardson (1993)—still appeal to the functions of entities to do the required explanatory work. For example, Bechtel and Abrahamsen (2005) define a mechanism as "a structure performing a function in virtue of its components parts, component operations, and their organization," where "The orchestrated functioning of the mechanism is responsible for one or more phenomena."

It is evident, then, that substantivalists will not eschew the idea that mechanisms do things and that their doing things is productive of phenomena. However, substantivalists are likely to eschew the idea that interactions are state changes over time; that is, that interactions constitute changes in the state of a system that amount to more than a mere change in the system's properties. The real point of dispute, then, is with whether to conceive of interaction in a Humean sense or not, where the substantivalist does and the dualist and/or advocate of process ontology does not. Thus, we find that the dispute between substantivalists, dualists, and advocates of process ontologies has as much to do with extraneous issues in philosophy as it does with analysing the concept of *mechanism*.

In the interests of progress, therefore, we can make three general—and universally accepted—claims about mechanisms. First, that all mechanisms have a *causal aspect*, because causal relations obtain between a mechanism's components or somehow "in" a mechanism's activities/processes. Second, that all mechanisms have a *phenomenal aspect*; namely, that they do things; that they are mechanisms of the things that they do in the sense that the mechanism of a watch is for the phenomenon of keeping time; just as the mechanism of a chemical synapse is for the phenomenon of chemical transmission. (Craver and Bechtel, 2006, p. 469).[32] And, third, that all mechanisms will have a *componential* or *organisational aspect* in that they are composed of some subset of set of {*entities, (inter)activities, processes*}.

Thus, we arrive at a clearer picture of what mechanisms are: causally interactive systems that are composed of organised parts. This characterisation can function as a framework from which to consider how a mechanism is specified in the process of formulating a mechanistic explanation.

When specifying a mechanism, it is necessary to begin by specifying both the set-up and termination conditions at that mechanism. Descriptions and/or other representations of set-up conditions are typically idealised, because they assume that such conditions are static time slices of the "beginning stage" of the mechanism (Machamer, Darden, and Craver, 2000, p. 11). By thinking in these idealised terms, questions about the processes giving rise to set-up conditions are circumvented. It is then possible to give an account of set-up conditions in terms of, say, the structural properties and/or spatial relations of the entities that enable the first stage of interaction of a mechanism. Set-up conditions, therefore, are crucial for showing "what comes next" (Machamer, Darden, and Craver, 2000, p. 11).

Analogously, termination conditions are "states or parameters describing a privileged endpoint, such as rest, equilibrium, neutralization of a charge, a repressed or activated state, elimination of something, or the production of a product" (Machamer, Darden, and Craver, 2000, p. 12). These, too, will often be idealised, because the notion of an end point or final product is typically arbitrary—there is nothing special about any given time slice that is taken to be the "end stage" of a mechanism, because the productive relations (partly) constituting the mechanism will not cease to exist at this point in time. Still, thinking in terms of "end stages" makes it possible to conceive of a mechanism as productive of the kind of entity or state of affairs that we expect it to produce.

Any attempt to specify a mechanism is, of course, part and parcel of an attempt to give a mechanistic explanation. Mechanistic explanations are epistemic products of human ingenuity, which represent—whether by linguistic description, diagrammatically, or even formally—component entities/parts, their organisation, and their interactions. As we have seen, the role of (causal) laws in mechanistic explanation is controversial. One may debate, then, whether or not mechanistic explanations fit the deductive-nomological model of explanation, whereby the "ex-

---

32 As I have said, differences may be apparent in the conception of what doing something amounts to, but all will agree that "There are no mechanisms *simpliciter*—only mechanisms for phenomena" (Craver and Bechtel, 2006, p. 469).

planans [of any given explanandum] must contain at least one "law of nature" and this must be an essential premise in the derivation in the sense that the derivation of the explanandum would not be valid if this premise were removed" (Woodward, 2017). Some think that they do. Others, however, prefer to think of mechanistic explanations as a distinct kind of explanation; one that explains by giving an account productive effects giving rise to a phenomenon.

In any case, the central feature of mechanistic explanations is that they *decompose* a system that is responsible for the production of the phenomena to be explained. Decomposition delivers an account of the organisational structure of the entities and/or interactions constituting the mechanism. In other words, decomposition is tantamount to the process of identifying the component parts and interactions of a mechanism; where the interaction of these component parts is what generates the phenomena that the mechanistic explanation is put forward to explain. Decomposition, however, can take one of two forms. It may be *functional*—in the sense that it breaks down a mechanism into "activities that, when properly organized, exhibit the phenomenon" (Craver and Bechtel, 2006, p. 473)—or it may be *structural*—in the sense that it "begins by breaking the mechanism apart into component entities and only then investigating what the components do" (Craver and Bechtel, 2006, p. 473).

Functional decomposition begins with a general characterisation of the functioning or behaviour of the mechanism, and then works downwards, so to speak, to give a characterisations of the lower-level entities that constitute the mechanism. In their discussion of functional decomposition, Bechtel and Abrahamsen (2005, p. 433) give the example of the biochemical system that performs metabolism in cells, where decomposition involves characterising the "individual chemical reactions on a series of substrates" responsible for the catabolisis of glucose to carbon dioxide and water; without paying attention to structural features that realise such reactions. The point of functional decomposition, therefore, is to decompose by paying attention to what a mechanism does.

Structural decomposition, in contrast, can be performed independently of a determination of the function of a mechanism. In this way, structural decomposition aims to specify the component entities of a mechanism—whether lower-level or higher-level—without paying too much attention to their operation. For instance, mechanistic explanations of cell organelle such as mitochondria depended on structural decomposition, because "finer features of [mitochondrial] structure were discovered through electron microscopy several years before their functional significance was recognized" (Bechtel and Abrahamsen, 2005, p. 433). The results of this kind of structural decomposition are displayed in Fig. 4.3, which was influenced by an earlier explanation from Palade (1952).

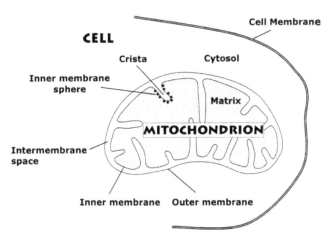

Fig. 4.3: A partial structural decomposition of the cell (Bechtel and Abrahamsen, 2005, p. 434). The mitochondrion is an organelle located in the cell cytoplasm. The inner membrane of the mitochondrion folds into the inner part (matrix) of the mitochondrion. This creates cristae, on which are located small spheres that contain the enzyme ATPase.

In an ideal scenario, structural decomposition will complement functional decomposition by charactering the components that perform the operations identified by functional decomposition. In practice, however, things may not be so easy.

Getting started with either functional or structural decomposition requires first that one has identified, and in some sense characterised, the phenomena to be mechanistically explained. The problem is that phenomena do not come in pre-defined and pre-specified packages; it is the job of researchers to define, specify, and so characterise the phenomena for which an explanation is sought. This point is put clearly by Craver and Bechtel (2006, p. 473) as follows:

> Phenomena are often subdivided, consolidated, or reconceptualized entirely as the discovery process proceeds. Researchers may recognize the need to subdivide a phenomenon into many distinct phenomena, as when learning and memory researchers were forced to recognize that there were many different kinds of memory requiring more or less distinct mechanisms to explain them. Alternatively, researchers may be forced to consolidate many different phenomena into a single phenomenon, as when it became understood that burning, respiring, and rusting were all due to a common mechanism and thus are examples of one phenomenon, oxidation. Finally, investigators may need to reconceptualize the phenomenon to be explained entirely. For example, early physiologists focused on the fact that animals burn foodstuffs and release heat. But after further investigation, researchers recharacterized this phenomenon as transforming energy into usable forms (e.g., ATP bonds).

In short, then, the prospect of undertaking a decomposition of a mechanism—and, hence, the prospect of providing a mechanistic explanation—depends first on identifying and characterising the phenomenon that is the result of what the mechanism doing the explaining does. This is true for both structure or functional decomposition.

Thus, there is an interplay between the act of characterising the phenomenon to be explained and undertaking a decomposition of the mechanism that is taken to be responsible for the production of that phenomenon. Typically, any characterisation of a phenomenon will be guided by a collection of notions well understood by a given science. For example, characterising the phenomenon of burning in terms of oxidation or characterising the phenomenon of increased supply in terms of decreased demand. In this way, "conceptions of the activities thought to be performed guide the identification of components, and vice versa" (Craver and Bechtel, 2006, p. 474).

Of course, it is not always possible to be sure which mechanisms are operative in the production of a given phenomenon. Here scientists adopt working hypotheses, whereby a single mechanism or a set of mechanisms is/are taken to generate the phenomenon to be explained. For example, the working hypothesis that fear is generated by a mechanisms that activates the amygdala nuclei within the limbic systems. In developing working hypotheses, then, scientists may function like engineers in the sense that they:

> attempt to organize known components and activities in such a way that they might possibly produce the phenomenon [through a process that] may involve reasoning analogically from other mechanisms (discovered in nature or human artifacts) and the activities performed in them (Craver and Bechtel, 2006, p. 474).

The interrelation of decomposition and phenomena-characterisation places some constraints on the discovery of mechanisms. This is because phenomena, by definition, occupy spatial or temporal dimensions, which, in turn, mandates that mechanisms should be organised at some level into collections of interacting spatial and/or temporal parts. Consider, for instance, how "the rate and duration of the phenomenon places time constraints on the activities of the components of mechanisms" (Craver and Darden, 2001, p. 115).

Importantly, however, these constraints are not all one-way. In fact, the decomposition of mechanisms into spatio-temporally organised components often feeds back into the process of mechanism discovery. For example, when discovering the size, shape, position, orientation, etc. of the components of a mechanism is taken as a guide for preferring some mechanisms and for ruling others out; or when uncovering the order, rate, and duration of the interaction of the components in a mechanism provides important clues into how the mechanism works in general (Craver, 2006).[33]

The task of discovering and decomposing a mechanism can involve a variety of experimental procedures. But, in general, understanding of the organisation and function of a mechanism is unlikely to be achieved without the aid of experimentation. Some experiments may be natural in the sense that they are "interventions into a mechanism are performed "by nature," through accidental damage, disease, or genetic mutation or variation" (Bechtel and Abrahamsen, 2005, p. 435). However, in most cases experiments will be well-designed procedures that perturb or somehow disturb or intervene on some component or activity in the mechanism under study. This may involve:

> inhibiting a component to observe its effect on the overall functioning of the mechanism or recording conditions internal to the mechanism when it is operative under various conditions (e.g., neuroimaging techniques such as fMRI) (Bechtel and Abrahamsen, 2005, p. 435).

A clear taxonomy of the different kinds experimental approaches to developing and testing descriptions of mechanisms has been given by Craver and Bechtel (2006, p. 475). They begin by making a distinction between intervening at the phenomenal level (L_P) and the mechanistic level (L_M). It then follows that experiments can intervene at either L_P or L_M; or that they can intervene in such a way that bridges L_P and L_M (see Fig. 4.4). According to Craver and Bechtel, interventions at L_P involve varying "the inputs to a mechanism or the conditions under which it operates (e.g., temperature) and record[ing] variations in the phenomenon"; interventions at L_M involve "excit[ing] or inhibit[ing] some component or activity in the mechanism and then record[ing] the results of that intervention elsewhere in the mechanism; and, finally, interventions bridging L_P and L_M "may be top-down (intervening at L_P and recording at L_M)or bottom-up (intervening at L_M and recording at L_P), and the experimental intervention may be either excitatory (somehow stimulating the target of the intervention) or inhibitory (somehow removing or impairing the target of the intervention)."

Mechanistic explanations can, therefore, be corroborated by a range of experimental procedures. Such procedures can be operative in both the discovery and testing of a mechanism. For sure, there are epistemological difficulties with such procedure—for instance, difficulties with interpreting the results of "excitatory and inhibitory interventions" where little or no change to the phenomenon is

---

33 It may even be that this feedback process of mechanism discovery influences later attempts at phenomena-characterisation, because certain kinds of phenomena may be ruled our or re-conceived as a result of considerations of a mechanism's spatial or temporal organisation.

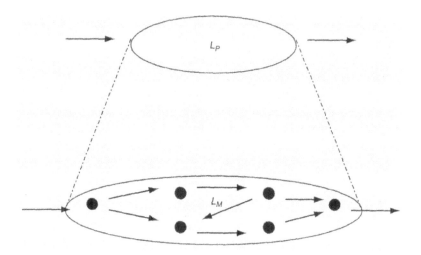

Fig. 4.4: Phenomenal level (top) and mechanism level (bottom) (Craver and Bechtel, 2006, p. 475).

observed or where the intervention has "unclear effects" on other components in the mechanism (Craver and Bechtel, 2006, p. 476). Such problems, however, are not unusual in the sciences and so insofar as a mechanistic explanation is able to predict the phenomenon, we can be confident that the mechanism put forward to explain the generation of the phenomenon provides an adequate—if, potentially, imperfect—explanation.

In cognitive science, mechanistic explanations are put forward in a range of disciplines and (sub-)disciplines. Most notably, perhaps, mechanistic explanations are devised to account for neurological activity in, say, (cognitive) neuroscience. A good neurobiological example of a mechanistic explanation is the explanation of the action potential of a neuron. Referring to this example, Craver and Bechtel (2006, p. 471) argue that:

> The components of this mechanism include the cell membrane, positively charged sodium ($N_A{}^+$) ions, positively charged potassium (K^+) ions, and two types of voltage-sensitive ion channels that selectively allow, respectively, $N_A{}^+$ or K^+ ions to diffuse through the membrane. It is the temporally organized activities of these channels that produce the action potential phenomenon.

The final mechanistic explanation—making reference to, among other things, (de-polarisation and hyperpolarisation of the) membrane and the activities along ion channels—is complex. But it can still serve to make one point concrete: that mechanistic explanations now play an important role in explaining the phenomena that are part of the explananda of cognitive science. This is not to say, however, that there are not further questions about the form and scope of mechanistic explanations. This topic becomes particularly relevant as we move away from neurobiological explanations to those kinds of explanations formulated within the domain of psychology.

4.1.2 Psychological Explanation

Referring to an explanation as "psychological" is, at first blush, vague at best. One may be inclined to think that such an explanation will attempt to explain intelligent behaviour related to the operations of the brain or mind. Such a view is widely accepted among psychologists and philosophers of psychology (cf. Fodor, 1974). But this does not provide a precise definition of what a psychological explanations is or how a psychological explanation explains. It is helpful, therefore, to spell-out the basic assumptions underpinning psychological explanations. By doing this, I will consider a widely accepted account of psychological explanations as a sub-species of mechanistic explanations; albeit a sub-species that explains by appeal to mechanisms with specific kinds of parts and interactions.[34] This leads to further questions about how such psychological mechanisms are specified and discovered; and, moreover, how such psychological mechanisms can be related to explanations of non-psychological phenomena.

The most important hypothesis of psychology is that "thinking can best be understood in terms of representational structures in the mind and computational procedures that operate on those structures" (Thagard, 2018). A representation, on the standard formulation, is a mental state—such as a belief, desire, imagining, perception, etc.—that refers to or is about something; and that has so-called semantic properties that make it evaluable in terms of, say, accuracy, consistency, truth, etc. These semantic properties place constraints on the kind of mental states that are possible or correct. For example, the constraint that one cannot consistently think that someone is both dead and alive; and the constraint that one should correctly perceive a ripe banana to be yellow.

The representational theory of mind—as it is commonly known—has a long philosophical history stretching back to at least Aristotle (Barnes, 2014). One reason for its longevity is because it provides a straightforward way of making sense of mental processes (e.g. thinking, reasoning, etc.). From this perspective, it is possible to think of, say, imagining your favourite footballer scoring the winning

---

34 It should be noted that this is not the only way to conceive of psychological explanations as I will explain in 4.2 below.

goal at the world cup as entertaining a series of representations of that footballer scoring such a goal. Similarly, it is possible to think of, say, the competency of (conditional) reasoning as a sequential manipulation of representations; e.g. "To infer a proposition q from the propositions p and if p then q is (*inter alia*) to have a sequence of thoughts of the form p, if p then q, q" (Pitt, 2018). Many different kinds of operations over mental representations have been proposed in cognitive science including, but not limited to, deduction, retrieval, matching, rotating, and search (cf. Eliasmith and Anderson, 2004; Holyoak and Morrison, 2012).

The representational theory of mind, however, has some serious shortcomings. For starters, it is not clear what kind of representational structure mental representations have. The concern here relates to the discussion I undertook in chapter two with regards to the various standard view theories of CONCEPT. Accordingly, one finds many different accounts of representational structure in cognitive science, including the imagist, definitionist, prototype, exemplar, and theory-theory accounts. At this time, no consensus has been reached about the representational structure of the mind and debate continues as to which representational format is preferable.

The second shortcoming of the representational theory of mind is that it relies on the idea that mental representations are *intentional*; that is, that they have a content in virtue of referring to or being about something. This assumption in and of itself is not a problem, but it is a problem if we hope to be able to explain all mental facts in terms of physical facts, because we have no good story of how intentional states can be explained in terms of physical states. A number of attempts have been made to *naturalise* intentionality in this regard, but all face difficulties and none have been accepted unequivocally. For example, causal-information theories (e.g. Dretske, 1981)—which hold that the content of a mental representation is grounded in the information it carries about what does (Devitt, 1996) or what would cause it to occur (Fodor, 1987)—face problems, because:

> [...] causal-informational relations are not sufficient to determine the content of mental representations. Such relations are common, but representation is not. Tree trunks, smoke, thermostats and ringing telephones carry information about what they are causally related to, but they do not represent (in the relevant sense) what they carry information about (Pitt, 2018).

Of course, causal-informational theories are not the only attempts to naturalise mental content. Other relevant theories include, but are not limited to, teleological theories (e.g. Fodor, 1990; Milikan, 1984; Papineau, 1987; Dretske, 1988; Dretske, 1995) and functional theories (e.g. Block, 1986; Davies, 2003). But each of these theories has limitations of their own. I do not have space to discuss these problems at length here, but for further discussion see Pitt (2018).

The shortcomings of the representational theory of mind are intricate and would require a book length discussion in their own right. For my purposes, however, it is sufficient to note that even with this uncertainty, the representational theory of mind continues to play a central role in any explanation that could be considered psychological. As a consequence, psychological explanations can be defined as those explanations that appeal to representations and representational contents to explain intelligent behaviour.

In almost discussions of psychological explanations it is assumed that "representations, processes and operations, and resources that they employ" are "the psychological entities [that] constitute the basic explanatory toolkit of cognitive modeling" (Weiskopf, forthcoming, p. 4). According to Weiskopf (forthcoming, p. 4):

> Representations include symbols (perceptual, conceptual, and otherwise), images and icons, units and weights, state vectors, and so on. Processes and operations are various ways of combining and transforming these representations such as comparison, concatenation, and deletion. Resources include parts of the architecture, including memory buffers, information channels, attentional filters, and process schedulers, all of which govern how and when processing can take place

Crucially, however, framing an explanation in terms of representations, processes and operations, and resources is a necessary, but not sufficient, condition for psychological explanation. For psychological explanation in terms of representations, processes and operations, and resources must also be interpretable as capturing the causal structure of cognition. That is, any putative psychological explanation must be able to be interpreted as showing how interactions among representations are causally responsible for the production of the phenomenon being explained. In what follows, I presuppose that these two conditions are individually necessary and jointly sufficient for psychological explanation. Having made this clear, I can move on to consider following two questions: what form do or can psychological explanations take?; and how do psychological explanations explain?

A clear and exhaustive survey of the forms that psychological explanations can take has been given by Weiskopf (2017). He identifies the following four different forms of psychological explanation, which I will consider in turn:
– Verbal descriptions
– Mathematical formalism
– Diagram and Graphics
– Computational models or simulations

Verbal descriptions involve the use of words—e.g. natural language—to specify what is ordinarily a very simple cognitive model. Consider, for instance, the verbal specification of the model of the levels of processing framework in memory modelling (e.g. Cermak and Craik, 1979). According to this model, "(1) [...] novel stimuli are interpreted in terms of a fixed order of processing that operates over a hierarchy of features, starting with their superficial perceptual characteristics and leading to more conceptual or semantically elaborated characteristics; (2) that depth of processing, as defined in terms of movement through this fixed hierarchy, predicts degree of memory encoding, so that the more deeply and elaborately a stimulus is processed, the more likely it is to be recalled later" (Weiskopf, forthcoming, p. 5). In this way, verbal descriptions are used to roughly specify a model or a model's general features, where that model is given in representational terms and is taken to capture the causal structure of some aspects of cognition.

Mathematical formalism involve more complex and precise means of specify a cognitive modelling than verbal descriptions. Such specifications can be made by appealing to, say, state-spaces and/or geometric models, which have a range of potential applications in cognitive science. For example, models can be developed that represent the state (and changes in the state) of cognition. On this account, cognitive processes can be viewed as trajectories through a state-space and changes to the cognitive systems itself (e.g. through brain damage) can be viewed as changes to the structure of the state-space itself. Mathematical modelling practices of this kind have already found favour in some areas of cognitive science, but I will deal with them later under the heading of a different kind of explanation entirely: dynamicist explanation.

Mathematical formalism—such as equations—are often exploited in psychological explanations. Weiskopf (2017, 6), for example, refers to the Contrast Rule developed by Tversky (1977) as an example of how "Equations may also be used to specify the form cognitive processes take." This rule—which has obvious relevance to explanations of the cognitive process of categorisation—is that "the similarity of two objects belonging to different categories (a and b) is a weighted function of their common attributes minus their distinctive attributes" (Weiskopf, forthcoming, p. 6). Formally:

$$Sim(a, b) = \alpha f(a \cap b) - \beta f(a - b) - \gamma f(b - a). \qquad (4.1)$$

If an explanation based upon a piece of mathematical formalism such as (4.1) is to count as psychological, then it must be interpreted as specifying a causal process involving representational states. For instance, the Contrast Rule could be interpreted as, say, specifying a causal process of computing similarities between two representations to determine if they belong in the same category. Whether or not such interpretations are justified is a question for future science. There are a number of experimental methods that allow us to determine if a causal interpretation should be modified or abandoned entirely. An effective way of arriving at a conclusion in this regard is to "use [the formalism in question] to design manipulations that have systematic effects" (Weiskopf, forthcoming, p. 6); that is, to develop experiments that put the causal interpretation of the formalism to the test.

An example of mathematical modelling in psychological explanations

It is helpful to take a brief aside to consider an example of a mathematical model exploited in a psychological explanation. One clear example of this kind of modelling comes from Bayesian approaches to cognitive science. Although Bayesian models have be developed to account for a range of cognitive competencies, here I will focus on one competency in particular: categorisation.

Bayesian models of categorisation typically assume that there is both an input to categorisation—the stimulus to be categorised—and an output from categorisation—the (cognitive) behaviour of the categoriser (Kruschke, 2008). But in order to count as cognitively adequate, the model must also represent the cognitive processes that mediate between input and output, and take these representations to be informative about the hypothesis space over which Bayesian inference operates. There are a number of possible candidates that could be sourced from cognitive scientific theories—e.g. prototypes, bundles of exemplars, or theory-like structures (Carey, 1985; Lakoff, 1987; McClelland and Rumelhart, 1981; Nosofsky, 1988; Rehder, 2003b). However, it has become standard practice to assume that Bayesian models operate over representations of unstructured lists of features; e.g. feature list representations (Anderson, 1991; Shafto et al., 2011).

An important question for Bayesian models of categorisation, however, is how models should represent input feature spaces, and, furthermore, how the representation of feature spaces influences the process of Bayesian categorisation. On many approaches to Bayesian category learning, feature inputs are represented as unordered lists of features, where categorisation proceeds by making the most probable categories those that group input stimuli together around a maximally optimal number of shared features (Sanborn, Griffiths, and Navarro, 2006; Goodman et al., 2008). But, unless weights are added to lists of features in some principled way, this approach can be criticised for failing to provide an account of the relative importance of the features around which categorisation occurs. For example, on this approach the features of **colour, shape, texture, genus**, and **region of first domestication** all count as equally relevant for the differentiation of, say, bananas and oranges.

In order to resolve the problem of uniformly diagnostic features, weights have been added to Bayesian models of categorisation, which make different features more or less diagnostic for specific categories. Such weighted models, however, face the challenge of finding a principled way to assign weights to individual features. For example, Hall (2007) and Wu et al. (2014) makes use of "decision tree-based filter method for setting [feature] weights," where feature weights are estimated by constructing an unpruned decision tree and looking at the depth at which features are "tested in the tree" or at the dependence of certain features on others (Hall, 2007, p. 121). These example models—and many others like them—have contributed to a growing literature that aims to improve the performance of naive Bayesian models while retaining their simplicity and computational efficiency.

Another addition to this literature comes from (Taylor and Sutton, 2020), who develop a model that is able to assigns weights to features without appealing to weighting schemas derived from a period of supervised learning. They do this by supposing that the input data is in the representational format of frames and not of feature lists (see Fig. 4.5 as an example of a frame). As attribute-value structures, frames represent both the "general properties or dimensions by which the respective concept is described (e.g., COLOR, SPOKESPERSON, HABITAT ...)" and the *values* that each property or dimension takes in any given instantiation "(e.g. [COLOR: **red**], [SPOKESPERSON: **Ellen Smith**], [HABITAT: **jungle**] ...)" (Petersen, 2015, p. 151).

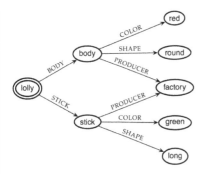

Fig. 4.5: Lolly frame (Petersen, 2015).

The reason that frames are useful and relevant to categorisation is that they can be used to constrain information. In the first place, frames provide constraints on the range of values at any given node, because "information represented in a frame does not depend on the concrete set of nodes. It depends rather on how the nodes are connected by directed arcs and how the nodes and arcs are labelled" (Petersen, 2015, p. 49). For example, if the value of COLOUR is given as square—e.g. [COLOUR: **square**]—then it is clear that the established 'category' is, in fact, no category at all (**square** is not a possible COLOUR value).

A second way in which frames constrain information derives from the fact that they are recursive (the value of one attribute can itself have attributes). The central node (graphically, the double-ringed node) indicates what the frame represents (i.e., lollies in the case of Figure 4.5). Attribute-value pairs 'closer' to the central node encode relatively important, but general, information; and attribute-value pairs 'further' from the central node encode relatively less important, but more specific, information.

This insight led Taylor and Sutton (2020) to their development of new kind of frame-theoretic, Bayesian model of categorisation that replaced feature lists with frames to make the matrix of input data D richer. Their proposal was that, in general, the importance of the similarity of feature-values of objects within categories is proportional to how 'close' these feature values are to the central node of a frame measured by (minimum) path distance. Take the frame from Petersen (2015) in Fig. 4.5 as an example. The type of value for the BODY and STICK attributes will be very similar across different lollies. Indeed, if something had, e.g., lolly properties but no stick, one might judge it to be a sweet, not a lolly. However, the shape, colour, and producer for each lolly component may vary to a greater extent without giving one cause to judge, e.g., that two differently coloured objects belong to different categories qua *lolly* or *not a lolly*.

Using unweighted feature lists alone, one cannot formally capture the idea that similarity between values is more important for more central nodes. With frames this idea can be formally captured and data sets can be minimally changed to include a distance measure. By recognising this state of affairs, Taylor and Sutton (2020) were able to formulate the following model, making use of two parameters that allow us to calculate $p(w|D, \alpha, \delta)$:

$$p(w|D, \alpha, \delta) \propto p(w|\alpha) \times p(D|w, \delta) \qquad (4.2)$$

In (4.2), $p(w|\alpha)$ contains the parameter α which sets the extent to which the number categories should be minimised. $p(D|w, \delta)$ contains the parameter δ which sets the extent to which features of objects within categories should be similar (i.e., that members of categories should have the same feature/attribute values).

A full specification of the model developed by Taylor and Sutton (2020) is given in the appendix. In brief, their model calculates the value for $p(w|\alpha)$ from the sum of the entropy of the set of categories in w with respect to the assignment of objects to categories in w, weighted by α. In other words, in terms of the average amount of information required to determine which object a category is in, give a set of categories. Values of $p(D|w, \delta)$ are calculated from the *delta*-weighted entropy of each category with respect to the features of objects within that category. If all objects within each category have the same features, then entropy will be minimised (one would need no information to know which features an object has given the category it is in). This translates into a high value for $p(D|w, \delta)$. If objects in the same category differ with respect to their attribute values, then, depending on the setting for δ, this probability will be lower.

Therefore, the difference between the frame-based model developed by Taylor and Sutton (2020) and models based on feature lists is that unsupervised feature list models do not have a principled way to weight similarity with respect to some features more heavily than similarity with respect to others. Frame-based models, on the other hand, do. The open question, then, is whether or not Tayor and Sutton's frame-theoretic, Bayesian model of category learning captures causal structure. This is an empirical question that must be tested in the course of further research. However, it is at least plausible to interpret the frame-theoretic, Bayesian model of category learning as specifying a causal process involving representational states, because the model does seem to describe a causal process that results in the organisation of input stimuli into category structures.

Diagrams and graphics provide a simpler and more intuitive way of modelling cognition than do mathematical formalisms and, perhaps, verbal descriptions. The most common kind of graphical representation exploited in psychological explanations are so-called "boxological models." According to Weiskopf (2017, 6-7) again: "The main components of these models are boxes, which stand for distinct functional elements, and arrows, which stand for relationships of control or informational exchange. A cognitive architecture can be described at one level of functional analysis by a directed graph made of such elements." One finds boxological models in psychological explanations of many different phenomena. As an example, consider the use of boxological models in psychological explanations of working memory. For instance, in the psychological explanation developed by Baddeley, Allen, and Hitch (2011) (see Fig. 4.6).

Baddeley, Allen, and Hitch (2011, p. 1399) describe their model as follows:

> At the heart of the current model is the episodic buffer, a purely passive system, but one that serves a crucial integrative role because of its capacity to bind information from a number of different dimensions into unitized episodes or chunks. We speculate that smell and taste may also have access to the system, although currently know of no direct evidence on this issue. Our current speculations continue to assume that conscious access to the phonological loop or sketchpad may operate via the buffer. The visuo-spatial and verbal subsystems are themselves assumed to act as lower level buffers allowing, in one case, information from visual, spatial, kinaesthetic and tactile information to be combined. In the case of the phonological loop, language-related information from a number of sources may be combined, including not only speech, but also written, lip read and signed language.

Given the ease with which they can be understood, pictorially represented models involving graphics and diagrams often serve as point of departure for more complex modelling practices in psychology. For instance, modelling practices involving mathematical tools. As clear representations of functional relationships between components of cognition, diagrammatic or graphical models often serve as a necessary first step towards modelling the kinds of information exchange that are productive of the phenomena to be explained. Of course, even with simple diagrammatic or graphical models there are heuristics at play. For example, a heuristic to focus on functions at a particular level of grain. This is not to say that further investigation could not attempt to explain the inner working of, say, a particular box in a boxological model. Nor is it to say that further investigation

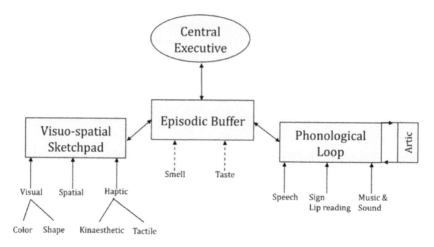

Fig. 4.6: A revised model of working memory (Baddeley, Allen, and Hitch, 2011, p. 1399).

could not subsume many boxes in a boxological model into one higher-order box with a higher-order function. Such recursive (de)composition is commonplace and would be expected to deliver greater detail about how exactly each representation (e.g. box) carries out the function that it has within the causal structure being modelled.

If it is true that diagrammatic or graphical models are often extended and/or supplemented by mathematical models, then it is also true that mathematical models are often taken as the source of the last form of psychological explanations I will consider here: explanations involving *computational models or simulations*. A computational model is a procedural model—typically cashed out in terms of the development and application of an algorithm—that takes the form of an executable program. The reason, therefore, that mathematical models are often the source of computational models is because "a set of mathematical equations can be manipulated or solved using many different computer programs implemented on many types of hardware architecture" (Weiskopf, forthcoming, p. 9). However, in principle any type of model—even a verbal description or a diagrammatic model— can be used to construct a computer simulation; with the only condition being that the operations described by the model must be succinct enough to be written into a program that executes them.

Computer modelling has a long history in cognitive science. Consider, for instance, simulations of cognitive processes that have involved the development of large-scale cognitive architectures like Soar (Newell, 1990) and ACT-R (Anderson et al., 2004). Furthermore, consider recent attempts to simulate neural networks by applying the methods of computational modelling (Rogers and McClelland,

2004). In each of these examples (and the many others like them), the purpose of computer modelling is to enable us to compare different models of cognition; particularly with respect to how well they are able to account for a given body of data. For instance, in the context of the example of mathematical models of Bayesian category learning given above, a computational model could be put to work to test which available categorisation model is best able to account for the data about people's success on categorisation tasks.

It is important to recognise that computational models are able to achieve results that could not be replicated by humans. Thus, we must be careful in our interpretations of computational models. It is important to keep in mind that a program executing a model—e.g. an algorithm or set of algorithms—is not the same things as the model itself. That is, that the properties of the program differ from the properties of the executed model. Weiskopf (forthcoming, p. 10) makes this clear, in the context of a discussion of the cognitive architecture ACT-R, when he says:

> ACT-R assumes that psychological operations consist of the application of production rules (which the program simulates), but not that they involve the execution of lines of compiled C code, and neural network models assume that cognition involves passing activation in parallel through a network of simple units, despite the fact that this activity is almost always simulated on an underlying serial computational architecture. Turning a model into a program is something of an art, and not every aspect of the resulting program should be interpreted either as part of the model that inspired it or as part of the target system itself.

The point, then, is that just because computer models have to be written into the form of a program in order to be simulated does not mean that we should equate programs and the models they are running. The psychological explanation follows from the model with its representational state and causal interpretation. The executed program is merely a test of the model and, hence, a means by which the model can be compared with its competitors.

With this cautionary tale out of the way, we are free to reap the rewards of computational modelling and simulation. Perhaps the greatest justification of computational modelling was set out by (McClelland, 2009, p. 16) as follows:

> The essential purpose of [computational] cognitive modeling is to allow investigation of the implications of ideas, beyond the limits of human thinking. Models allow the exploration of the implications of ideas that cannot be fully explored by thought alone

McClelland's idea is simple: that computational modelling and simulation is important, because it allows us to test our (verbal, mathematical, and/or diagrammatical) models of cognition against idealised scenarios and states of affairs. In this way—so the story goes—we can come to a clearer understanding of which of our models best approximates the actual state of affairs and make progress in our explanations of cognition.

Still, one may be uncomfortable with the idea that computational models are really explanatory. One might contend, instead, that it is the model—whether verbally, mathematically, or diagrammatically specified—implemented by the computational program that explains. This claim—while potentially valid—depends on a certain view of what explanation amounts to; for instance, that the "core notion" of explanation:

> does not require reference to features of the psychology of explainers or their audiences and that it can be characterized in terms of features that are non-contextual in the sense that they are sufficiently general, abstract and "structural" that we can view them as holding across a range of explanations with different contents and across a range of different contexts (Woodward, 2017).

If this claim is correct, then computational models do not seem to count as explanations, because they merely implement those models with the required general, abstract and "structural" properties. However, if one takes the view that explanations will necessarily involve contextual features and/or the psychology of explainers, then computational models may well count as explanations; albeit "pragmatic" explanations that are used to help us achieve certain goals. One's perspective on whether or not computational models are a genuine case of psychological explanation will, then, be sensitive to one's views about explanation in general.

I have now considered the four different kinds of psychological explanation: verbal descriptions, mathematical formalism, diagram and graphics, and computational models or simulations. This discussion makes clear what kinds of explanatory practices in cognitive science can be understood as "psychological." However, it does not provide an answer to the question of how psychological explanations explain in the first place. And this question must be answered if we want to know how psychological explanations are able to account for intelligent behaviour related to the brain.

Bechtel and Wright (2009) identify two different "models" of explanation in psychology: the nomological model of psychological explanation and the mechanistic model of psychological explanation. A nomological model of psychological explanation is one that affords a central role to laws and law-like generalisations. Perhaps the most well-known nomological model of explanation is the deductive-nomological model developed by Hempel and Oppenheim (1948). On this account of explanation, an explanandum—e.g. a sentence "describing the phenomenon to be explained"—is explained by an explanans—"the class of those sentences which are adduced to account for the phenomenon"—when "the explanandum must be a logical consequence of the explanans" and "the sentences constituting the explanans are true" (Hempel and Oppenheim, 1948, pp. 247–248). Crucially, however, the "explanans must contain at least one "law of nature," because the explanation would not be valid if this premise were removed (Woodward, 2017).

The deductive-nomological model can seem to make sense in domains such a (theoretical) physics, where laws play a central role in explaining empirical regularities (consider, for instance, the role that Newton's laws play in explaining the empirical regularities of pendulums or falling apples). But, in psychology, laws are referred to rarely if at all. While it is true that the intelligent behaviour (and other psychological phenomena) are realised in "brains comprised of neurons that generate action potentials, and the electrical currents that constitute the action potential are governed by principles such as Ohm's law,", it is often unclear which physical laws should be appealed to in order to explain the phenomenon under scrutiny (Bechtel and Wright, 2009).

Attempts have been made to formulate so-called "empirical laws" that describe the relations between empirically measured variables. But this does not amount to the same thing as specifying "theoretical laws" from which empirical observations can be "derived," because empirical laws typically count as nothing more than a re-telling of "what happens" by "restat[ing] the phenomenon in more general terms" (Cummins, 2000, p. 119). As a result, the nomological model of psychological explanation is hamstrung by its reliance on laws and our inability to either find psychological laws or to adequately bridge the gap between psychological explanations and law-based explanations in, say, physics.

We thus need another workable model of how psychological explanations explain. Exactly what form this model should take is still up for debate—as I will demonstrate in section 4.2 below—, but one model of psychological explanation has come to the fore in recent years: the mechanistic model of psychological explanation. I have given a lengthy account of what mechanistic explanations are above. Broadly speaking, mechanistic explanations explain by specifying a mechanism responsible for the production of a given phenomenon. Crucially, however, psychological explanations must be of a particular sub-type of mechanistic explanations: the subspecies in which the components (or entities or parts) of the mechanism are mental representations that interact according to rules of computation.

If psychological explanations are mechanistic, they are in the sense that they characterise the "mediating states of an intelligent system that carry information," which coordinates the organism's behaviour in light of the represented environmental contingencies (Markman and Dietrich, 2000, p. 471). This point is put clearly by Bechtel and Wright (2009), who say:

> the mechanisms appealed to by many psychologists are of a distinctive kind. Rather than serving to transform chemical substances as in basic physiology (e.g., the process of synthe-

sizing proteins from free amino acids), many of the mechanisms appealed to in psychology are those that serve to regulate behavior or process information. Reward mechanisms, for example, figure in control systems responsible for the information relevant to approach and consummatory behavior. Other psychological mechanisms, especially in primates, are a stage removed from the actual regulation of behavior, and are instead involved in tasks like planning future behaviors or securing information about the world.

Now, we have seen already in section 4.1.1 that a central feature of giving a mechanistic explanations is decomposing the system responsible for the the production of the phenomena to be explained. Such a decomposition is tantamount to the process of identifying the components and interactions of the mechanism being put forward in the explanation. In the context of psychological explanations, however, decomposition would have to deliver the explanatorily-interesting parts of the information-processing mechanism that produces and regulates behaviour. That is, the "operative parts" that figure in mechanistic interactions that are productive of the psychological phenomena to be explained. Such a project was eschewed by Behaviourists on the grounds that explanation needs make no reference to the "internal," mental states of individuals (cf. Rey, 1997; Skinner, 1974). But has become a central feature of psychological explanations in cognitive science.

In cognitive psychology, for example, the standard way to undertake mechanistic decomposition has been to posit different "types of operations that transformed representations so as to produce the overall information-processing activity" (Bechtel and Wright, 2009). Building upon developments in computer engineering and computational theory, early cognitive psychologists postulated activities such as retrieving, storing, and operating on representations (Neisser, 2014). In this way, psychological explanations appealing to mechanisms proceed by specifying a representations and the rules of interaction governing their operation. Such explanations deliver "representation-operation mechanisms," which can themselves be presented verbally, mathematically (formally), or diagrammatically or graphically; and can be "tested" via computational modelling and/or simulations. Here, then, we see a direct link between how psychological explanations explain—e.g. by specifying a mechanism responsible for producing the phenomena—and the form they take.

Of course, arriving at a consensus about the componential organisation of a mechanism in terms of representation and operations is not straightforward. In fact, this topic remains a bone of contention to this day. In general, cognitive psychologists hypothesise—by appeal to metaphors and other intuitions—about how a psychological mechanism might perform activities such as remembering, problem-solving, language processing, and reasoning. Having formulated such hypotheses, it is then possible to make predications and test the hypotheses by appealing to empirical data about, say, reaction times and errors departing from normal performance. However, this does not guarantee that cognitive psychology develops successful explanations, because:

> Although their explanatory aim was to identify the task-relevant mental operations, cognitive psychologists more often succeeded in establishing differences between psychological phenomena and showing that they rely on different mental operations without thereby specifying them. For example, in addition to the distinction between declarative and procedural memory, Endel Tulving (1983) advanced a distinction within declarative memory between memory for factual information, including facts about oneself (*semantic memory*) and memory that involves reliving episodes in one's own life (*episodic memory*) (Bechtel and Wright, 2009).

Questions remain, therefore, about the explanatory import of psychological explanations, whether mechanistically construed or not. In particular, there are concerns about how and, indeed if, it is possible to show how the representation-operation mechanisms postulated in psychological explanations are realised in the neural hardware of the brain. This process of relating psychological components to brain components is often called *localisation*; and it represents one of a number of difficulties that threaten to undermine the intelligibility of a mechanistic model of psychological explanations altogether. I will return to this discussion in section 4.2 below, but first I will consider one final kind of explanation in cognitive science.

4.1.3 Dynamicist Explanation

Aside from mechanistic explanations and their (putative) subspecies psychological explanations, another kind of explanation has been developed in cognitive science: dynamicist explanations. Dynamicist explanations were first introduced as an alternative to the "computational theory of mind," which aligns with the mechanistic model of psychological explanation introduced above in its commitment to the view that explaining cognition is a matter of modelling mental representations that interact according to rules of computation (Van Gelder, 1995). The central idea of dynamicist explanations is that "Rather than computers, cognitive systems may be dynamical systems; rather than computation, cognitive processes may be state-space evolution within these very different kinds of systems" (Van Gelder, 1995, p. 346).

In the first place, dynamicist explanations were formulated to respond to the "what else could it be?" argument. This argument was set-out by Newell (1990, p. 56) as follows:

> [...] although a small chance exists that we will see a new paradigm emerge for mind, it seems unlikely to me. Basically, there do not seem to be any viable alternatives. This position is not

surprising. In lots of sciences we end up where there are no major alternatives around to the particular theories we have. Then, all the interesting kinds of scientific action occur inside the major view. It seems to me that we are getting rather close to that situation with respect to the computational theory of mind.

By embodying the response to the "what else could it be?" argument, dynamicist explanations were taken by many to support an alternative and equally viable conception of cognition: one not in terms of computation; but in terms of the dynamic evolution of a total system.

The first question that we must attend to in order to better understand dynamicist equations is very basic indeed; namely, what are dynamical systems? And here we run straight into a problem, because there are a number of different definitions available. This state of affairs was commented on by Van Gelder (1998, p. 618), who introduced a table to give a brief overview of the different perspectives on dynamical systems (see table 4.1). These definitions take a number of forms; from definitions in terms of bodies (e.g. particles) governed by forces; to definitions in terms of properties (e.g. diachronicity) that many or even all dynamic systems share. For this reason, Van Gelder (1998, p. 618) argues that "There is no single official definition waiting to be lifted off the shelf" and that cognitive scientists should conceive of dynamical systems in whatever sense "matters for them."

But what, then, is the understanding of dynamical systems that plays a role in cognitive science? Van Gelder (1998) highlights three key ingredients to this understanding: that dynamical systems are quantitative in state, have quantitative state/time interdependence, and have rate dependence. The first ingredient asserts that a dynamical system assume "that [cognitive] behavior is systematically related to distances as measured by that metric" Van Gelder (1998, p. 618). This idea, therefore, is that the properties of a dynamical system can be represented by abstract mathematical magnitudes whose values are real numbers. The second ingredient asserts that dynamical systems are both quantitative in time and quantitative in state, and that these properties are interdependent. The idea here, then, is that "the behavior of the system is such that amounts of change in state are systematically related to amounts of elapsed time." Finally, the third ingredient asserts that dynamical system's rates of change depend on current rates of change. The idea here is that the variables of dynamical systems "include both basic variables and the rates of change of those variables," where the relationship between the two can be mostly conveniently expressed by (a set of) differential equations (Van Gelder, 1998, p. 618).

Working from these three key ingredients of the understanding of dynamical systems at play cognitive science, Van Gelder (1998, p. 619) defines a dynamical system as a system that is quantitative and can be modelled accordingly. This

Tab. 4.1: Some examples of common definitions of the term "dynamical system" from outside cognitive science (Van Gelder, 1998, p. 618).

Guiding Idea	Example
1. A system of bodies whose motions are governed by forces. Such systems form the domain of dynamics considered as a branch of classical mechanics.	"A collection of a large number of point particles." (Desloge, 1982, p. 215) Webster's: "Dynamics … a branch of mechanics that deals with forces and their relation primarily to the motion … of bodies of matter."
2. A physical system whose state variables include rates of change.	"In the original meaning of the term a dynamical system is a mechanical system with a finite number of degrees of freedom. The state of such a system is usually characterized by its position … and the rate of change of this position, while a law of motion describes the rate of change of the state of the system" (Bingham, Goldie, and Teugels, 1989, p. 328).
3. A system of first-order differential equations; equivalently, a vector field on a manifold.	A dynamical system is "simply a smooth manifold M, together with a vector field v defined on M" (Casti, 1992, p. 109).
4. Mapping on a metric space.	"A dynamical system is a transformation $f:Zt \to Z$ on a metric space (Z, d)" (Barnsley, 1988, p. 134).
5. State-determination.	"A dynamical system … is one whose state at any instant determines the state a short time into the future without any ambiguity" (Cohen and Stewart, 1994, p. 188).
6. Any mapping, equation, or rule.	"A dynamical system may be defined as a deterministic mathematical prescription for evolving the state of a system forward in time" (Ott, 1993, p. 6).
7. Change in time.	"A dynamical system is one which changes in time" (Hirsch, 1984, p. 3). "The term dynamic refers to phenomena that produce time-changing patterns … the term is nearly synonymous with time-evolution or pattern of change" (Luenberger, 1979, p. 1).

definition is taken to reflect the actual practices of dynamicist cognitive scientists, because it emphasises the quantitative character of dynamicist explanations and the idea that quantitative modelling is able to capture "deep and theoretically significant properties of systems." For Van Gelder, this understanding is equivalent to the view that:

> a system that is quantitative in state is one whose states form a *space*, in a more than merely metaphorical sense; states are *positions* in that space, and behaviors are paths or trajectories. Thus quantitative systems support a geometric perspective on system behavior, one of the hallmarks of a dynamical orientation.

Having set out the general understanding of dynamical systems in cognitive science, it is possible to scrutinise the so-called "dynamical hypothesis" (Van Gelder, 1995). The dynamical hypothesis has two aspects: firstly, that cognitive systems are dynamical systems and, secondly, that we can and should explain cognition dynamically. These two aspects are interrelated—since a proof of the second aspect could be said to corroborate the first—, but they can be differentiated.

With respect to the first aspect of the dynamical hypothesis, a number of issues should be clarified. For example, the dynamical hypothesis should not be read as making the claim that cognitive *agents* are necessarily identical to dynamical systems. Instead, as Van Gelder (1998, p. 619) puts it:

> the relationship [...] is not identity but *instantiation*. Cognitive agents are not themselves systems (sets of variables) but, rather, objects whose properties can form systems. Cognitive agents instantiate numerous systems at any given time. According to the nature hypothesis, the systems responsible for cognitive performances are dynamical

The idea, then, is that cognitive agents may be taken to *emerge* from one or many dynamical systems (Kelso and Engstrøm, 2006, p. 109). These systems need not be thought of as operative only at the neuronal level, because the variables of dynamical systems may be "macroscopic quantities at roughly the level of the cognitive performance itself" (Van Gelder, 1998, p. 619). In this sense, it would also be a mistake to think of dynamical systems as giving rise to cognitive agents. In fact, the dynamical system responsible for a given kind of cognitive competency might include variables that depend on features of the environment or on organism-environment interactions; e.g. optic flow (cf. Warren, 1995).

With respect to the second aspect of the dynamical hypothesis, the big problem is to understand how and why dynamical modelling can and should be used to explain cognition. Typically, the "why question" is answered in the form of a critique of non-dynamical approaches to explanation in cognitive science. The general idea of this critique—which I will elaborate upon further in section 4.2

below—is that non-dynamical explanation incur the hefty explanatory baggage of taking representations and representational-contents to be explanatory primitives in cognitive science. The "how question" can be answered in many ways, since there are many different schemas for dynamical explanation at work today in cognitive science.

As an example, consider explanations based on *coordination dynamics*. Such explanations are described by (Kelso and Engstrøm, 2006, p. 90) as:

a set of context-dependent laws or rules that describe, explain and predict how patterns of coordination form, adapt, persist and change in natural systems. ... [C]oordination dynamics seeks to identify the laws, principles, and mechanisms underlying coordinated behavior among different types of components in different kinds of systems at different levels of description.

Such coordination dynamicist explanations proceed by first discovering "the key coordination variables and the dynamical equations of motion that best describes how coordination patterns change over time"; then by "identify[ing] the individual coordinated elements (such as neurons, organs, clapping hands, pendulums, cars, birds, bees, fish, etc.) and discern[ing] their dynamics" (Chemero and Silberstein, 2008, p. 10).

Chemero and Silberstein (2008, pp. 10–11) consider an example of an explanation based on coordination dynamics given by (Oullier et al., 2005). Oullier et al. (2005) conducted an experiment where participants were asked to sit opposite from another, close their eyes, and raise and lower their fingers at a comfortable rate. The experiments showed that "When the subjects have their eyes closed, their finger movements were out of phase with one another. When subjects are asked to open their eyes, their finger movements spontaneously synchronize, only to desynchronize when the subjects are asked to close their eyes again" (Chemero and Silberstein, 2008, pp. 10–11). This phenomenon was best explained in terms of a "spontaneous coordination of brain activity and behavior with an external source (in this case the other subject)," which abstracts away from details about the "mechanisms by which finger movements structure light, which impacts retinal cells, which impacts neural cells, which impacts muscles, which move fingers, and so on"; and simply posits "that the movements of the fingers are non-mechanically or informationally coupled" in a way that can be modelled dynamically.

Advocates of the dynamical hypothesis take a flexible view about the indicators of cognition. They accept that such indicators may include, but are not necessarily limited to, knowledge, intelligence, adaptability, and coordination with remote states of affairs. Thus, a dynamical system responsible for a given kind of cognitive competency might also include variables that depend on features of the environment or on organism-environment couplings. This state of affairs makes dynamical explanations particularly well suited to "extended" explanations of cognition, because a dynamical system (or a set of dynamical systems) can have variables and parameters accounting for properties and states of affairs on either side of the skull (Clark, 2008; Clark and Chalmers, 1998).

This last point is clear in the work of Beer (1995) and later in Beer (2000). To clarify this point, consider the following model from Beer (1995), who says:

> I will model an agent and its environment as two dynamical systems α and ε, respectively. I will assume that α and ε are continuous-time dynamical systems: $x_\alpha = \alpha(x_\alpha; u_\alpha)$ and $x_\varepsilon = \alpha(x_\varepsilon; u_\varepsilon)$. In addition, I will assume that both α and ε have convergent dynamics, that is, the values of their state variables do not diverge to infinity, but instead eventually converge to some limit set.
>
> [...]
>
> An agent and its environment are in constant interaction. Formally, this means that α and ε are coupled nonautonomous dynamical systems. In order to couple two dynamical systems, we can make some of the parameters of each system functions of some of the state variables of the other. I will represent this coupling with a sensory function **S** from environmental state variables to agent parameters and a motor function **M** from agent state variables to environmental parameters. $\mathbf{S}(x_\alpha)$ corresponds to an agent's sensory inputs, while $\mathbf{M}(x_\varepsilon)$ corresponds to its motor outputs. Thus, we have the following:
>
> $$x_\alpha = \alpha(x_\alpha; \mathbf{S}(x_\varepsilon); u'_\alpha),$$
> $$x_\varepsilon = \alpha(x_\varepsilon; \mathbf{M}(x_\alpha); u'_\varepsilon), \qquad (4.3)$$
>
> where u'_α and u'_ε represent any remaining parameters of α and ε respectively that do not participate in the coupling. I will assume that this coupled agent-environment system also exhibits only convergent dynamics.

This point about the inclusion of extra-organismic variables connects to another typical feature of dynamical explanations: the lack—or, at least, the downplaying of—representations. As I said above, this anti-representationalist flavour of dynamical modelling is often taken to be a reason for "why" dynamical modelling can and should be used to explain cognition. But anti-representationalism is not a necessary feature of dynamic modelling, since one can just as well model the dynamic relations between representational structures. However, having a preference for dynamical explanation can bias one against representations for one of two reasons. Firstly, because "it seems unnecessary to call on internal representations of environmental features when the [environmental] features themselves are part of the cognitive system to be explained" (Chemero and Silberstein, 2008, pp. 11–12). Secondly, because if "the dynamic structure of the brain is determined by the brain itself," then there is no need to assume that it represents the environment.

Of course, endorsing the dynamical hypothesis and developing dynamicist explanations means more than just appealing to certain kinds of models and

Tab. 4.2: General characteristics of dynamicist explanations (inspired by Van Gelder, 1998, p. 621).

Characteristic	Idea
1. Change.	Emphasis in how variables constituting cognitive states/processes change.
2. Geometry.	Understand cognitive states/processes geometrically, in terms of its "position with respect to other states and features of the system's dynamical landscape such as basins of attraction."
3. Structure in time.	"Cognitive structure laid out temporally" and "seen as the simultaneous, mutually influencing unfolding of complex temporal structures."
4. Ongoing.	Cognitive states/processes seen as "always ongoing, not starting anywhere and not finishing anywhere."

modelling techniques—it means that one conceives of cognition, cognitive competencies, and wider cognitive performance *dynamically*. As Van Gelder (1998, p. 620) puts it, developing dynamicist explanations in the first place "means taking the resources of dynamics—as opposed, for example, to mainstream computer science—as the basic descriptive and explanatory framework."

I have already given three key ingredients of dynamical systems above, but the general idea is worth reiterating: to conceive of a system dynamically is to conceive of that system as a collections of quantities and magnitudes that can be conveniently expressed by (a set of) differential equations. Perhaps the most straight forward way to think about a system in these terms is to think of it *geometrically*, whereby it is conceived "in terms of positions, distances, regions, and paths in a space of possible states [and dynamic modelling] aims to understand structural properties of the *flow*, that is, the entire range of possible paths" (Van Gelder, 1998, p. 621).

With this point in mind, we can consider how it is that dynamicist explanations purport to explain cognition. We can once again follow Van Gelder (1998, p. 621) in identifying the "general characteristics of a broadly dynamical perspective" towards explaining cognition. The most important of these characteristics are presented in table 4.2. In short, the idea is that dynamicist explanations explain cognition in virtue of being quantitative, change-oriented, and continuous. This idea was set-out by Van Gelder (1998, p. 622) in the following short manifesto:

for every kind of cognitive performance exhibited by a natural cognitive agent, there is some quantitative system instantiated by the agent at the highest relevant level of causal organization, so that performances of that kind are behaviors of that system; in addition, causal organization can and should be understood by producing dynamical models, using the theoretical resources of dynamics, and adopting a broadly dynamical perspective.

Dynamicist explanations now feature prominently in many areas of cognitive science; particularly in systems and cognitive neuroscience (cf. Bressler and Kelso, 2001; Carson and Kelso, 2004; Fuchs, Jirsa, and Kelso, 2000; Jantzen, Steinberg, and Kelso, 2009; Jirsa, Fuchs, and Kelso, 1998; Schoner and Kelso, 1988, as examples of a vast body of literature). As an explanatory trend in cognitive science, dynamicism can be understood as a reaction against the dominant representationalist and computationalist paradigm. The appeal of dynamicist explanations is that—unlike representationalist and computationalist explanations—they take the nature of change in time as the primary explanatory focus (Van Gelder, 1995). Dynamical systems are the best way to represent and express such temporal situated transitions. And the hope is that by formulating dynamic systems-based explanations, we will be able to better understand the emergence and stability of cognition as a temporally extended and self-organising system.

4.2 Explanatory Pluralism in Cognitive Science

On the face of it, there is no problem with a single discipline employing different kinds of explanations. In botanist biology, for example, we have explanations that are taxonomical (e.g. when organising plants into "seed plants" (gymnosperms) and "free-sporing" plants (cryptograms)), mechanical (e.g. when undertaking a biochemical study of the chemical processes used by plants, such as the photosynthetic Calvin cycle and crassulacean acid metabolism (Lüttge, 2006)), and evolutionary (e.g. when charting the development of plants from algae mats to complex angiosperms (Lewis and Brodie, 2007)). Difficulties only arise if the different kinds of explanation cannot be made consistent with one another.

In (the philosophy of) cognitive science, debate about the coherence between mechanistic, psychological, and dynamicist explanations is on-going and tendentious. Some take the view that the different kinds of explanations are coherent; the task is just to show how. Consider, for instance, the view defended by Clark (2008). Clark (2008) develops a so-called an "integrative explanatory framework," which couples a dynamic account of the gross behaviour of the agent-environment system with a psychological-mechanistic explanation of how the components of the agent-environment system interact to produce the phenomena relevant to cognitive science. For Clark, some explanations are "representation-hungry" and others are not, dependent upon the extent to which the explananda (e.g. the cognitive competencies to be explained) are behaviours that coordinate "with specific environmental contingencies" Clark (2008). Where so-called "environmentally decoupling" is a feature of the explananda, Clark claims that we must turn to mechanisms defined as operations on representations; but we can develop dynamic explanations of the "adaptive hookup" between cognitive systems and their environments in those cases where the explananda depends directly on environmental contingencies.[35]

The problem with positions such as the one endorsed by Clark (2008)—and many others like it (cf. Bechtel and Richardson, 2010)—is that they partition the explanatory work according to whether the explananda are more suited to one or another kind of explanation. It remains to be seen, therefore, if it is possible to explain the gross behaviour of the agent-environment system in purely mechanistic terms; just as it remains to be seen if it is possible to explain decoupled behaviours such as, say, memory in dynamic terms. The upshot is that the project of making different kinds of explanations coherent risks being nothing more than a grouping together of different kinds of explanations. The question, then, is whether this grouping deserves to be called an all-encompassing and coherent explanatory framework at all. The argument that it does faces the problem of responding to two trends in cognitive science:

1. Hegemonisation
2. Autonomisation

Hegemonisation occurs when only one kind of explanation is taken to be genuinely explanatory and other putative kinds of explanation are made subservient to this dominant kind of explanation or eschewed entirely. The two clearest examples of hegemonisation in practice are Kaplan and Craver (2011) and Piccinini and Craver (2011), who argue for the pre-eminence of mechanistic explanation over dynamicist and psychological explanations respectively. For Kaplan and Craver (2011, p. 623), "the explanatory force of dynamical models, to the extent that they have such force, inheres in their ability to reveal dynamic and organizational features of the behavior of a mechanism." And, similarly, Piccinini and Craver (2011) argue that "there is no functional analysis that is distinct and autonomous from mechanistic explanation because to describe an item functionally is, *ipso facto*, to describe its contribution to a mechanism."

The working idea of Craver, Kaplan, and Piccinini is that psychological and dynamicist "explanations" contribute to explanation only insofar as they make

---

35 Clark calls this explanatory strategy "minimal representationalism," and situates it within a wider theoretical framework: "active externalism" (cf. Clark, 1997; Clark, 2003; Clark and Chalmers, 1998).

possible mechanistic explanations. They argue that psychological and dynamicist explanations are not *de facto* explanatory, but only help us to arrive at genuinely explanatory mechanistic explanations in virtue of providing "sketches" of such explanations. In this vein, they argue:

> Descriptions of mechanisms—mechanism schemas (Machamer, Darden, and Craver, 2000) or models (Glennan, 2005; Craver, 2006)—can be more or less complete. Incomplete models—with gaps, question-marks, filler-terms, or hand-waving boxes and arrows—are mechanism sketches. Mechanism sketches are incomplete because they leave out crucial details about how the mechanism works. Sometimes a sketch provides just the right amount of explanatory information for a given context (classroom, courtroom, lab meeting, etc.). Furthermore, sketches are often useful guides to the future development of a mechanistic explanation. Yet there remains a sense in which mechanism sketches are incomplete or elliptical (Piccinini and Craver, 2011, p. 293).

On their arguments, then, genuine explanations must discover mechanisms, because cognitive science cannot content itself with mere functional and/or dynamic descriptions "that fail to correspond to the structural components to be found in the brain" (Piccinini and Craver, 2011, p. 307).

Now, one may think that this mechanistic hegemonisation threatens the integrity of dynamicist explanations but not the integrity of psychological explanations, since psychological explanations can be thought of as a subspecies of mechanistic explanation in which the components of the mechanism are mental representations that interact according to rules of computation. But this line of reasoning comes under attack from those who defend and initiate the trend of autonomisation in cognitive science.

Autonomisation is the process of differentiating kinds of explanation and of showing how each is able to do explanatory work in its own right. Some of the earliest attempts at autonomisation were concerned with showing how certain sciences are autonomous from others. Famously, Fodor (1974) argued that the explanatory domains of the special sciences—including psychology—should be autonomous from underlying physical details. This line of reasoning —which argued for the autonomy of explanations in psychology from explanations in physics—has been further expanded and expounded by those resisting hegemonisation in cognitive science.

Following Fodor, those resisting the hegemonisation of, for instance, mechanistic explanations over psychological and dynamicist explanations have argued for the taxonomic and explanatory autonomy of different kinds of explanations. The idea of taxonomic autonomy is taken directly from Fodor himself, who argued that;

> Physics develops the taxonomy of its subject-matter which best suits its purposes: the formulation of exceptionless laws which are basic in the several senses discussed above. But this is not the only taxonomy which may be required if the purposes of science in general are to be served: e.g., if we are to state such true, counterfactual supporting generalizations as there are to state. So, there are special sciences, with their specialized taxonomies, in the business of stating some of these generalizations.

In short, then, taxonomic autonomy obtains when a given kind of explanation has the freedom to posit a range of entities, states, and processes independent of the explanatory work done by other kinds of explanations. Explanatory autonomy builds upon taxonomic autonomy by adding a further condition: that any kind of explanation is sufficient by itself to give an adequate explanation of its own explanatory domain (Weiskopf, forthcoming).

In the context of cognitive science, some have undertaken the project of autonomisation to differentiate and fortify the independence of psychological and dynamicist explanations. Weiskopf (forthcoming), for example, argues that psychological explanations "are capable by themselves of meeting any standards of taxonomic legitimacy and explanatory adequacy." Likewise, advocates of dynamicist explanations—such as Van Gelder (1995) and Chemero and Silberstein (2008)—have sought to show that such explanations need not be constrained by the norms governing successful mechanistic explanation. The upshot is that autonomisation pulls in the opposite direction to hegemonisation: one that drives and substantiates diversification. In contrast, hegemonisation undermines diversification by seeking to strictly define what a cognitive scientific explanation should look like and how it should explain.

The opposing forces of hegemonisation and autonomisation are driven by deeper disagreements about the nature of explanation. Those in favour of hegemonisation are also likely to be in favour of a certain kind of explanatory reductionism. The kind of explanatory reductionism, for instance, that affirms the thesis that the same rules that determine what makes for a good explanation should apply to all cases of explanation (Strevens, 2008). This kind of explanatory reduction should be thought of as the kind of reduction that is methodological in the sense that it strives to find the necessary components for any case of explanation. For example, in the case of cognitive science, that all explanations should describe structural components that correspondence to feature found in the brain.

Those in favour of autonomisation will likely reject explanatory reductionism. But this leads to a further problem, because then it is unclear what components are, in fact, necessary for genuine explanation. Weiskopf (forthcoming, p. 21) argues that psychological explanations are autonomous from mechanistic explanations, but that they still capture causal structure. However, for Weiskopf, psychological explanations only capture causal structure by "abstracting away many or most aspects of the physical, biological, and neural architecture that support it." Thus, the capturing of causal structure by psychological explanations is divorced from any story about implementation in the brain. Chemero and Silberstein (2008, p. 12) argue that dynamicist explanations are autonomous in an even more obvious way, because they "abstract away from causal mechanical [...] details" to explain the behaviour of cognitive systems in terms of dynamic changes over time.

In cognitive science, therefore, autonomisation will only succeed if no stipulation is made about what is required for genuine explanation. In fact, autonomisation will require that we leave open the possibility that there may not be a single necessary component of explanation at all. This strikes many—e.g. Kaplan and Craver (2011) and Piccinini and Craver (2011)—as unacceptable. But the question is: is there any principled reason why autonomisation could not succeed? It will not be enough to simply suppose that all cognitive scientific explanations must have some necessary components in common, because advocates of autonomisation can always respond that what matters in only that each kind of explanation does some of the explanatory work required in cognitive science.

The philosophical debate about what is required for explanation—both within and without cognitive science—is divisive. Those in favour of hegemonisation have brought forward arguments for why we should think that there is at least one necessary component to genuine explanation (cf. Piccinini and Craver, 2011). But it is not clear that one must assent to these arguments (I will discuss this at greater length in the following chapter), and so autonomisation remains a live position. What is clear, however, is that there are a number of different kinds of explanation being formulated in cognitive science. These include the mechanistic, psychological, and dynamicist kinds of explanations elucidated above. Evidently, then, there already exists a kind of *plurality* of cognitive scientific explanation.

Still, one may think that this plurality obtains only at the level of explanatory *schemas* and does not provide evidence for the fundamental disunity of explanations in cognitive science. The problem here is that it is not straightforwardly clear what is meant by "pluralism" in this context. On the one hand, one may think of pluralism in a metaphysical sense such that there cannot be "some ultimate victor in competing scientific theories," because the reality to be explained is fundamentally dis-unified (Dale, 2008, p. 156). On the other hand, one may think of pluralism as obtaining only at the level of explanation, whereby different explanatory strategies are employed to answer different explanatory question, and where the explanations "delivered by science depend on our practical and epistemic interests" (Ruphy, 2016, p. 82).

The first of these two interpretations of pluralism can be attributed to Cartwright (1999) and Dupré (1993) (or, more generally, to the so-called Stanford school of pluralists). This kind of "external pluralism" commits one to a metaphysical claim that is independent from the actual explanatory practices in science. The second interpretation of pluralism can be attributed to Kellert, Longino, and Waters (2006) and Ruphy (2016) (or, more generally, the Minnesota school of pluralists). This kind of "internal pluralism" commits one only to an epistemological claim about the contingent plurality of explanations in science. Whereas the first interpretation is willing to accept the claim that "some parts of the world (or situations in the world) are such that a plurality of accounts or approaches will be necessary for answering all the questions we have about those parts of situations"; the second interpretation does not characterise pluralism by reference to any metaphysical doctrine (Kellert, Longino, and Waters, 2006, p. xxii).

Dupré (1993) prefers the first, metaphysical interpretation of pluralism. He claims that pluralism is consistent with the view that there are mind-independent facts or kind, but that there are a plurality of ways these facts and kinds can be categorised depending upon social context. Ruphy (2016), by contrast, defends the second, epistemological interpretation by arguing that pluralism "merely amounts to a general methodological prescription and is too weak to yield uncontroversial metaphysical lessons [...] external to scientific practice" (Cat, 2017). Ruphy, then, is at pains to reject the "separatist" (read: metaphysical) "tendency to "freeze" [...] situations of plurality, closing the door to possible evolution and reconfiguration of the articulations of the pieces of knowledge and practice involved" that may lead us back to monism (Ruphy, 2016, p. 133).

For my purposes here, the important point is about what pluralism entails about our capacity to arrive at a consensus about the explananda of cognitive science (cf. Jordi, 2012; Kellert, 2008; Rescher, 1993). Above, I set-out the two problems for making the different kinds of explanation in cognitive science coherent: hegemonisation and autonomisation. The upshot of this discussion was that we do not yet know what is required of (genuine) explanation in cognitive science and we are still in the middle of a larger debate about how and even if this question can be resolved. It follows that, for now at least, we must be willing to accept a plurality of different kinds of explanations in cognitive science, regardless of whether we take this plurality to have metaphysical implications.

With this in mind, I assent to the following argument for the "possibility of pluralism" put forward by Dale (2008, pp. 162–163):

C. The argument for the possibility of pluralism:

1. No theory in cognitive science yet has actual comprehensiveness in application.(Premise)

2. It is possible that cognitive theories do not have the representational where-withal to contact explanatory needs in all contexts of inquiry.[36] (Premise)

3. It is therefore possible that cognitive scientists face theoretical diversity to have comprehensive coverage of their problem domains. (From C1 and C2)

Both Premise 1 and Premise 2 follow from the fact that different kinds of explanations are differently suited to explaining different explananda in cognitive science. For example, cognitive neuroscientists will invariably develop mechanistic explanations to give a causal and neural-implementational account of some phenomenon. However, other higher cognitive capacities—e.g. reasoning or memory—will be best explained in psychological terms, whereby abstraction from the details of implementation is required. And explanations of cognitive competencies as environmentally-embedded contingencies will be best explained by another explanatory framework altogether: dynamicist explanations.

The point, then, is that we cannot necessarily expect any single kind of cognitive scientific explanation to account for all of the explananda that cognitive scientists now want to explain. Dale's (2008, 163) comparison of psychological explanations involving "discrete symbols" (read: representations) and dynamicist explanations describing "dynamical systems" makes this point clear. He says:

> it may simply not be possible to use some theories in a domain that others are in the habit of explaining. Sharply discrete symbolic descriptions have now been thoroughly discarded as explanations of gait and posture; instead, formalisms from dynamical systems have clearly more relevance and application in that domain (e.g. Kelso and Jeka, 1992). Conversely, understanding transitions from equation to equation in a complex algebraic problem in a high-school student is currently more thoroughly explored by these symbolic systems (e.g. Nathan, Kintsch, and Young, 1992). Both are valid and important problems in cognitive science, but may require different explanatory schemes. Thus, given the statement that scientific theories are inherently, deliberately limited in their scope, urging comprehensiveness may be pressing their limits of representation (in the sense of Giere, 2004).

Few, if any, think that mechanistic, psychological, and dynamicist explanations of, say, reasoning or memory can be put together to arrive at a global picture of these explananda. Rather, the tendency is to undermine one or more of the other kinds of explanation (hegemonisation) or to carve out an independent explanatory niche for each kind of explanation with their own subject-matter and explanatory success conditions (autonomisation). And until the debate between these opposing forces

---

36 The term "representation" used here is meant to refer to scientific representation and not to the representations posited in psychological explanations.

is resolved, we must accept the possibility of cognitive science being a irreducibly pluralistic explanatory enterprise. The question, then, is whether or not we should welcome this pluralistic state of affair or strive for a unified explanatory framework? The uncertainty about how to answer this question is representative of explanatory ambiguity in cognitive science.

4.3 Problem 1 and the Meta-Explanatory Challenge

In chapter three, I introduced the "meta-explanatory challenge to new theories of CONCEPT," which argued that we cannot simply appeal to cognitive science to decide between eliminativist, pluralist, and hybrid theories of CONCEPT, because each theory endorses a different interpretation of the explananda of cognitive science. Progress, therefore, would depend upon the reaching of a consensus about cognitive science as an explanatory project. In this chapter, however, I have shown that reaching a consensus about *how* cognitive science explains will not be easy. In fact, by introducing and elucidating different kinds of explanation in cognitive science—i.e. mechanistic, psychological, and dynamicist kinds of explanation—, I have shown that it is more plausible to think of cognitive science as a pluralist, explanatory program, where no one explanatory schema is favoured above all others.

Now, one may think that questions of *how* cognitive science explains are orthogonal to the concerns raised by the "meta-explanatory challenge," because all theories of CONCEPT could take the same view on how cognitive science explains and still disagree about the explananda of cognitive science. For example, all theories of CONCEPT could endorse a hegemonic, mechanistic view of genuine cognitive scientific explanation and still disagree about whether CONCEPT is a single, unifying kind. But, crucially, another possibility cannot be ruled out: that different theories of CONCEPT take different views on how cognitive science explains. And if this second option is even a possibility, then the "meta-explanatory challenge" is fortified, because it is possible that different "new" theories of CONCEPT take different views on which kinds of cognitive scientific explanations are genuinely explanatory.

5 Problem 2: Explananda Ambiguity

In the last chapter, I argued that the possibility of interpreting cognitive science as a pluralist explanatory enterprise risks strengthening the "meta-explanatory challenge to new theories of CONCEPT," because it is possible that "new" theories of CONCEPT disagree about which cognitive scientific explanations are genuinely explanatory.[37] However, one could push back against this argument by arguing that it is equally as likely that different "new" theories of CONCEPT agree about which kinds of cognitive scientific explanations are genuinely explanatory. From this perspective, the meta-appeal to cognitive science to decide between "new" theories of CONCEPT may once again find traction, because the different "new" theories of CONCEPT would be in agreement about how cognitive science explains.

In this chapter, I will reject this counter-argument by demonstrating that the different "new" theories of CONCEPT are likely to take different views on which cognitive scientific explanations are genuinely explanatory. This argument will be spelled-out in the context of a discussion of *explanatory integration* in cognitive science. What I will demonstrate is that one's view about whether to favour integrations of a single kind of explanation or integrations of many kinds of explanations will, ultimately, depend on one's interpretation of the explananda of cognitive science. It follows that one's views about which cognitive scientific explanations are genuinely explanatory will also depend on one's views about the explananda of cognitive science. This, in turn, seals the "meta-explanatory challenge to new theories of CONCEPT."

5.1 Integrating Mechanistic Explanations: An Example

The debate about what is required from cognitive scientific explanation is long and convoluted. As Weiskopf (forthcoming) points out, modelling cognition can involve various abstractions and idealisation as we, say, "neglect the brain's intricate internal organization and treat it simply as a suitably discretized homogeneous mass having certain energy demands (Gaohua and Kimura, 2009)"; or focus on "detailed structural and dynamical properties" revealed by "the distribution of various neurotransmitter receptor sites (Zilles and Amunts, 2009)." There is an open question, however, about how—if at all—we are to integrate various models of cognition into one coherent picture of the operation and organisation of the

---

[37] This chapter contains some material that is a re-working of Taylor (2019b).

https://doi.org/9783110708165-005

mind/brain. This issue was brought out in chapter four during my discussion of the plurality of mechanistic, psychological, and dynamicist explanations in cognitive science, and the opposing forces of hegemonisation and autonomisation.

One possibility, however, is to focus on the integration of a single kind of explanations; say, mechanistic explanation. I noted in the last chapter that a mechanism is "a structure, responsible for one or more phenomena, that performs a function in virtue of its component parts, component operations, and their organization" (Bechtel and Abrahamsen, 2005). A mechanism, therefore, need not be *deterministic* (it's components may be stochastic) (Bogen, 2005; Bogen, 2008); *reductionistic* (it may be, e.g., a multilevel explanations spanning a range of spatio-temporal levels of grain) (Bechtel, 2009); *sequential* or *linear* (it may include feedback loops wherein the output of the mechanism or components in turn influences the input of the mechanism or components in a subsequent iteration) (Bechtel, 2011); or *localisable* (components of mechanisms might be widely distributed (as are many brain mechanisms) and might violate our intuitive sense of the boundaries of objects (as an action potential violates the cell boundary) (cf. Craver and Tabery, 2017, for a thorough account of what mechanisms are and are not). It need only be a collection of "entities and activities organized such that they are productive of regular changes from start or set-up to finish or termination conditions" (Machamer, Darden, and Craver, 2000, p. 3).

Miłkowski (2016) has argued that the integration of mechanistic explanations is an absolute ideal in cognitive science. An integration of two mechanistic explanations will show how two sets of causally efficacious entities and interactions—e.g. two mechanisms—are co-organised to generate the phenomena for which both are co-responsible. Such integration can occur, for example, when one mechanism is shown to be a part of another mechanism. According to Piccinini and Craver (2011, p. 284), developing "multilevel mechanistic explanations of neural systems" will lead to an increase in explanatory power. The problem, however, is that open questions remain about how mechanistic explanations can be integrated into one coherent account of the states and processes responsible for cognition (Newell, 1990).

Broadly speaking, any integration of mechanistic explanations will aim to arrive at the best set of cohering, mechanistic explanations of the explananda. With respect to cognitive science and in the maximally explanatory case, an integration of mechanistic explanations would hope to account for all of the phenomena associated with (human) cognition. Piccinini and Craver (2011, p. 284), for example, argue that the explananda explained by a maximally explanatory integration of mechanistic explanation will exhaust all of the explananda of cognitive science. It is an open question if this hegemonistic view is correct, but we can assume that those in favour of mechanistic explanations will, at the very least, take integrations of these explanations to be able to explain phenomena including cognitive competencies such as language comprehension, memory, and categorisation; but also flexible behaviours, as well as the processes of learning and development.

Concerns about the integration of mechanistic explanations in cognitive science arise whenever we are uncertain how to "fit together" two or more mechanistic explanations in a way that gives us insight into a cognitive system's organisation and operation (Weiskopf, forthcoming). Piccinini and Craver (2011, p. 307) argue that cognitive science has "advanced to the point that [...] there are tremendous potential benefits from affecting such integration." According to Craver (2007), integrating mechanistic explanations involves integrating three perspectives: the "isolated perspective (level 0)" that characterises the mechanism with respect to the causal processes (input-output relations) that the mechanism is meant to explain. The "contextual perspective (level +1)" that locates the mechanism as a contributing part of another mechanism. And, finally, the "constitutive perspective (level -1)" that breaks down the mechanism into its constitutive parts and interactions to make perspicuous how the interactions of these parts give rise to the causal story told at the level 0.

It is clear, therefore, that the integration of mechanistic explanations will entail the telling of an "inter-level" story that relates, in one way or another, two or more mechanistic explanations (Miłkowski, 2016). An almost canonical example of this kind of integration is given in the discussion of explanations of Long-Term Potentiation (LTP) and spatial memory in Bechtel (2009), Craver (2005), and Craver (2007). Marraffa and Paternoster (2013, p. 14) provide a clear summary of Craver's (2007) account as follows:

> Craver (2007) examines the development of the explanations of Long-Term Potentiation (LTP) and spatial memory. He distinguishes at least four levels. At the top of the hierarchy (the behavioral-organismic level) are memory and learning, which are investigated by behavioral tests. Below that level is the hippocampus and the computational processes it is supposed to perform to generate spatial maps. At a still lower level are the hippocampal synapses inducing LTP. And finally, at the lowest level, are the activities of the molecules of the hippocampal synapses underlying LTP (e.g., the N-methyl Daspartate receptor activating and inactivating). These are "mechanistic levels" or "levels of mechanisms": the N-methyl D-aspartate receptor is a component of the LTP mechanism, LTP is a component of the mechanism generating spatial maps, and the formation of spatial maps is a part of the spatial navigation mechanism. Integrating these four mechanistic levels requires both a "looking up" integration, which will show that an item (LTP) is a part of a upper-level mechanism (a computational-hippocampal mechanism); and a "looking down" integration, which will describe the lower-level mechanisms underlying the higher-level phenomenon (the molecular mechanisms of LTP) [(See Fig. 5.1)].

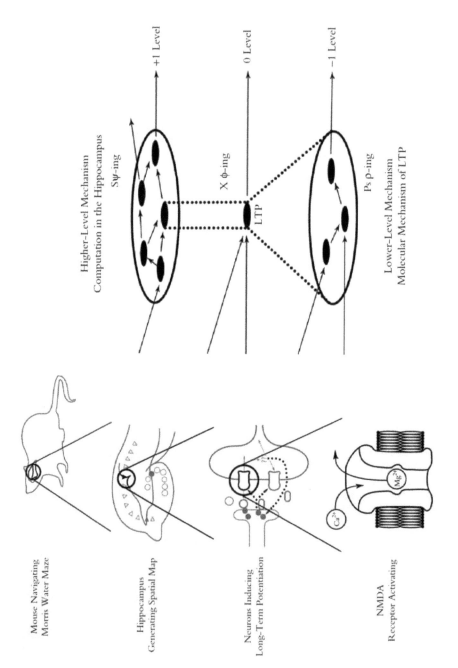

Fig. 5.1: Levels of spatial memory (left) and integrating levels of mechanisms (right) (Craver, 2007).

For Craver, the integration of mechanistic explanations entails giving a causal explanation of a cognitive phenomenon (e.g. cognitive competency or cognitive system) that spans various levels. For example, that spans behavioural traits (memory and learning), brain regions (hippocampus), and neural structures (hippocampus synapses). In this sense, integrations of mechanistic explanations demonstrate how mechanisms have other mechanisms as their interacting parts and so are "intrinsically organized in multilayers" of mechanisms. In other words, integration of mechanistic explanations show how two or more mechanisms are hierarchically organised in such a way that organisations of lower level entities and activities are the component parts of higher level organisations of entities and activities (Craver, 2001). The integration of mechanistic explanations will, therefore, be "multilevelled" in the sense that it accounts for the way that mechanisms produce a certain cognitive competency or behaviour in virtue of being themselves composed of causally efficacious mechanisms.[38]

5.2 Two Virtues of Integrating Mechanistic Explanations

Craver's account supposes that an integration of mechanistic explanations takes all the mechanisms specified by the explanations being integrated and locates them in a single, hierarchically organised mechanism. Suppose, then, that e_1 were a mechanistic explanation of the visual processes responsible for edge detection, e_2 were a mechanistic explanation of depth perception, and e_3 were a mechanistic explanation of colour perception. According to Craver's account, e_1, e_2, and e_3 would only be integrated when the mechanisms specified by all three explanations were located in a single, hierarchically organised mechanism that accounts for edge detection, depth perception, and colour perception. The upshot is that the integration of mechanistic explanations will be a process that takes a set of explanations $\{e_1...e_x\}$ specifying different mechanisms and *unifies* them within a single, multilevel explanation specifying one, hierarchically organised mechanism.

Contra Craver, Miłkowski (2016, p. 16) has argued that unification is not a virtue of the integration of mechanistic explanations, because it can only be cashed out in terms of "simplicity, invariance and unbounded scope, and non-monstrosity."

---

[38] Note that all integrated explanations must do some relevant explanatory work. This could be achieved if an integrated explanation helps to explain a previously unexplained explanandum, thereby increasing the number of explananda accounted for by the hierarchically organised mechanism (e.g. make the explanation more complete); or if it contributes to an existing explanation of some explanandum, thereby consolidating and/or furthering the explanatory power attained by specifying the hierarchically organised mechanism (e.g. making the explanation more deep).

Simplicity, he argues, is not a virtue of integrated mechanistic explanations because "maximally non-redundant representations may be difficult to decipher"
and so "mechanisms should be simple and parsimonious only as far as it aids
their uses" (Miłkowski, 2016, p. 27). Neither is invariance and unbounded scope,
because the target explananda of cognitive scientific models may occur "only in
certain spatiotemporal locations" where "causal explanations seem mostly local."
And neither is non-monstrosity, because "structures may exist that are composed
of relatively independent subsystems," and explaining these systems may require
multifaceted models.

However, Miłkowski's view of unification as definable in terms of either simplicity, invariance and unbounded scope, or non-monstrosity is too superficial.
Consider, for instance, the different virtues of *ontological unifications*—e.g. unifications that spell out causal or reductive relations—and *epistemological unifications*—e.g. unifications that satisfy particular epistemic or pragmatic goals (cf.
Cartwright, 1999; Cat, 2017). No doubt, the virtues of epistemological unification
may be threatened by Miłkowski's account of the failings of simplicity, invariance
and unbounded scope, and non-monstrosity with respect to integrations of mechanistic explanations. However, the virtues of ontological unification will not be
impugned by these failings, because an integration of mechanistic explanations
can have the virtue of unifying causal or reductive relations between entities whatever the cost to simplicity, invariance and unbounded scope, or non-monstrosity.

This point can be equally well made by considering the differences between
the virtues of *global* and *local unification*. Global unifications unify all explanations, whereas local unifications unify only a subset of explanations. Armed with
this distinction, it is clear that some local unifications are more likely to have the
virtues of simplicity, invariance and unbounded scope, and/or non-monstrosity.
For example, a local unification of two mechanistic explanations—one specifying
a computational-hippocampal mechanism, another specifying molecular mechanisms of LTP (see Fig. 6 above)—will likely be at least simple and non-monstrous.
Global unification, however, is much less likely to have such virtues, because
the simplicity, invariance and unbounded scope, and non-monstrosity will likely
decrease as a function of the number of explanations being integrated. These examples demonstrate that Miłkowski's fails to take into consideration difficult and
unsolved problems about how to conceive of the theoretical virtue of unification
(cf. Cat, 2017, for an overview of discussions about unification).

Therefore, when we properly disentangle the virtues of simplicity, invariance
and unbounded scope, and non-monstrosity and the virtue of unification *tout
court*, it is far from clear that Miłkowski gets things right. And when it comes
to Craver's account of the integration of mechanistic explanations, the virtue of
unification is clearly playing an important role, because it is only via unification

in a hierarchically organised mechanism that we are able to make sense of the coherence between integrated mechanistic explanations. That is, it is only via unification in a hierarchically organised mechanism that one mechanistic explanation's (causal) descriptions of entities and interactions is made consistent with another's. Miłkowski (2016, p. 16) recognises this point and admits that this is why "many defenders of mechanistic explanation conflate the issues of integration and unification."

Still, one may think that it should possible to give an account of the integration of mechanistic explanations that does not ascribe to them the virtue of unification. Such an account may, perhaps, conceive of integrated mechanistic explanations as "hanging together" in some shape or form (BonJour, 1985). But any integration of this kind will be so weak as to be of no value at all. To see why, suppose I have a mechanistic explanations e_1 of edge detection and another mechanistic explanation e_2 of the movements of planets in the solar system. It is clear that these two explanations are consistent with each other and can be "hung together" to give us insight into a strange system involving the perception of edges and the movements of, say, Jupiter and Saturn. But what use is this "hanging together" and why should we think that it constitutes integration? Intuitively, it does not appear to give us any greater insight either perceptual capacities or celestial motion, because the two mechanisms introduced by e_1 and e_2 cannot be unified in a hierarchically organised mechanism responsible for both phenomena.

There must, therefore, be a stricter condition on the integration of mechanistic explanations. But all attempts to spell out what this condition could be without ascribing to integrations the virtue of unification are controversial at best. Constraint-based accounts of integration have been put forward in terms of, e.g., restrictions on "the boundaries of the space of plausible mechanisms" (Craver, 2007, p. 247) and in terms of the requirement that all integrated explanations being true at the same time (Thagard, 2007). However, it is not clear that these accounts eschew the virtue of unification nor is it clear that they adequately deal with the problem of futile "integrations" discussed above. The reason is because they offer no clear limit on the space of plausible mechanisms or demarcation of the relevant true explanations, which risks making integration "more art than science" (Miłkowski, 2016, p. 19).[39] The virtue of unification plays exactly this role on Craver's account by stipulating that integrations must result in the spec-

---

[39] One may want to define integration as a complex concept incorporating a number of individually necessary and jointly sufficient conditions. Following this line of reasoning, Thagard (2002) introduced his "principles of explanatory coherence" as a guide to what integration must entail. Whether or not such complex accounts can be made to work and can avoid ascribing to integrations the virtue of unification is still up for debate (Miłkowski, 2016).

ification of a single hierarchically organised mechanism. This alone is a good reason for thinking that it is a theoretical virtue of the integration of mechanistic explanations.

Integrations of mechanistic explanations also have the virtue of *greater qualitative parsimony*. Qualitative parsimony concerns the number of types (or kinds) of thing postulated by an explanations; whereas quantitative parsimony concerns the number of individual things postulated. For example, the explanation that the damage to my car was caused by 10 children is more qualitatively parsimonious but less quantitatively parsimonious than the explanation that it was caused by 2 children, 1 bear, and 1 dog. The idea that qualitative parsimony is theoretical virtue is well-established in the literature and in the history of philosophy (cf. Quine, 1964; Sober, 1994, as examples of why qualitative parsimony (e.g. Occam's razor) is a theoretical virtue).[40] To say that integrations of mechanistic explanations have greater qualitative parsimony is just to say that such integrations do the same explanatory work by positing fewer kinds of things.

Prima facie, it seems that the number of kinds of mechanisms specified by a set of mechanistic explanations will not be affected by whether or not that set is integrated. For example, it seems that mechanistic explanations of, say, Long-Term Potentiation and spatial memory will always appeal to at least four mechanisms: a behavioural-organismic mechanism, a hippocampus-computational mechanism, a hippocampus-synapses mechanism, and molecular mechanism. However, we can see that this conclusion is mistaken when we factor in my discussion of the virtue of unification above. For then we see that only in the case of an integration of mechanistic explanations will those mechanisms be mereologically subsumed as parts of one hierarchically organised mechanism. Therefore, integrations of mechanistic explanations postulate only one *superordinate kind* of mechanism that subsumes all other mechanisms as its parts.

For any integration of mechanistic explanations, the only kind of thing postulated is a hierarchically organised mechanism that has other mechanisms as its parts. For instance, spatial mechanisms (cf Wimsatt, 1997), temporal mechanisms (cf Bechtel, 2013), stable and ephemeral mechanisms (cf Glennan, 2009) neural mechanisms, or computational mechanisms (cf Miłkowski, 2013), etc.[41]

---

40 Lewis (1973, p. 87), for instance, subscribed "to the general view that qualitative parsimony is good in a philosophical or empirical hypothesis." For historical discussion of the theoretical virtue of qualitative parsimony see Sober (2015).

41 These different kinds of mechanisms are individuated as classes by their different entities and interactions (cf. Miłkowski, 2013, for an illuminating discussion of this idea with respect to computational mechanisms in particular).

One could argue that there are other kinds of things postulated in such cases; namely, "bottoming-out" types of entities and activities that are the parts of the lowest level mechanisms. In cognitive science, such 'bottoming-out" entities and activities may include, for instance, the "descriptions of the activities of macro-molecules, smaller molecules, and ions" provided by neurobiology (Machamer, Darden, and Craver, 2000, pp. 13–15). However, these entities and activities must be accepted as "fundamental" in the sense that they demarcate where the "field stops when constructing mechanisms" (Machamer, Darden, and Craver, 2000, pp. 13–15). Thus, for all sets of mechanistic explanations in cognitive science— whether integrated or not—these entities and activities must be presupposed and so will not vitiate the increase in qualitative parsimony following integration.

There are open question about the "independence" or "objecthood" of the parts of mechanisms. Simon (1996) argues that the parts of a mechanism have stronger and more abundant causal relations with other components in the mechanism than they do with items outside the mechanism, and that the decomposition of mechanisms into parts will depend, in some way, on the intensity of interaction among components. Others—such as Craver (2007)—argue that a part of a mechanism is only defined relative to what one takes the mechanism to be doing. In any case, all agree that an integration of mechanistic explanations will result in the specification of a hierarchically organised mechanism that has other mechanisms as its parts. This is just what Craver (2007) means when he talks about the "levels" of a hierarchy of mechanisms following integration. Moreover, it is clear that a mechanism that subsumes others will be of a superior order within the classification of mechanisms, because the kind of things grouped in that class are mechanisms of mechanisms.

Consider the following toy example to see how integrations of mechanistic explanations have the virtue of greater qualitative parsimony. Suppose that we have a set of mechanistic explanations specifying four mechanisms— e.g., a behavioural-organismic mechanism, a hippocampus-computational mechanism, a hippocampus-synapses mechanism, and molecular mechanism —accounting for a kind of categorisation judgement; say, the judgement of whether or not individual c belongs in category C in terms of similarity between the properties of c and typical members of C. Now, if we compare this set of mechanistic explanations both before and after their integration (supposing that integration is possible), we find that following integration the set of explanations is more qualitatively parsimonious, because it explains the relevant kind of categorisation judgement by specifying only one kind of mechanism: a hierarchically organised mechanism that has the behavioural-organismic, hippocampus-computational, hippocampus-synapses, and molecular mechanisms as its parts.

Thus, I maintain that the virtue of greater qualitative parsimony is part and parcel of what makes the integration of mechanistic explanations valuable. Consequently, I think that we can identify greater qualitative parsimony as a second theoretical virtue of the integration of mechanistic explanations; which is just to say that such integrations have the virtue of being more qualitatively parsimonious than any un-integrated set of mechanistic explanations with equivalent explanatory power.

It is possible to give formal rendering of this virtue as follows. First let $IM(x)$ stand for an integrated set of mechanistic explanations x and let $UM(y)$ stand for a set of un-integrated mechanistic explanations y. Then let $EP(e, y)$ stand for a function that delivers the explanatory power of y with respect to some explanandum or set of explananda e. Finally, let $QP(x, e)$ be a function which delivers the qualitative parsimony of x with respect to its explanation of e, such that:

$$\forall x \forall y (IM(x) \wedge UM(y) \rightarrow \forall e(EP(e, x) \equiv EP(e, y)$$

$$\rightarrow QP(x, e) > QP(y, e))) \tag{5.1}$$

My claim, therefore, is that unification and greater qualitative parsimony are two of the theoretical virtues of integrations of mechanistic explanations (although there are likely many others). Each of these virtues can be appealed to as reasons for enacting an integration of mechanistic explanations in cognitive science.

5.3 Cross-Explanatory Integration

As I argued in chapter four, however, mechanistic explanations are not the only kind of explanations available in cognitive science; we also have psychological and dynamicist explanations. Here I will give a very quick re-fresh of both psychological and dynamicist explanations, while also re-stating and further expanding upon the differences between such explanations and mechanistic explanations. This will allow me to briefly consider the possibility of another kind of integration in cognitive science: the cross-explanatory integration of psychological and/or dynamicist and/or mechanistic explanations.

Dynamicist explanations posit variables that are "not low level (e.g., neural firing rates) but, rather, macroscopic quantities at roughly the level of the cognitive performance itself" (Van Gelder, 1998, p. 619). As a reminder of dynamicist explanation, consider the HKB model of the dynamics involved in human bimanual coordination developed by Haken, Kelso, and Bunz (1985). The HKB model "accounts for behavioral data collected when experimental subjects are instructed to repeatedly move their index fingers side to side in the transverse plane in time with a pacing metronome either in phase (simultaneous movements toward the midline of the body) or antiphase (simultaneous movements to the left or right of the body midline)" (Kaplan and Craver, 2011, p. 614). To do this, the HKB model—as with all dynamicist explanations—introduces a differential equation, which describes the coupled dynamics of these cognitive performances:

$$\phi = -a \sin \phi - 2b \sin 2\phi \qquad (5.2)$$

where "ϕ is the so-called collective variable representing the phase relationship (relative phase) between the two moving index fingers (when $\phi = 0$, the fingers are moving perfectly in phase), a and b are coupling parameters reflecting the experimentally observed finger oscillation frequencies, and the coupling ratio b/a is a control parameter since relatively small changes in its value can have a large impact on system behavior" (Kaplan and Craver, 2011, p. 614)

Dynamicist explanations were inspired by developments in the modelling of continuum systems (Chemero and Silberstein, 2008). Modelling an object as a continuum involves assuming that the object is continuously distributed (e.g. non-discrete) and fills the entire region of space it occupies. Examples of objects that can be modelled as continuum include gases, liquids, crowds, and car traffic. Continuum mechanics relies on a number of governing equations, which account for "relations of dependency" in the system being modelled. For example, for sufficiently dense and relatively slow moving continuum (e.g. Newtonian fluids) the Navier–Stokes equations account for the linear relation of dependency between stress and other and pressures (e.g. gravity, inertial accelerations, etc.) with respect to the continuum's "flow velocity."[42] Dynamacist explanations do not explain why these dependencies hold, but do show how the behaviours of all continuum systems depend on these dependencies. The HKB model, for instance, "exemplifies a law of coordination that has been found to be independent of the specifics of system structure" by "captur[ing] the coordination between behaving components of the same system" (Bressler and Kelso, 2001, p. 28).

The central difference between mechanistic and dynamicist explanations concerns how they carry explanatory force. Mechanistic explanations carry explanatory force "to the extent, and only to the extent, that they reveal (however dimly) aspects of the causal structure of a mechanism" (Kaplan and Craver, 2011). Dynamicist explanations, in contrast, carry explanatory force not by respecting the underlying causal structures that give rise to system-level dynamics, but by characterising the behaviour of systems in terms of emergent or higher-level variables

---

42 For further reading about the Navier-Stokes equations and their role in continuum mechanics see Acheson (1990) and Smits (2000).

describing (changes to) the global state of the system (cf. Van Gelder, 1995; Van Gelder, 1998; Chemero and Silberstein, 2008). This allows dynamicist explanations to "abstract away from causal mechanical and aggregate micro-details to predict the qualitative behavior of a class of similar systems" (Chemero and Silberstein, 2008, p. 12).

Integrating dynamicist and mechanistic explanations is a highly prized long-term goal for those who recognise both kinds of explanations. As an example of an attempt at this kind of cross-explanatory integration, consider the work of Bechtel (2008, 2011). In a series of papers, Bechtel argues that the best cognitive scientific explanations will introduce a continuum between fully decomposable (or highly modular) systems that are apt for mechanistic explanations and holistic, un-decomposable systems that are apt for dynamicist explanations (Bechtel, 1998; Bechtel, 2008; Bechtel, 2011). The idea here is that cognition be thought of as a "functionally integrated system" with mechanistic parts (subsystems) that are constantly interacting and influencing one another in the form of dynamic feedback loops and other non-linearities. Thus, he claims that there will be a division of labour between mechanistic and dynamicist explanation reflecting the division between two explanatory tasks: explaining interactions *within* and *between* subsystems, and explaining the feedforward, feedback, and collateral connections that characterise the dynamic behaviour of the system as a whole.[43]

The problem with Bechtel's picture is that "it is by no means obvious how to link the output of modules to the relevant dynamical variables of the whole system" (Marraffa and Paternoster, 2013, p. 34). While Bechtel claims that mechanistic explanation at the level of subsystems provides the foundation for dynamicist explanation, the two kinds of explanations still do independent explanatory work. For instance, mechanistic explanations explain interactions between and within subsystems; whereas dynamicist explanations account for patterns of dynamic organisation characterising the state of the cognitive system as a whole. As Marraffa and Paternoster (2013, p. 34) point out, this means that Bechtel's cross-explanatory integration remains incomplete, because no account is given of how to connect the states and processes described by mechanistic explanations with the global states described by dynamicist explanations. Thus, Bechtel's attempted cross-explanatory integration seems to be nothing more than a "tacking together" of mechanistic and dynamicist explanations.[44]

---

43 The outcome of these two tasks can then be "tightly coupled together" as an integrated "dynamic mechanical explanation" (DME) (cf. Bechtel and Abrahamsen, 2010, for the canonical formulation of DME's).

44 Issad and Malaterre (2015) try to make sense of Bechtel's account by arguing that mechanistic explanations and dynamic mechanical explanations can be subsumed under a new category of

Alongside dynamicist explanation, we also have psychological explanations. Psychological explanations are "defined in terms of the functional coupling of their components," which is neutral with respect to the physical (e.g. spatio-temporal) organisation of those components. (Weiskopf, forthcoming). The central difference between mechanistic and psychological explanations—if there is a difference at all—concerns how they capture the causal organisation of cognitive systems. In contrast to standard mechanistic explanations, psychological explanations are taken to capture the causal structure of a "relatively restricted aspect or subsystem of the total cognitive system" by employing "relatively few variables or factors" (e.g. representations and operations over representations). Moreover, they are taken to individuate their explanatory targets—their explananda—in a way that is neutral with respect to the physical structure of the system that realises them (Weiskopf, forthcoming, pp. 10–11). The idea of psychological explanations, then, is that the explain by abstracting away from decomposable aspects of the biological and neural architecture to capture the "causal organization of a psychological system by representing it in terms of abstract relationships among functional components" (Weiskopf, forthcoming, p. 37).

Aside from their neutrality with respect to the underlying physical, biological, and neural architecture, another distinctive feature of psychological explanations is their positing of contentful representations and interactions over these representations. Psychological explanations stipulate that the functional components represented must be intentionally interpreted states. In this way, psychological explanation is committed to "intentional internals" in the sense of Egan and Matthews (2006). Their account of how "cognitivist" explanation (read: psychological explanations) featuring intentional internals works runs as follows:

> The cognitive capacity to be explained—e.g., recovering the three dimensional structure of the scene, recognizing faces, understanding speech—is typically decomposed into a series of subtasks, each of which is itself characterized in intentional terms. The intentional internals posited by the cognitive theory are presumed to be distally interpretable, i.e., to represent such external objects and properties as the orientation of surfaces, facial features, spatial

---

explanation: "Causally Interpreted Model Explanations" (CIME's). CIME's are taken to explain "neither in virtue of displaying a mechanism nor in virtue of providing a causal account, but in virtue of mathematically showing how the explanandum can be analytically or numerically derived from a model whose variables and functions can be causally interpreted" (Issad and Malaterre, 2015, p. 288). However, this forces Issad and Malaterre to admit that "supplying a causal-story is no longer seen central in providing explanatory force" and so "providing a mechanism *per se* is also not so central when it comes to explanatory force" (Issad and Malaterre, 2015, p. 289). This view, then, does not seem like a case of cross-explanatory integration at all, but, rather, a reduction of the mechanistic explanation to dynamicist explanation.

locations, etc. It is thought that if these intentional internals are not distally interpretable, then the account is unlikely to yield an explanation of the organism's successful interactions with its environment. Moreover, cognitive processes must preserve certain epistemic and semantic relations defined over these representations. The outputs of these processes should *make sense*, should be *rational*, given the inputs. This rich cognitive structure constrains theorizing at the lower levels. Cognitive theorists then look for computational and neural states to realize the intentional internals. The outcome, if things go well, will be a mapping between the causal structure of the mind and the causal structure of the brain (Egan and Matthews, 2006, p. 382).

As I said in chapter four, psychological explanations may represent systems in terms of, e.g., verbal descriptions, diagrams and graphics, mathematical formalism, or computational models or simulations. Verbal descriptions give a rough descriptions of simple cognitive models. For example, to elaborate the levels of processing framework in memory modelling as in Cermak and Craik (1979). Mathematical formalisms give a more precise description of cognitive models. Diagrams or graphics—such as boxological models—provide pictorial representations of the relationships between functional components, typically in terms of schematic representations of informational exchange. And computational models or simulations investigate of "the implications of ideas, beyond the limits of human thinking"; that is, they "allow [for] the exploration of the implications of ideas that cannot be fully explored by thought alone" (McClelland, 2009, p. 16). In all cases, however, the language (whether verbal or not) will be couched in representational terms and so will focus on the manipulation of intentional states without concern for the underlying physical structure.

Some who defend the explanatory role of psychological explanations argue for their autonomy from mechanistic explanations (cf. Fodor, 1974). All, however, accept that a complete understanding of the mind/brain will involve "perfecting cognitive models and coordinating them with neurobiological ones" (Weiskopf, forthcoming, p. 37). It is not yet clear what this "coordination" should look like, but we can suppose that it will entail a fitting together of mechanistic and psychological explanations to give us insight into a cognitive system's operation. Such an account would likely include a specification of the causal relation between structures at the level of neural-biology and intentional structures that "that hover at some remove from the neural organization of the mind/brain" (Weiskopf, forthcoming, p. 33). Such an integration would, therefore, connect different kinds of causal explanation to show how functionally characterised elements of psychological explanations relate to neural structures and processes.[45]

---

45 Weiskopf (2011) makes as start on providing this taxonomy by subsuming both mechanistic and psychological explanations under a single kind of explanation: componential causal explanation.

Having now recapitulated dynamicist and psychological explanation, it is possible to give a brief definition of a *cross-explanatory integration*. A cross-explanatory integration will be any integration that somehow fits together two or more different kinds of explanation. In cognitive science, therefore, a cross-explanatory integration will somehow fit together mechanistic and dynamicist explanations (as Bechtel (2008) attempts to), mechanistic and psychological explanations (as Weiskopf (forthcoming) alludes to), dynamicist and psychological explanations, or mechanistic, dynamicist, and psychological explanations. Of course, there are open questions about how such an integration is to be enacted, just as there are open questions about how any integration in cognitive science is enacted (Miłkowski, 2016). I will not engage with these questions, but, rather, will consider whether or not cross-explanatory integrations can be said to be worthwhile at all.

5.4 Two Views of Cognitive Scientific Explananda

Kaplan and Craver (2011) argue that dynamicist explanations do not have a role to play in cognitive science. They defend "a mechanistic approach to thinking about explanation at all levels of explanation in neuroscience," by arguing that "Dynamical models do not provide a separate kind of explanation subject to distinct norms," because "the explanatory force of dynamical models, to the extent that they have such force, inheres in their ability to reveal dynamic and organizational features of the behavior of a mechanism" (Kaplan and Craver, 2011, p. 623). Similarly, Piccinini and Craver (2011) argue that "there is no functional analysis that is distinct and autonomous from mechanistic explanation because to describe an item functionally is, *ipso facto*, to describe its contribution to a mechanism." The upshot of these hegemonic views is that there is no added benefit from recognising either dynamicist or psychological explanations in cognitive science.

One reason for thinking that Craver, Kaplan, and Piccinini are right is because by introducing non-mechanistic explanations we are confronted with the problem of cross-explanatory integration. To some, cross-explanatory integrations seem futile, because they cannot have the virtues of unification and greater qualitative parsimony. This is case because cross-explanatory integrations must integrate explanations that postulate inconsistent kinds; e.g. spatio-temporally organised components and activities (mechanistic explanations), non-decomposable global states (dynamicist explanations), and non-spatio-temporally organised intentional internals (psychological explanations). Therefore, unification and greater qualitative parsimony will not be virtues of cross-explanatory integrations, because no reduction or subsumption of the kinds postulated is possible without impugning the explanatory postulates of one kind of explanation or another.

Thus, there seems to be a good case against non-mechanistic explanation: the fact that cross-explanatory integrations lack the virtues of integrations of mechanistic explanations. It is important to recognise, however, that only explanatory integrations over certain kinds of explanations will have the virtues of unification and greater qualitative parsimony. Mechanistic explanations are perfect in this respect, because the postulate "mechanism" can be unified with other postulated mechanisms and can be subsumed by one superordinate kind: a hierarchically organised mechanism. However, things become more difficult when integrating over explanations that do not have straightforwardly unify-able or subsume-able postulates. In this way, the view which rejects cross-explanatory integrations because they lack the virtues of unification and greater qualitative parsimony appears biased towards a certain kind of explanation from the start. That is, explanations whose postulates are consistent and enough alike in kind.

The motivation for this bias, I think, is an attitude towards cognitive scientific explananda that is *fundamentalist* in Weiskopf's (2017) terms. Fundamentalists assume that the end-goal of explanation is the specification of one fundamental structure, which unifies and subsumes all other structures captured in explanation. My claim is that those who take issue with cross-explanatory integration do so because they think they have identified a kind of explanation that specifies such a structure in cognitive science: mechanistic explanation. They think this because they suppose that hierarchically organised mechanisms are all that is needed to make sense of the connection between, say, higher-level computational cognition and lower-level, implementational cognition. Notably, however, a fundamentalist attitude towards cognitive scientific explananda is not the only option on the table. According to an *anti-fundamentalist* view, cognitive science is not in the business of specifying a fundamental structure, but of capturing a variety of structures via a diversity of explanatory strategies.

Those who defend an exclusively mechanistic approach to cognitive scientific explanation are fundamentalists in the sense defined above. However, it is important to recognise that there is one good reason for supposing that this view is flawed: because mechanistic explanations are unlikely to be able to do the work of explaining cognition on their own. To see why, Weiskopf (forthcoming, p. 1) asks us to:

> [...] consider protein folding, a process which starts with a mostly linear native state of a polypeptide and terminates with a complexly structured geometric shape. There does not appear to be any mechanism of this process: for many proteins, given the initially generated polypeptide chain and relatively normal surrounding conditions, folding takes place automatically, under the constraints of certain basic principles of economy. The very structure of the chain itself plus this array of physical laws and constraints shapes the final outcome.

This seems to be a case in which complex forms are produced not by mechanisms but by a combination of structures and the natural forces or tendencies that govern them.

Weiskopf's example demonstrates that not all aspects of cognition are going to be easily explained by mechanistic explanations. This, in turn, threatens the claim that hierarchically organised mechanisms are the fundamental structure of cognition, because it demonstrates that we have good reason to believe that "mechanistic explanations come to an end at some point, beyond which it becomes impossible to continue to find mechanisms to account for the behavior of a system's components" (Weiskopf, forthcoming, p. 31). At this point, the "description of lower-level mechanisms would be irrelevant" and other explanatory strategies would need to be found (Machamer, Darden, and Craver, 2000, p. 13).

A mechanistic fundamentalist can respond that "To accept as an explanation something that need not correspond with how the system is in fact implemented at lower levels is to accept that the explanations simply end at that point" (Piccinini and Craver, 2011, p. 307). But this is just to say that explanations are only explanations if mechanistic; which is a claim that finds its justification in the doctrine of mechanistic fundamentalism itself. From an anti-fundamentalists perspective, this argument is circular and should be rejected out of hand. Accordingly, anti-fundamentalists will argue that different kinds of explanations should have the taxonomic autonomy to define their own range of entities, states, and processes as target explananda; and the explanatory autonomy to develop independently sufficient and adequate explanations of the target explananda they identify (Weiskopf, forthcoming). Such an idea finds its articulation in the doctrine of autonomisation discussed in chapter four.

One's choice between fundamentalism and anti-fundamentalism will directly influence one's views about the legitimacy of different kinds of cognitive scientific explanations. If one sides with the fundamentalist, then one will assume that at the endpoint of cognitive scientific inquiry the distinctions between different kinds of explanations will be dissolved and a fundamental structure will be specified. For example, that we will come to recognise that as well as having mechanistic explanations of neural structure and representational operations we are able to have mechanistic explanations of, say, psychological, social, and even ecological dimensions of cognition as well. On this view, ironing out the differences between different kinds of explanations will be a matter of homogenising our explanatory practices to reflect the real ontological state of affairs.[46]

---

46 Note here that I have been discussing mechanistic fundamentalism in order to critically examine the claim that cross-explanatory integrations should be judged according to the standards of

Conversely, if one sides with the anti-fundamentalist, then one will assume that different kinds of explanations are responsible for explaining different aspects of cognitive systems; e.g. neuronal cognition, psychological cognition, and environmentally-embedded cognition. On this view, cognitive systems would be multi-dimensional, but not in the mechanistic sense where we have the embedding of lower-order mechanism within higher-order mechanisms. Rather, the cognitive system would be such that one dimension (say, the dimension of functional states) could not be reduced to another dimension (say, the dimensions of interactions between spatio-temporally organised components) even if what exists in one dimension is in some way dependent on what exists at another.[47] The different kinds of explanation would, then, each be tasked with explaining one of these dimensions on their own terms and according to their own standards of success.

Choosing between fundamentalism and anti-fundamentalist will influence the interpretation one gives to the predicates deployed in different kinds of explanations in cognitive science. All will agree that predicates—such as "is a mechanism," "is an intentional internal," or "is a global state"—are deployed under the assumption that they designate genuine properties possesses by (some aspects of) cognitive systems. But if one takes a fundamentalist view, then one will deny that some of the predicates deployed actually designate genuine properties. For instance, one could deny that a predicate such as "is an intentional internal" designates genuine properties or ague that it only designates causally operative and spatio-temporally organised properties, which could, in fact, be best designated by another predicate entirely (e.g. "is a mechanism"). The diametrically opposite view is that all predicates deployed in all kinds of explanations in cognitive science designate genuine properties possessed by (some aspects of) cognitive systems. If one takes this anti-fundamentalist view, then the different kinds of explanations in cognitive science are much more than mere methodological distinctions; they each explain a different ontological dimension of cognitive systems with their own irreducible properties.

In summary, the fundamentalist argument that cross-explanatory integration is disqualified because it lacks virtues such as unification and greater qualitative

---

integrations of mechanistic explanations. However, one could equally espouse 'dynamicist fundamentalism' or 'psychological fundamentalism,' whereby the fundamental structure of cognition is, say, some un-decomposable system or a collection of functional/intentional states.

47 This second view is analogous to the kind of "non-reductive" view endorsed in the philosophy of science/physics (cf. Poland, 1994, for discussion about "non-reductive physicalism"). Thus, this view would entail a rejection of "crass scientistic reductionism" and the endorsement of the ontological autonomy of all dimensions of cognitive systems recognised by cognitive scientific explanations (Heil, 2003).

parsimony is not decisive. Anti-fundamentalists need not assume that theoretical virtues are uniform across cognitive science, because they can endorse the autonomy of different kinds of explanations. Fundamentalists, however, cannot share this view, because they will be convinced that the virtues of explanatory integration in cognitive science are indexed to the explanatory specification of one fundamental structure. From this perspective, explanatory legitimacy obtains only when we make progress in specifying a fundamental structure, which *ipso facto* mandates that all genuine explanations must be apt for specifying such a structure. The surest route to reaching such a specification is by ensuring that all cognitive scientific explanations postulate kinds that are, in principle, unify-able and subsume-able under a superordinate kind. Kinds, that is, like "mechanism."

It is important to note, however, that the fundamentalist has not won the day yet. It follows that, at this time at least, any repudiation of cross-explanatory integration on the grounds that it lacks the virtues of unification and greater qualitative parsimony is premature. Another possibility is still available: that cross-explanatory integrations have virtues in their own right.

5.5 Two Virtues of Cross-Explanatory Integration

Note first that those who accept cross-explanatory integration and endorse anti-fundamentalism will recognise diverse kinds of cognitive scientific explanations, but will still conceive of cognition as somehow unified. If this were not true, then integration would be entirely without purpose. In line with this way of thinking, Weiskopf (forthcoming, p. 14) argues that different kinds of explanations do not have a privileged evidential bases (whether neurophysiological, behavioural, introspective etc.); what is always being explained is our evidence for cognitive competences, even if explanations differ in kind. For its advocates, therefore, cross-explanatory integration can be understood as an attempt to give a "multi-dimensional" explanation of the same thing—cognition—without prioritising one dimension or another.[48]

---

48 Multi-dimensional explanation should not be confused with multilevel explanation, since the idea of levels may be relevant from one perspective (mechanistic explanations), but not from another (dynamicist explanations).

When we understand this point, we can recognise that for anti-fundamentalists cross-explanatory integrations will exhibit one theoretical virtue to a higher degree than integrations of one kind of explanation: *explanatory depth*. According to Keas (2018, p. 2766), an explanation exhibits explanatory depth "when it excels in causal history depth or in other depth measures such as the range of counterfactual questions that its law-like generalizations answer regarding the item being explained." Clearly, a cross-explanatory integration will not excel in causal history depth, because it may integrate dynamicist explanations which do not aim to capture causal structure at all.[49] However, cross-explanatory integration will exhibit a high level of "law-focused" explanatory depth, which Hitchcock and Woodward (2003, p. 182) define as a "generality with respect to other possible properties of the very object or system that is the focus of explanation."

The idea of "law-focused" explanatory depth is complex. Put simply, it holds that an "explanation is deeper insofar as it makes use of a generalization that is more general" (Hitchcock and Woodward, 2003, p. 181). Hitchcock and Woodward (2003, 182) argue that the "right sort of generality is generality with respect to other possible properties of the very object or system that is the focus of explanation." Such generality can be identified by undertaking "testing interventions," which probe the "counterfactual dependencies" of an object or system by intervening to manipulate—perhaps in an idealised way—the system's behaviour under various conditions. The counterfactual dependencies of an object or system, therefore, are just the manipulable dependencies that are constitutive of the behaviour of the system. To make this clear, consider Hitchcock and Woodward's helpful example:

suppose that the height (Y) of a particular plant depends upon the amount of water (X_1) and fertilizer (X_2) it receives according to the following formula:

$$Y = a_1X_1 + a_2X_2 + U \tag{5.3}$$

where U reflects unknown sources of error [...and...] for some change ΔX_1 and ΔX_2 [(5.3)] correctly 'predicts' that if X_1 and X_2 had been changed by those amounts, then the height of the plant would have changed by (approximately) the amount $a_1\Delta X_1 + a_2\Delta X_2$. [...]

the low-level generalization [(5.3)] relating water and fertilizer to plant height strikes us as explanatory, but only minimally so: the explanations in which it participates are shallow

---

49 Keas (2018, p. 2766) says that "Causal history depth is often characterized in a causal-mechanical way by how far back in a linear or branching causal chain one is able to go. Evidently, then, this is not the kind of explanatory depth that cross-explanatory integrations could have as a virtue.

and relatively unilluminating. If we had a theory—call it (*T*)—describing the physiological mechanisms governing plant growth it would provide deeper explanations. Such a theory would presumably be invariant under a wider range of changes and interventions than [(5.3)]; that is, we would expect (*T*) to continue to hold in circumstances in which the relationship between height, fertilizer and water departed from the linear relationship [(5.3)]. (Hitchcock and Woodward, 2003, pp. 183–184).

"Law-focused" explanatory depth, therefore, should be understood in terms of the "range of invariance of a generalization," where "Explanatory generalizations allow us to answer what-if-things-had-been different questions: they show us what the value of the explanandum variable depends upon" (Hitchcock and Woodward, 2003, p. 182). This idea was further elucidated by Keas (2018) by means of the following example:

Newton's account of free fall possessed more explanatory depth than Galileo's. Newton explained not just free fall very near earth's surface (the restricted range of Galileo's theory), but also free fall toward earth starting from any distance. Furthermore Newton could explain free fall toward a hypothetically "altered earth"—perhaps if there is a change in its mass and radius, or if one works with another planet or a star that has such an alternative mass and radius. So the Newtonian explanation of free fall remains invariant through a larger range of investigator interventions. In short, Newton's "free fall" account is explanatorily deeper than Galileo's because it handles a larger range of counterfactual (what-if-things-had-been-different) questions about the same kind of phenomena (free fall in various circumstances).

The multi-dimensional explanations engendered by cross-explanatory integrations will handle a range of counterfactual (what-if-things-had-been-different) questions about cognition. For example, counterfactual cases involving differences in neural structure (brought about, for instance, via brain legions), differences in the global state of the cognitive systems (brought about, for instance, as the result of environmental contingencies), and differences in the intentional states of the cognitive system (brought about, for instance, as a result of the availability of external objects able to be represented). Supposing, then, that the "explanandum variable" for cognitive science is cognition—call it *C*—it is evident that cross-explanatory integrations will make use of a generalisation that is very general indeed: the generalisation that cognition is multi-dimensional.

Working from Hitchcock and Woodward's example, we can say that a multi-dimensional explanations engendered by cross-explanatory integration will have the following form:

$$C = a_1 M_1 + a_2 D_2 + a_3 P_3 \qquad (5.4)$$

where M_1 is some entities and interaction specified by a mechanistic explanation, D_2 is some global state specified by a dynamicist explanation, and P_3 is some functional/intentional states specified by a psychological explanation; and for some change ΔM_1, ΔD_2, and/or ΔP_3, (4) correctly 'predicts' that if M_1, D_2, and/or P_3 had been changed, then the behaviours of the cognitive systems would be different. Thus, (4) just says that explaining the explanandum 'cognitive behaviours' (C) depends on identifying some dependencies between whatever is explained by mechanistic, dynamicist, and psychological explanations.[50] From this perspective, it is clear that (5.4) will have greater explanatory depth than any exclusively mechanistic, dynamicist, or psychological explanation, because it will make use of a generalisation that is more general: that cognitive behaviours depend on the dependencies between the various dimensions explained by different kinds of cognitive scientific explanations.

A fundamentalist could respond that we have no good reason to think that the dependencies expressed by (5.4) are constitutive of the behaviour of cognitive systems. This amounts to the same thing as arguing that only one kind of explanation (typically, mechanistic explanation) is needed for a complete explanation of cognitive behaviours. But the anti-fundamentalist will deny that this fundamentalist response has force. And this denial is at least plausible, since it is obvious—at least from the perspective of folk psychology—that cognitive behaviours can be affected equally by changes to the components and activities involved in cognition (e.g. from the destruction or degeneration of brain cells), the global state of cognition (e.g. in twin earth cases where environmental contingencies matter), or the functional/intentional states of cognition (e.g. when we rationally hold two distinct singular beliefs about one and the same object; say, Venus). For sure, difficult questions remain about how these dependencies work and about the scope of such dependencies. But trying to give an answer to these questions just is the reason for doing cognitive science in the first place.

From an anti-fundamentalist perspective, a further virtue of cross-explanatory integrations is *applicability*. Applicability is a diachronic virtue in Keas' (2018, 2780-2787) sense, which is to say that it "can only be instantiated as a theory is cultivated after its origin." Some—e.g. Strevens (2008)—think that, in Keas' terms again, "Successful scientific theories constitute knowledge of the world (knowing that), not control over the world (which is mainly knowing how) for practical (non-theoretical) purposes." However, it is clear that practical applicability does not

---

50 It is important to recognise that the nature of such dependencies is not necessarily linear. We should not expect a change to, say, M_1 to affect D_2 or P_3; just as we would not expect a change in the amount of water to affect the amount of fertiliser in Hitchcock and Woodward's example. This is true even if we would expect changes to either the amount of water or the amount of fertilizer to affect plant height; and if we would expect changes to whatever is explained by either mechanistic, dynamicist, or psychological explanations to affect cognitive behaviours.

detract from the value of a theory, even if it only depends on the understanding or knowledge that theory provides. In accord with this sentiment, Douglas (2014, p. 62) argues that "With the pure versus applied distinction removed, scientific progress can be defined in terms of the increased capacity to predict, control, manipulate, and intervene in various contexts." For the anti-fundamentalist, cross-explanatory integrations will be taken to increase this capacity to a greater extent than integrations of only one kind of explanation.

It is an open question how a pragmatic virtue like applicability relates to epistemic concerns about the knowledge or understanding. Keas points to Agazzi's (2014) claim that:

> the existence of technological applications is the last decisive step that assures that [theories] have been able to adequately treat those aspects of reality they intended to treat.

that technological applications:

> are designed or projected in advance, as the concrete application of knowledge provided by a given science or set of sciences.

and hence, with a mechanistic perspective assumed, that theories:

> contains not only prescriptions as to the way of realising the structure of the machine but also as to its functioning. [...] it is a state of affairs that constitutes a confirmation of the theories used in projecting the machine Agazzi (2014, pp. 308–10).

Although Keas takes Agazzi's position to afford an "inflated epistemic role for applicability," he notes that this view is consistent with Hacking's (1983) loudly italicised argument that:

> *We are completely convinced of the reality of electrons when we regularly set out to build—and often enough succeed in building—new kinds of device that use various well understood causal properties of electrons to interfere in other more hypothetical parts of nature* Hacking (1983, p. 265).

Whether or not concrete applications of cognitive scientific explanations really are planned in advance and have epistemic import, it is clear that cross-explanatory integrations will have a high level of applicability. This follows because they will explain a number of putative "properties"—both causal and non-causal—of a cognitive systems. A greater number of technological innovations will, therefore, be made possible by supposing that cognition can be best explained as the result of cross-explanatory integrations (Vincenti, 1990). What, exactly, these technological innovations will confirm or deny about our explanations of cognition remains to be seen. From the anti-fundamenatalist perspective, however, there is reason to think that technological innovations inspired by cross-explanatory integrations in cognitive science really are a test for multi-dimensional understandings of cognition.

Of course, this only makes sense if we have technological innovations inspired by cross-explanatory innovations in cognitive science. But this does not seem far-fetched. To underscore this point, consider the development of AI systems; for example, the development of self-propelled robotics such as Tesla's cars equipped with autopilot systems. Systems such as these certainly do involve many parts and components, but also operate over functional/intentional states (for example, representations of locations) and will transition between global states according to governing equations accounting for relevant dependencies (for example, equations that account for the angle of turning as a relation of dependency between, say, speed, radial load, and axial load) (Yang, Lu, and Li, 2013). For the anti-fundamentalist, then, the successes of these technologies demonstrate that we should have sufficient confidence in the application of cross-explanatory integrations "as the basis for a new or improved technology" (Keas, 2018, p. 2785).

The fundamentalist will, of course, dispute the claim that cross-explanatory integrations are a better guide to successful action and are better able to enhance our technological control. Once again, however, this criticism is grounded in an assumption about the aim of cognitive scientific explanation and the failure or cross-explanatory integrations to contribute to that aim. It is clear that one will not think that cross-explanatory integrations can function as the basis for better technology if one also thinks that they do worse as explanations than integrations of a single kind of explanation. But since the anti-fundamentalist takes the opposite view, we find once again that the deciding factor is the attitude one takes towards to explanatory ambitions of cognitive science. Given an anti-fundamentalist viewpoint, the applicability of cross-explanatory integrations will far outstrip the applicability of integrations of a single kind of explanation.

The preceding discussion of the virtues of cross-explanatory integrations illustrates that such integrations can be taken to have some virtues to a greater extent than integrations of a single kind of explanation; e.g. explanatory depth and applicability. For sure, this claim depends upon the adoption of an anti-fundamentalist perspective, but there is no *a priori* reason that such a perspective could not be correct. Thus, I have shown that any evaluation of different kinds of explanatory integration in cognitive science in terms of their respective virtues will depend on the perspective one adopts towards the explanatory task of cognitive science. A more detailed study could be undertaken to show which other theoretical virtues align with which perspective. However, this first requires that we have agreement about which theoretical virtues exist and are relevant. This task is beyond the scope of this chapter. It is enough, however, to have shown that the importance and weight of *some* theoretical virtues of explanatory integrations—e.g. unification, greater qualitative parsimony, explanatory depth, and applicability—will depend on one's views about what cognitive science hopes to explain.

5.6 Problem 2 and the Meta-Explanatory Challenge

My argument in this chapter has shown that one's view about the theoretical virtues of explanatory integration in cognitive science cannot be conveniently segregated from one's view about the explanatory task of cognitive science. The general thrust of this idea has been nicely formulated by Cat (2017) in his discussion of unification. He says:

> Philosophically, assumptions about unification help choose what sort of philosophical questions to pursue and what target areas to explore. For instance, fundamentalist assumptions typically lead one to address epistemological and metaphysical issues in terms of only results and interpretations of fundamental levels of disciplines. Assumptions of this sort help define what counts as scientific and shape scientistic or naturalized philosophical projects. In this sense, they determine, or at least strongly suggest, what relevant science carries authority in philosophical debate.

In much the same way, perspectives on what we should expect from explanatory integration in cognitive science will cohere with our assumptions about what questions cognitive science should pursue, what target areas cognitive science should explore, and, ultimately, what kind of explanations cognitive science should put forward.

What one expects from explanatory integration will cohere with one's views about the explananda of cognitive science (e.g. fundamentalism vs. anti-fundamentalism). Where one expects explanatory integrations to have the virtues of unification and greater qualitative parsimony, one may suppose, say, that a single fundamental structure is responsible for cognition. This, in turn, may lead one to countenance only a single kind of explanation—say, mechanistic explanation—in cognitive science. However, where one expects explanatory integrations to have the virtues of explanatory depth and applicability, one may suppose that a number of irreducible structures are responsible for cognition. This, in turn, will lead one to countenance many kinds of explanations in cognitive science.

Transposing this discussion back onto the task of deciding between different "new" theories of CONCEPT, we find that the "meta-explanatory challenge" is unassailable. The reason is because different "new" theories of CONCEPT will likely take different views on what is expected from explanatory integration in cognitive science, which will cohere with their divergent views about what cognitive science explains. Eliminativists, for example, will eschew the theoretical virtues of unification and greater qualitative parsimony, because they will suppose that the representational structure of the mind is disunified. In contrast, pluralist or hybridists will expect integrations to have the theoretical virtues of unification and/or greater qualitative parsimony, because they will assume that there is some unity between different kinds of representation/information.[51]

To make this point concrete, consider again explanations of categorisation judgements. For the eliminativist, there will be many different explanations of categorisation judgements positing at least the kinds PROTOTYPE, EXEMPLAR, and THEORY-LIKE STRUCTURE respectively. For the pluralist, however, categorisation judgements will be explained by the shared functional properties of all representational kinds. And, for the hybridist, categorisation judgements will be explained by one, richly structured representational kind. Eliminativists, therefore, will not expect integrations of the various explanations of categorisation judgements to possess the virtues of unification and greater qualitative parsimony; pluralists will; and hybridists will be unconvinced that integration is even necessary (since the explanations can all be understood as appealing to (different parts of) integrated representations anyway).

This example highlights that the different "new" theories of CONCEPT will likely expect different things from explanatory integration in cognitive science. If this correct—as I think it is—, then their coming to an agreement about how cognitive science explains seems highly unlikely. And this is not surprising, since, to reiterate, what one expects from explanatory integration will cohere with one's views about the explananda of cognitive science, and the different "new" theories of CONCEPT cohere with different views on the explananda of cognitive science. Thus, the "meta-explanatory challenge" is sealed and we seem to be left without an empirical arbiter to help us decide on the "best" theory of CONCEPT.[52] Does this mean that mere intuition will play the decisive role in one's decision about which theory of CONCEPT to uphold? Avoiding this state of affairs is essential for any naturalistically-inclined theorist of CONCEPT.

---

51 It is clear that the differences between eliminativist, pluralist, and hybridist specifications of the explananda obtain at a finer level of grain than does the difference between fundamentalism and anti-fundamentalism. Nevertheless, the different specifications will still cohere with different interpretations of how cognitive science explains and what theoretical virtues we should expect explanatory integration in cognitive science to possess.

52 Recall here that appealing to cognitive science cannot help us to decide between theories of CONCEPT adhering to the standard view either. In fact, appealing to cognitive science seems to undermine the standard view entirely.

6 CONCEPT as a Working Hypothesis

In chapters four and five, I argued that we must take seriously the "meta-explanatory challenge to new theories of CONCEPT," because there is unlikely to be a consensus between the "new" theories of CONCEPT about how or what cognitive science explains.[53] But if this is right, then we find ourselves in the dark as to both what we should expect from a theory of CONCEPT and how to decide between available theories of CONCEPT. In this chapter, I begin by giving a brief recapitulation of the reasons why we should not endorse standard view theories of CONCEPT, before considering why we should not accept any "new" theories of CONCEPT either. Thus, I quickly recapitulate both the "explanatory challenge to the standard view" and the "meta-explanatory challenge to new theories of CONCEPT," and find that both are compelling.

The standard view holds that theories of CONCEPT will be theories of single kind of mental representations. On this view, the claim that "Concepts are K" must be reinterpreted as "Concepts are mental representations of the kind X," where the placeholder X can be substituted by any viable representation (Komatsu, 1992). Such representations include, but are not limited to, images (Fodor et al., 1980), definitions (Russell, 1921), prototypes (Lakoff, 1987), bundles of exemplars (Nosofsky, 1988), and theory-like structures of some sort (Carey, 1985; Rehder, 2003b). Until recently, the debate in the literature has focused on which of these representations is best able to satisfy what is required—both empirically and methodologically—of a general theory of concepts in cognitive science (Laurence and Margolis, 1999; Murphy, 2002).

Theories of concepts as one or another of these representations have typically assumed that there are certain properties common to all objects falling under the kind CONCEPT. For example, that all such objects falling under the kind CONCEPT have a single kind of structure and store a single kind of information (cf. Machery, 2009). According to this standard view, a theory of CONCEPT is to be evaluated on how well it accounts for these properties to explain the formation and application of concepts in higher cognition (Machery, 2006). Thus, the standard view holds that "all concepts share a general common structure and that a single model could, in principle, be developed, which would account for the formation and application of all concepts" (Bloch-Mullins, 2017).

---

53 This chapter contains some material that is a re-working of Taylor (2019a).

https://doi.org/9783110708165-006

It is now widely accepted, however, that the standard view cannot be correct. The line of argument that ends with this conclusion takes as a premise an analysis of the explanatory results of cognitive science. Recall that the argument itself—which I justified in chapter two and set out in chapter three—runs as follows:

D. The explanatory challenge to the standard view:

1. The standard view holds that a theory of CONCEPT should be a theory of a single kind of representation. (Premise)
2. No theory of CONCEPT taking concepts to be a single kind of representation has been successful in accounting for all, or even most, of the phenomena related to the formation and application of concepts. (Premise)

---

3. Indicates: We should reject the standard view claim that a theory of CONCEPT should be a theory of a single kind of representation. (From D1 and D2)

What is notable about the "explanatory challenge to the standard view" is that it does not offer a solution to the failings of the standard view. However, philosophers have responded by developing "new" theories of CONCEPT, which either do not take all concepts to have the same representational structure or do not take concepts to have the same representational structure in the traditional sense. For example, eliminativist theories of CONCEPT take the members of CONCEPT to be variously structured representations and, hence, to be useless in cognitive science (cf. Machery, 2009). Pluralist theories of CONCEPT take the members of CONCEPT to be the shared functional properties of representations (cf. Weiskopf, 2009). And hybrid theories of CONCEPT take the members of CONCEPT to be a single kind of complexly structured representation (cf. Vicente and Martínez Manrique, 2014).

Much of the recent literature has been dedicated to analysing and evaluating these "new" theories of CONCEPT (cf. Bloch-Mullins, 2017). However, I have argued that these "new" theories of CONCEPT face an explanatory challenge of their own, because they differently interpret the explananda of cognitive science leading them to different conceptions of CONCEPT's explanatory role. This "meta-explanatory challenge"—which I spelled out at the end of chapter three—runs as follows:

E. The meta-explanatory challenge to new theories of CONCEPT:

1. "New" theories of CONCEPT disagree about explananda of cognitive science and how to interpret relevant bodies of data. (Premise; from chapter three)

2. Indicates: Cognitive science cannot help us to decide which new theory of CONCEPT to favour. (From E1)

3. Indicates: Even after rejecting the standard view, appealing to cognitive science does not help us to decide on the "best" theory of CONCEPT. (From E2)

In chapters four and five, I made the case that the "meta-explanatory challenge" cannot be overcome, because the disagreement between "new" theories of CONCEPT about the explananda of cognitive science is pernicious. I have paid little attention, however, to the question of the validity of the "meta-explanatory challenge to new theories of CONCEPT" (or, for that matter, the "explanatory challenge to standard view theories of CONCEPT"). Like others in the literature, I have simply assumed that the "meta-explanatory challenge"—and the appeal to cognitive science it represents—will function as an appropriate basis for theorisation about CONCEPT (cf. Bloch-Mullins, 2017; Machery, 2009; Weiskopf, 2009). No-one, that is, has yet taken the time to clear up the commitments of this challenge nor to ask if it really does help us to better theorise about CONCEPT. In this final chapter, I do just that and arrive at new—and radically different—perspective on theorisation about CONCEPT and on what it means to appeal to cognitive science.

6.1 Difference and Identity

In his pioneering work, Machery (2009) argued that we should mark the difference between the "philosophy of concepts" and the "psychology of concepts." According to Machery:

> "Concept" in psychology refers to a specific class of bodies of knowledge, assumed to be used by default in the processes underlying most higher cognitive competences, and a theory of concepts in psychology attempts to describe the properties of these bodies of knowledge in order to explain the properties of the higher cognitive competences. "Concept" is used in various ways in philosophy. Of particular relevance here is the idea that a theory of concepts spells out the conditions under which one can have propositional attitudes about the objects of one's attitudes. When the goals of theories of concepts in philosophy and in psychology

are clearly explained and properly distinguished , most philosophical attacks against the psychological theories of concepts are decisively undermined.

The point of Machery's distinction is to show that attempts to bring together the psychology of concepts and the philosophy of concepts, or to somehow argue that the philosophy of concepts plays a foundational role in grounding any psychology of concepts, cannot be made to work. And his overarching conclusion is radical: that the psychology of concepts should be cast adrift from the philosophy of concept, because psychological research on the kinds typically grouped together as concepts cannot be organised into coherent framework.

Machery's larger project is to show that the psychology of CONCEPT is not worth undertaking at all; hence his eliminativist theory of CONCEPT. Thus, Machery thinks that a theory of CONCEPT should not be a theory adhering exclusively to the either the standard view or, in fact, a theory of representational kinds. In short: Machery holds that a theory of CONCEPT should not be a theory of representations. This idea is not new. In fact, many philosophers have denied that concepts should be identified exclusively with mental representations and, as a result, that a theory of CONCEPT should be a theory of representations (cf. Peacocke, 1992; Zalta, 2001).

Two contrasting views can be taken on Machery's distinction between the philosophy and psychology of CONCEPT: accept or reject. And these two views correspond to two different accounts of what theorisation about CONCEPT entails: the difference account and the identity account.

According to the difference account, "it is justified and important to distinguish between that which constitutes our beliefs and that which explains our higher cognitive processes, such as categorization"; where theorisation about each of these things cannot be conflated (Löhr, 2018, p. 7). Unsurprisingly, the difference account has been most strongly defended by Machery (2009), who holds that philosophers' and psychologists' theorisation about CONCEPT differs in important respects. According to Machery (2006, pp. 99–100):

> In philosophy, a concept of an *x* is that which it is necessary and sufficient to possess in order to have propositional attitudes about *x* as *x*. For instance, the concept of dog is that which it is necessary and sufficient to possess in order to have propositional attitudes about dogs as dogs.

Whereas:

> Psychologists interested in concepts attempt to characterize [representations used in our higher cognitive competences], because their properties explain various features of our higher cognitive competences—they explain why we categorize the way we do, why we tend to draw the inductions we tend to draw, and so on.

As Löhr (2018) has shown, defenders of the difference account take the view that the philosophical theorisation about CONCEPT cannot be reduced to psychological theorisation about CONCEPT without loss of explanatory power. For instance, Lalumera (2010) argues that the philosophical theories of CONCEPT cannot be abandoned, because of the need to explain how we can possess identical beliefs despite widely varying experiences. Similarly, Rey argues that philosophical theories of CONCEPT are needed to explain why our categorisation of individuals (e.g. as doctors) does not always align with our beliefs about members of those categories (e.g. as wearing white coats) (Rey, 2010); and to explain how we are able to represent phenomena (e.g., the Müller-Lyer illusion) that depend on the possession of beliefs (e.g. x is longer than/the same length as y) (Rey, 2009). The idea underlying each of these arguments, then, is that philosophical theories of CONCEPT are necessary to account for those propositional attitudes that seem to be unaffected by higher cognitive competences or that make such competences possible.

Advocates of the identity account reject these arguments and contend that "to have a concept about x in the philosophical sense consists of having a concept about x in the psychological sense" (Machery, 2006, p. 99). Thus, the identity account collapses the distinction between concepts as the necessary and sufficient conditions for propositional attitudes and concepts as those things—e.g. representations—that explain higher cognitive competences. One plausible advocate of the identity account is Prinz (2002). On his view, concepts just are "perceptually derived representations used in category detection" (Prinz, 2002, p. 237).[54] It follows that any x that is necessary and sufficient for the possession of propositional attitudes about x as x must have some "perceptual basis." And since explaining perceptually based categorisation is the remit of a psychological theory of CONCEPT, there is no need to endow philosophical theories of CONCEPT with their own explanatory task.

Some baulk at the very idea of the identity account, because they assume that an independent "semantic theory" is necessary to explain how people can have attitudes towards the objects that are represented in higher cognition (cf. Rey, 2009). In this way, the identity account is highly controversial, because it states that psychological theories of CONCEPT *ipso facto* deliver philosophical theories of CONCEPT as well. Machery (2009, p. 36), for one, rejects this idea as "unconvincing" by arguing that "psychologists' semantic claims are in fact psychological claims under disguise." In support of this view, he argues that we should "disentangle"

---

[54] It is important to recognise that the identity account is concerned exclusively with concepts. The claim is not, therefore, that individuals have no innate endowment whatsoever. Rather, it is that anything that we denote with the term "concept" is, in an important sense, perceptually-derived.

psychologists' theories of reference from their theories of the what best explains higher cognitive competences. For instance, that we should disentangle a descriptivist theory of reference—e.g. in the case of Carey's work on concepts—from any psychological theory of why we categorise the way we do, why we reason the way we do, and so on. The identity account takes the opposite view. In Machery's terms, it holds that a single theory of CONCEPT:

> ought to satisfy both philosophers' and psychologists' interests: it ought to explain what type of knowledge is used in the processes underlying the higher cognitive competences, and it ought to explain how we can have propositional attitudes about the objects of our attitudes.

Now, the tension between the difference and identity accounts has repercussions for the "meta-explanatory challenge," because the "meta-explanatory challenge" contains the premise that ""New" theories of CONCEPT disagree about explananda of cognitive science and how to interpret relevant bodies of data." As we have seen, however, it is possible to conceive of the explananda of theories CONCEPT in two different ways. From the perspective of the difference account, only psychological theories of CONCEPT have the explananda of cognitive science as their explananda. Whereas, from the perspective of the identity account, all theories of CONCEPT have the explananda of cognitive science as their explananda. As a consequence, the two accounts disagree about whether the "meta-explanatory challenge" is to be interpreted as taking scope only over psychological theorisation about CONCEPT or over theories of CONCEPT *tout court*.

Therefore, it is unclear how the "meta-explanatory challenge to new theories of CONCEPT" should inform our search for a best theory of CONCEPT, because it is unclear if the "meta-explanatory challenge" is to be read as having unqualified implications for *all* theories of CONCEPT. Thus, there are at least two different interpretations of the "meta-explanatory challenge" available: one aligned with the difference account; the other aligned with the identity account. These two interpretations can be presented as follows:

F. The difference account meta-explanatory challenge to new theories of CONCEPT:

1. "New" theories of CONCEPT disagree about explananda of cognitive science and how to interpret relevant bodies of data. (Premise; from chapter three)

---

2. Indicates: Cognitive science cannot help us to decide which new theory of CONCEPT to favour. (From F1)

---

3. Indicates: Even after rejecting the standard view, appealing to cognitive science does not help us to decide on the "best" *psychological* theory of CONCEPT. (From F2)

And:

G. The identity account meta-explanatory challenge to new theories of CONCEPT:

1. "New" theories of CONCEPT disagree about explananda of cognitive science and how to interpret relevant bodies of data. (Premise; from chapter three)

2. Indicates: Cognitive science cannot help us to decide which new theory of CONCEPT to favour. (From G1)

3. Indicates: Even after rejecting the standard view, appealing to cognitive science does not help us to decide on the "best" theory of CONCEPT *tout court*. (From G2)

6.2 Against the "New Consensus"

Bloch-Mullins (2017) argues that a "new consensus" has formed with respect to theorisation about CONCEPT. This "new consensus" is described as a "particular motivation" for rejecting theories of CONCEPT that take the objects falling under the kind CONCEPT to have a common representational structure.[55] However, the "meta-explanatory challenge" cannot hope to deliver any kind of consensus about theorisation about CONCEPT until we agree about its scope. That is, until we decide

---

[55] Note, that Bloch-Mullins rejects the "new consensus, because it fails to recognise that the explanatory force of prototype, exemplar, and theory theories of CONCEPT is "limited even with respect to the phenomena often cited to support it, as each fails to satisfy an important explanatory desideratum with respect to these phenomena" (Bloch-Mullins, 2017, p. 1). However, she thinks that a consensus can be reached by developing a theory of CONCEPT that accommodates "all important explanatory desiderata"; such as her "integrated model of concepts." I disagree, because I do not see how such a theory would resolve the tension between the difference and identity accounts about scope of—and, hence, the explanatory desiderata relevant for—theorisation about CONCEPT.

whether or not it should be read from the perspective of the difference (argument F) or identity (argument G) accounts.

Most engaged in the debate carry on as though this question has already been answered. As we have seen, Machery argues that:

> [...] psychological theories of concepts, do not attempt to explain how we can have attitudes about the objects of our attitudes.
> There is little point in blaming some philosophical theories of concepts, such as Fodor's theory, for being unable to explain how we reason, how we categorize, how we draw analogies, or how we induce (as does, e.g., Prinz, 2002). For, simply, a philosophical theory of concepts is not in the business of providing such explanations.

But the pertinent question is: why we should think that this is true? In defence of the opposite view, Margolis (1998, p. 68) refers to Carey's psychological (theory) theory of CONCEPT and argues that "The theory analogy, once plainly put, amounts to the view that concepts have their semantic properties by virtue of their roles in restricted knowledge structures." The problem, as Machery (2009, p. 36) notes, is that one can "endorse a similar interpretation of the psychological theories of concepts" and "conclude that as semantic theories, they are worthless" (cf. Fodor, 1994; Fodor, 1998, as examples of this view). The problem we face, therefore, is deciding which of the difference or identity accounts to endorse.

I do not think that this problem can be easily overcome, because the tension between the difference and identity accounts emerges from a deeper disagreement about whether or not it is possible to have an empiricist theory of CONCEPT at all. An empiricist theory of CONCEPT assumes that the properties of concepts are discovered *a posteriori* and can be revised and (re-)evaluated in the course of empirical research. In contrast, a non-empiricist theory of CONCEPT—hereafter a rationalist theory of CONCEPT—assumes that the properties of concepts are not discovered *a posteriori* and cannot be revised and (re-)evaluated in the course of empirical research. The point of dispute, then, concerns the question of whether or not the properties attributed to concepts by a theory of CONCEPT are empirically defeasible.

Empiricist theories of CONCEPT take the view that empirical science can and should inform our understanding of concepts. Typically, empiricist theories of CONCEPT hold that concepts are mental representations and that the properties of these representations—e.g. their structure and functional properties—are to be discovered empirically. Consequently, empiricist theories of CONCEPT will defer to empirical research to, say, determine the structure of concepts—e.g. prototype, exemplar, theory-theory etc.—; to determine if concepts are contentful (cf. Chomsky, 1995; Egan, 2014); and to determine if concepts are "in the head" (cf. Clark, 2008; Hutchins, 1995). Thus, concepts are taken to have properties that are, in principle, empirically defeasible. In this way, empiricist theories of CONCEPT place *a posteriori* restrictions on what concepts are, because concepts are conceived as tokened mental representations, typed according to the empirically-discovered role that they play in thought.

In contrast, rationalist theories of CONCEPT eschew the idea that concepts are mental representations for one of three reasons. Firstly, because mental representations are too fine-grained for philosophical purposes, since "It is possible for one and the same concept to receive different mental representations in different individuals" Peacocke (1992, p. 3). Secondly, because mental representations are "not quite the notion of a concept," because there are concepts, but not mental representations, that it is possible we will never entertain. In defence of this claim, Peacocke (2005a, p. 169) says:

> It can, for instance, be true that there are concepts human beings may never acquire, because of their intellectual limitations, or because the sun will expand to eradicate human life before humans reach a stage at which they can acquire these concepts. 'There are concepts that will never be acquired' cannot mean or imply 'There are mental representations which are not mental representations in anyone's mind'.

And, thirdly, because "mental representations are explanatorily idle because they reintroduce the very sorts of problems they are supposed to explain" (Margolis and Laurence, 2014). Dummett (1993, p. 98) makes this idea clear when he says:

> [T]here is really no sense to speaking of a concept's coming into someone's mind. All we can think of is some image coming to mind which we take as in some way representing the concept, and this gets us no further forward, since we still have to ask in what his associating that concept with that image consists.

For these reasons, rationalist theories of CONCEPT deny that mental representations are fit for purpose when theorising about CONCEPT. Instead, they conceive of concepts as *abstract objects*—as opposed to particular mental objects and/or states—, which mediate between thought and language, on the one hand, and the referents of our thinking and speaking, on the other; or as *abilities* possessed by cognitive agents—for instance, the ability to discriminate between objects or to draw inferences about such objects (Bennett and Hacker, 2008; Kenny, 2010). In any case, the idea is always that the properties of concepts—for instance, that they are the necessary and sufficient conditions of propositional attitudes—are not empirically defeasible. Rationalist theories of CONCEPT, therefore, place *a priori* constraints on what concepts *are*.

The problem is that both empiricist and rationalist theories of CONCEPT are consistent with the best current cognitive science, since evidence of the exercise of cognitive competences underdetermines the question of whether or not concepts *are* representations with empirically defeasible properties. To cement this point, consider a hypothetical cognitive scientific explanation of how we categorise an individual c in a category C, which posits some particular representational structure—e.g. a prototype (cf. Osherson and Smith, 1981) or an exemplar (Nosofsky, 1988)—and is entirely empirically adequate. Advocates of both empiricist and rationalist theories of CONCEPT will be able to endorse this explanation while taking entirely different views about whether concepts are, in fact, representations (e.g. prototypes) and about whether we should think that the properties of concepts are empirically defeasible.

This state of affairs can also be elucidated by considering two of the different kinds of explanations formulated in cognitive science. On the one hand, we have "psychological" explanations, which posit representations and hold that:

> Cognitive science consists mostly of working out the distinction between *representing as* and merely *representing*, which is to say that cognitive science is mostly about intentional states as such (Fodor, 2008, p. 13).

One the other hand, we have explanations that do not posit representations. For example, dynamicist explanations, which often take an extended or ecological perspective on cognition, and so argue that it is:

> unnecessary to call on internal representations of environmental features when the features themselves are part of the cognitive system to be explained (Chemero and Silberstein, 2008, pp. 11–12).

We certainly do not exhaust all discussion of explanation in cognitive science by considering only psychological and dynamicist explanations. However, given that we can easily find support for both kinds of explanations in the actual practice of cognitive researchers, it is clear that we cannot look to the explanatory results of cognitive science to help us to decide if cognitive science even *should* posit representations in explanation, let alone whether or not concepts *are* representations with empirically defeasible properties (cf. Carson and Kelso, 2004; Jantzen, Steinberg, and Kelso, 2009; Weiskopf, forthcoming, as examples of both kinds of explanations).

If one prefers an empiricist theory of CONCEPT, then one will endorse the identity account and argument G above. However, if one prefers a rationalist theory of CONCEPT, then one will endorse—at the very most—the difference account and argument F above.[56] Cognitive science cannot decide between these two opposing

---

56 It might be that an advocate of a rationalist theory of CONCEPT will deny that psychological theories of CONCEPT are actually theories of CONCEPT. In any case, they will accept that so-

views, because it has not settled the question of what concepts *are*.[57] It is judicious, therefore, for philosophers to not get ahead of themselves in the name of progress. The "new consensus" should be seen as a mirage, constructed upon the idea that we can have agreement about how to bring the explanatory results of cognitive science to bear on theorisation about CONCEPT without getting tangled-up in prior difficulties about what is the appropriate kind of theory of CONCEPT in the first place. While we are unable to reach an agreement in this regard, the "new consensus" will be a consensus in name only.

6.3 Putting Cognitive Science First (and Last)

The original purpose of the appeal to cognitive science was to bring the explanatory results of cognitive science to bear on theorisation about CONCEPT. However, to endorse either the difference or identity accounts of theorisation about CONCEPT is to leave cognitive science behind from the very start and to conjecture about whether the properties we attribute to concepts are empirically defeasible. One may wonder, then, why advocates of the difference or identity accounts bother appealing to cognitive science at all. But they do. When discussing the criteria for natural kind-hood, for example, Machery (2009, p. 232) argues that CONCEPT is:

> [...] a natural kind if and only if there is a large set of scientifically relevant properties such that *C* is the maximal class whose members tend to share these properties because of some causal mechanism

Just as Weiskopf (2009, p. 147)—a likely defender of the identity account—argues that natural kinds are:

> [...] groupings of entities that participate in our best empirically discovered reliable generalizations, and which participate in those generalizations due to some set of properties they have in common.

Still, I think that Machery and Weiskopf get one thing right; namely, that progress is to be made by concentrating on the efforts and results of cognitive science. But I think that this recommendation should be stronger: progress is to be made by concentrating *exclusively* on the efforts and results of cognitive science. The general

---

called psychological theories of CONCEPT are, at least, theories of representations (this is, in fact, Machery's (2009) view).

57 Perhaps this could be resolved by a 'final' cognitive science that fixes the explanatory strategy of cognitive science once and for all. But we are still quite a way from that.

idea of the appeal to cognitive science—e.g. to look to the explanatory results of cognitive science as a way to inform theorisation about CONCEPT—is a good one. The problem, however, is that this good idea is corrupted by an underlying—and resolutely philosophical—dispute about whether we should *expect* from our theories of CONCEPT. As a consequence of this dispute, the attempt to appeal to cognitive science to inform theorisation about CONCEPT is pre-scientifically sabotaged.

This kind of pre-scientific sabotage is clearly apparent in the case of the difference account, which endorses the rationalist view that we can theorise *a priori* about the properties of concepts. But the identity account is not innocent in this regard either, because it is forced to be unduly selective about which properties attributed to concepts are, in fact, empirically defeasible. For example, it is forced to suppose that theories of CONCEPT will be theories of mental representations even when there is a large body of empirical research that challenges the representational theory of mind as a research paradigm (cf. Elman, Bates, and Johnson, 1996; McClelland et al., 2010). Thus, the identity account endorses only a "selective empiricism," because it supposes that some of the properties attributed to concepts are empirically defeasible—e.g. representational structure—, but others are not—e.g. being representations.

Quine famously argued that philosophers can do no better than to adopt the "standpoint of the best available knowledge; i.e. science, in some suitably broad sense" (Hylton and Kemp, 2019). In this regard, he argued that "philosophy of science is philosophy enough" (Quine, 1953) and that:

> we do not try to justify science by some prior and firmer philosophy, but neither are we to maintain less than scientific standards. (Quine, 1974, 34f).

The dispute between advocates of the difference and identity accounts is exactly about how to establish a "prior and firmer philosophy." One defending an anti-representationalist and rationalist philosophy, the other a pro-representationalist and empiricist philosophy; but both "prior" philosophies nonetheless. It seems to me, therefore, that a lesson can be taken from Quine about how to correctly appeal to cognitive science to inform theorisation about CONCEPT; namely, to accept that theorisation about CONCEPT is not something external to—or "prior" to—cognitive science, but, rather, something *within* cognitive science.[58]

---

58 Some may argue that Quine's position is itself a sort of "prior and firmer philosophy"; namely, some form of scientism. Quine, however, defends a kind of "naturalism," whereby "Science is not a substitute for common sense but an extension of it" and the scientist "is indistinguishable from the common man in his sense of evidence, except that the scientist is more careful" (Quine, 1957,

I said above that cognitive science cannot help us to decide between the difference and identity accounts of theorisation about CONCEPT, because of the pre-scientific disagreement between the two about what concepts *are* and if concepts have empirically defeasible properties. One may conclude, then, that, for now at least, we can only take a pre-scientific stand on what we expect a theory of CONCEPT to deliver. This conclusion, I think, is premature, because it misses one important point: that while it might be true that cognitive science cannot decide between perspectives on theorisation about CONCEPT originating outside of cognitive science, this does not imply that we cannot search for common ground from *within* cognitive science. Recognising this state of affairs leads one to a radically different perspective on theorisation about CONCEPT. Before spelling-out this perspective, however, it is necessary to briefly consider the idea of a working hypothesis.

6.4 Working Hypotheses

A working hypothesis is a hypothesis that is provisionally accepted as a basis for further research in the hope that a tenable theory will be produced, even if the hypothesis ultimately fails. In this way, a working hypothesis is an accepted starting point for further research. As Dewey (1938, pp. 142–143) put it, working hypotheses are "provisional, working means of advancing investigation." They are statements of expectation that:

> direct inquiry into channels in which new material, factual and conceptual, is disclosed, material which is more relevant, more weighted and confirmed, more fruitful, than were the initial facts and conceptions which served as the point of departure (Dewey, 1938, pp. 142–143).

Thus, working hypotheses are put forward as a means of furthering and expediting a mode of explanation or a given research paradigm.

Evidently, then, working hypotheses have a practical dimension: they function as a kind of regulatory measure to guide and buttress particular avenues of inquiry. For instance, the unity of science has been conceived as a working hypotheses that substantiates a particular mode of inquiry. In accord with this line of thought, Oppenheim and Putnam (1958) argue that:

---

229 & 233). Any philosopher with an interest in putting (cognitive) science first and last should have no problem endorsing such a view. Any without such an interest will be unconvinced by my claims in any case.

> [...] the assumption that unitary science can be attained through cumulative micro-reduction recommends itself as a working hypothesis. That is, we believe that it is in accord with the standards of reasonable scientific judgment to tentatively accept this hypothesis and to work on the assumption that further progress can be made in this direction.

In this regard, working hypotheses are the "basis for further investigation that [...] always takes the form of a problem" (Mead, 1899, p. 370). Attempts to answer the relevant problem(s) are guided by the relevant working hypothesis, but there need be no presumption about the truth of the hypothesis. Rather, a working hypothesis is any hypothesis that we need not "believe to be altogether true, but which is useful in enabling us to conceive of what takes place" (Peirce, 1958, §534).

Still, it would be mistake to think of the purpose of working hypotheses as purely practical; they also help us to explain. By formulating working hypotheses in any domain of science, practitioners of science are able to engage with problems previously undefined (by means of both theorisation and experimentation); to proffer explanations of those problems; and, eventually, to revise the specification of the problems and the explanations given. Working hypotheses, therefore, provide a starting point for explanations and they prop-up the explanations formulated to explain the problems that they themselves have revealed.

To get to grips with working hypotheses, it is helpful to consider two examples. Firstly, consider conjectures in mathematics; that is, mathematical propositions that appear to be true, but which are formally unproven. Such conjectures are assumptions that are unjustified, but that are central for an explanation or exposition of a given mathematical explanandum. For example, Thurston's "geometrization conjecture," holds that every three-dimensional space (the explanandum) can be cut up, in a systematic way, so that each piece has one of only eight geometries (Thurston, 1979). The purpose of conjectures is to facilitate the investigation of their consequences, typically by formulating conditional proofs; e.g. proofs that accept a conjecture as an antecedent and prove what necessarily follows as a consequence. For instance, if we accept the geometrization conjecture as an antecedent, then it can be shown that the Poincaré conjecture—that "every simply connected, closed 3-manifold is homeomorphic to the 3-sphere"—follows as a consequence (Stewart, 2003).

Now consider the atomic hypothesis; namely, the hypothesis that "the phenomenal world around us is made up, ultimately, of minute constituent entities that cannot be further subdivided" (Bose, 2015).[59] This hypothesis has played a

---

[59] In the Western intellectual tradition, this hypothesis stretches back at least as far as Leucippus and Democritus (c. 460–c. 370 BC), and likely even earlier in heterodox Indian traditions that rejected the authority of the Vedas (cf. Bose, 2015).

central role in framing the investigation and explanation of the natural world. For example, Newtonian mechanics explained the putative force of gravity by asserting that "particles" attract one another "with a force which is directly proportional to the product of their masses and inversely proportional to the square of the distance between their centers" (Newton, 1999). Similarly, particle physics explained the interactions giving rise to, say, chemical reactions and radioactive decay by breaking objects down into their fundamental components (cf. Close, 2004). In this sense, the atomic hypothesis played a central role in isolating particular explananda and structuring explanations of these explananda.

Assenting to the truth of either mathematical conjectures or the atomic hypothesis is beside the point. Regardless of their truth, both make possible otherwise closed avenues of investigation and explanation. In this sense, they are working hypotheses that invite further investigation by framing a problem as an explanandum. In the case of mathematical conjectures, the problem might be how best to understand the geometry of three-dimensional space and the working hypothesis might frame the problem as an explanandum of topology. In the case of the atomic hypothesis, the problem might be how best to understand the experience of an apparently continuous distribution of matter and the working hypothesis might frame the problem as an explanandum of the finite divisibility of any given object. In both instances, the working hypothesis serves as the basis to theorise about types of properties and classes that are epistemically fruitful; e.g. three-dimensional geometries, chemical compounds, electromagnetism, and so on.

6.5 CONCEPT as a Working Hypothesis

In the last section, I argued that working hypotheses open up new avenues of investigation and explanation by framing problems as explananda. In the context of explaining the mind/brain, such problems include making sense of how we perceive, organise, reason, and communicate about our surroundings. The difficulty, however, is that the problem of explaining these cognitive competences arises from the fact that we have such competences: the problem of explaining the mind/brain is a problem for the mind/brain. This pre-theoretic circularity leaves us without a point of departure in our explanatory task.[60] To make progress, therefore, we routinely employ working hypotheses about the structure and operation of cogni-

---

60 When I use the term "pre-theoretic," I am referring to something like Sellars' "manifest image", which he defines as "the framework in terms of which man came to be aware of himself as man-in-the-world." (Sellars, 1963, p. 6).

tion. For example, the representational theory of mind (RTM) (cf. Thagard, 2018). These working hypotheses expedite the explanatory task of cognitive science by framing the pre-theoretically identified problems in new terms; e.g. in terms of representational structure and operations over representations.

On the traditional view, theories of CONCEPT fit into this picture as an attempt to *externally* validate different working hypotheses. For instance, to validate RTM by determining what kind of mental representations structure cognition. But, as I have argued, different perspectives on theorisation about CONCEPT (e.g. the difference and identity accounts) are available and the explanatory results of cognitive science are no help for deciding between them. The reason for this is because different working hypotheses can be accepted in cognitive science, which undermine one or another theory of CONCEPT. For example, one may accept a working hypothesis contradicting RTM and so undermine theories of concepts as representations; just as one may accept a working hypothesis contradicting the claim that the mind has semantic content and so undermine theories of concepts as the necessary and sufficient conditions for propositional attitudes.

But another perspective on theorisation about CONCEPT is possible: that theorisation about CONCEPT is *internal* to cognitive science. Recall that Quine recommends the "abandonment of the goal of a first philosophy prior to natural science" (Quine, 1981, p. 67). If this view is correct, then theorisation about CONCEPT cannot be "external" to cognitive science, because we must be ready "to see philosophy *as* natural science trained upon itself and permitted free use of scientific findings" (Quine, 1981, p. 85). By saying that theorisation about CONCEPT is internal to cognitive science, therefore, we are agreeing with Quine that there can be no extra-scientific theorisation about CONCEPT. This view certainly goes against the difference account given its defence of rationalist theories of CONCEPT. But it will also contravene the identity account given its "selective empiricist" tendencies.

On the view I want to defend, then, theories of CONCEPT should be understood as working hypotheses that expedite cognitive science. Consider four possible—and prominent—theories of CONCEPT that I argue should be understood as working hypotheses:

(a) Members of CONCEPT unify and structure cognition, and so support cognitive competences.
(b) Members of CONCEPT are mental items that play a role in conceptual, cognitive processing.
(c) Members of CONCEPT are representations.
(d) Members of CONCEPT are the necessary and sufficient conditions for propositional attitudes.

(a) is a very general working hypothesis indeed, which may now be outdated given that there are (perhaps) domains of cognitive processing that are non-conceptual (e.g. perception, motor control, etc.). For this reason, other, more restricted working hypotheses—e.g. (b)—may now be preferred. (c) is (part of) the working hypothesis endorsed by advocates of the identity account and empiricist theories of CONCEPT. And (d) is (part of) the working hypothesis endorsed by advocates of the difference account and rationalist theories of CONCEPT. Each of these working hypotheses is different and many more complicated working hypotheses are possible.[61]

The value of any working hypotheses about CONCEPT is best elaborated by analogy with the atomic hypothesis. The atomic hypothesis was formulated as a means of furthering our investigations into (some of) the explananda of physics—e.g. gravitational force or chemical reactions—in terms of indivisible units. Similarly, I argue that working hypotheses about CONCEPT are formulated as a means of furthering our investigations into (some of) the explananda of cognitive science—e.g. categorisation, reasoning, language comprehension etc. Depending on the working hypothesis in play, different investigations and explanations of the explananda can be carried out. For instance, some working hypotheses will facilitate explanations in representational terms (when (c) is established and defended) (cf. Rosch, 1975; Nosofsky, 1986, for two of many examples of such explanations); others in terms of relevant semantic properties (when (d) is established and defended) (cf. Dummett, 1993; Peacocke, 1992); and so on. In this sense, working hypotheses about CONCEPT operate as the basis for further investigation and explanation of the mind/brain by making a provisional claim about what (some aspect of) the mind/brain is like.

Consider again explanations of categorisation, which are typically taken to involve concepts. Some working hypotheses about CONCEPT—e.g. (c)—frame the explanandum of categorisation in representational terms, and so make possible explanations of categorisation in terms of a correspondence mapping between instances of a category and a represented category (cf. Hampton, 1995; Lakoff, 1987; Osherson and Smith, 1981). Others—e.g. (d)—frame the explanandum as possible only given the satisfaction of necessary and sufficient conditions for propositional attitudes, and so make possible the explanation of categorisation in terms of the "presentation" of referents by abstract objects mediating between mind and world (Peacocke, 1992).[62] And others still may frame the explanandum in terms of non-representational dependencies, and so make possible explanations

---

61 As a quick and easy example of a more complicated working hypothesis about CONCEPT, consider the working hypothesis that is the conjunction of (b) and (c); e.g. $(2) \wedge (3)$.

62 In this regard, Peacocke (1992, p. 2) argues that "Concepts C and D are distinct if and only if there are two complete propositional contents that differ at most in that one contains C substituted in one or more places for D, and one of which is potentially informative while the other is not."

of categorisation in terms of "neural dynamics" constrained by "Hebbian reinforcement learning" and "expectation maximization" (cf. Jamalabadi et al., 2012; Van Gelder, 1993).[63] In all cases, however, the development of different kinds of cognitive scientific explanations *cohere with* the acceptance of a different working hypothesis about CONCEPT.

Of course, after being established, some working hypotheses can then be put to the test. Consider, for example, Rutherford's working hypothesis that members of the kind ATOM are composed of sub-atomic particles, which stood in conflict with the working hypothesis that atoms are indivisible. This working hypothesis was eventually shown to be supported by the empirical data; for instance, data about the existence of an atomic nucleus where positive charge and (most) atomic mass are concentrated (Rutherford, 1914).[64] Thus, Rutherford's working hypothesis about the ATOM was shown to be more than a mere "provisional, working means of advancing investigation"; it was shown to be the best theory of ATOM available.

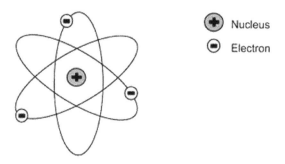

Fig. 6.1: Rutherford's model of the atom.

But there is a problem with testing working hypotheses about CONCEPT: that they invariably cohere with a specific view about *how* we are to appeal to cognitive science. Consider a test of the working hypothesis that members of CONCEPT are represen-

---

63 The working hypothesis here might be that members of CONCEPT are non-representational dependencies.

64 The relevant empirical data here was obtained in the Geiger-Marsden experiments, where a beam of α particles was directed at a thin foil of metal (gold) and a "scattering pattern" was measured using a fluorescent screen (cf. Geiger, 1910; Geiger and Marsden, 1913, for a detailed account of this experiment and its finding).

tations.[65] The relevant cognitive science against which to test such a hypothesis would have to be *representational* cognitive science, because non-representational cognitive science explicitly rejects the working hypothesis that members of CONCEPT are representations. But such a test would be theory-laden, because representational cognitive science already coheres with the working hypothesis that the psychological entities—e.g. concepts—operative in higher cognition are representations.[66] The same argument will generalise to the tests of all working hypotheses about CONCEPT, because the only relevant cognitive science that could (dis)confirm such a working hypothesis will be the cognitive science with which that hypothesis already coheres. The open question, then, is why it is of value to think of theories of CONCEPT as working hypotheses at all?

6.6 Internal and External Theories of CONCEPT

Recall that advocates of the difference and identity accounts do not agree about how we should theorise about CONCEPT in virtue of endorsing different —rationalist and selective empiricist—views about what we should expect a theory of CONCEPT to explain. As a result, the "meta-explanatory challenge" fails to inform our decision about the best CONCEPT, because we can disagree about its scope. One possibility is just to accept this state of affairs. However, if we do this, then we also have to accept that all hope of arriving at a best theory of CONCEPT is lost. The reason is because we would have to accept that every theorist of CONCEPT will be free to make a choice between rationalism and selective empiricism. But this conclusion depends, ultimately, on the assumption that theorisation about CONCEPT is *external* to cognitive science. This is not an assumption that we need to endorse.

As I have argued above, we need not assume that theorisation about CONCEPT is *external* to cognitive science,, because we can think of cognitive science and theorisation about CONCEPT as intertwined. On this view, developing a theory

---

65 As is clear from what I have said above, there may be disagreement about whether representations are the only things that are "conceptual" in kind—e.g. whether we should countenance both CONCEPT$_{psy}$ and CONCEPT$_{phil}$.

66 To be clear, I see no reason why any kind of cognitive science could not continue even after its practiners relinquish their commitment to any given working hypothesis about CONCEPT. This, in fact, is exactly what would follow for *representational* cognitive science if the relevant cognitive scientists were to follow Machery (2009) and abandon their commitment to the claim that members of CONCEPT are representations while maintaining a commitment to representational states in general.

of CONCEPT is a process *internal* to cognitive science, which amounts to establishing and defending a working hypotheses about the conceptual nature of the mind/brain. For example, hypotheses (a)-(d) introduced in the previous section. These working hypotheses then function as the basis for further investigation and explanation; for instance, as the basis for further investigation and explanation of cognitive competences—such as categorisation—in terms of, say, the representational structure (working hypotheses c) or semantic properties (working hypotheses d) of the mind/brain.

Perhaps the simplest way to come to terms with the idea of theorisation about CONCEPT that is internal to cognitive science is to think of such theorisation as the elaboration of a "story" in the technical sense of Hartmann (1999).[67] As Allen (2013, p. 257) argues, the development of such "stories" is important, because:

> in cases where the problems to be explained originate with phenomena that are understood pre-scientifically or pre-theoretically, a story must explain why a given model is relevant to the initial questions, even if sometimes the upshot is that these questions were based in confusion. Insofar as psychology, including comparative psychology, starts with questions about the nature of mental states and sometimes with the first-person nature of their possession, the "stories" about models that attribute contentful mental states (something that is done from the third-person perspective) are expected to bear on first-person perspectives on those states.

Theorisation about CONCEPT that is internal to cognitive science, therefore, enables us to do two things at once; that is, to make possible new investigations and explanations of cognitive competences, and to link such investigations and explanations back to the pre-theoretic assumptions with which they began.

Internal theories of CONCEPT can take many forms. Some may establish the working hypothesis that concepts are representations; others the working hypothesis that concepts are the conditions for propositional attitudes. Still, all internal theories of CONCEPT will afford concepts a role in the investigation and explanation of the mind/brain. And this is of the utmost important, because it implies that all theorists of CONCEPT take themselves to be, firstly, differentiating the study of the mind/brain (perhaps understood as cognitive science) from other practices

---

67 In the context of a discussion of Hadron Physics, Hartmann (1999) argues that:
   A story is a narrative told *around* the formalism of the model. It is neither a deductive consequence of the model nor of the underlying theory. It is, however, *inspired* by the underlying theory (if there is one). This is because the story takes advantage of the vocabulary of the theory (such as 'gluon') and refers to some of its features (such as its complicated vacuum structure). Using more general terms, the story fits the model in a larger framework (a 'world picture') in a non-deductive way. A story is, therefore, an integral part of a model; it complements the formalism. To put it in a slogan: a *model is an (interpreted) formalism + a story*.

of investigation and explanation; and, secondly, to be explaining the mind/brain by utilising CONCEPT as a way to carve the mind/brain at its structural joints (cf. Fodor, 1983, p. 128). Thus, from the perspective of all internal theories of CONCEPT, the kind CONCEPT is an invaluable part of the story that we tell ourselves to make explanations of the mind/brain possible and to ensure that such explanations cohere with our primitive understanding of the world.

There is, however, one big problem with taking the view that theorisation about CONCEPT is internal to cognitive science: that different theories of CONCEPT internal to cognitive science will by definition establish different working hypotheses. For example, the different hypotheses (a)-(d) above. Still, the working assumption of most cognitive scientists (and philosophers) is that the mind/brain is one thing, to be explained by one kind of cognitive science with one appropriate interpretation. If this is correct, then the various kinds of cognitive science inspired by different theories of CONCEPT cannot peacefully co-exist and there is work to be done in deciding which explanatory project ought be favoured. For instance, to decide on the relative merits of different kinds of explanation (e.g. causal-mechanistic explanations vs. dynamic explanations) and different explanatory posits (e.g. representations).

I do not have space to engage in work of this kind here. Rather, I want only to emphasise that when we think of theories of CONCEPT as working hypotheses, we can hold out hope that, at some point, the "best" kind of cognitive science, cohering with the "best" working hypotheses about CONCEPT, can be found. In contrast, when we deny that theories of CONCEPT are working hypotheses, we also abandon any hope of appealing to the explanatory results of cognitive science to decide on the best theory of CONCEPT, because we are forced to either endorse a "meta-explanatory challenge" applying to all theories of CONCEPT (Argument G) or a "meta-explanatory challenge" applying only to those psychological theories of CONCEPT that are sensitive to the results of cognitive scientific research.

It is, of course, an open question about how different kinds of cognitive science are to be compared. Some may argue that different kinds of cognitive science should be compared according to how well they explain a variety of different behavioural phenomena that we typically associate with the operations of the mind/brain. For example, behavioural phenomena evidencing the standard explananda of cognitive science—e.g. categorisation, reasoning, language comprehension etc.—, but also evidencing more fine-grained explananda such as cognitive dissonance, rationalisation, (implicit) biases and so on. Others, however, may argue that different kinds of cognitive science should be compared according to some set of theoretical virtues. For instance, their simplicity, unity, explanatory depth, applicability, consistency, coherence, evidential/causal accuracy, and beauty (cf. Keas, 2018, for a thorough examination of different theoretical virtues). If what I have said about theories of CONCEPT being working hypothesis is correct, then reaching an agreement in this regard will be the first steps of progress.

But even if one is inclined to agree with me on this point, one may still worry that my account fails to address a lingering problem: the question of how exactly we go about theorising about CONCEPT in the first place. Rationalist theorists might deny that our initial theories of CONCEPT have anything to do with cognitive science. Instead, they might claim that such theories arise out of another domain of inquiry; say, some *a priori* domain of "philosophy." This claim will enact a strict demarcation between philosophy and science, which some will find unpalatable. Another, empiricist possibility is that initial theories of CONCEPT are part of a "manifest" cognitive science, which later influences the development of different kinds of fully-fledged cognitive science.[68] This view dissolves the distinction between philosophy and science, but does so by augmenting the notion of science to include simpler practices undertaken in a potentially pre-theoretic setting.

If we are forced to take a stand on the issue of how theorisation about CONCEPT first gets going, then it seems that we collapse back into the tension between rationalist and empiricist theories of CONCEPT, because we are forced to specify whether theorisation about CONCEPT begins as an empirically defeasible enterprise. However, the value of taking theories of CONCEPT to be working hypotheses is that we do not have to take a stand on this issue. This follows because we can think of theories of CONCEPT as working hypotheses that further our explanations and investigations of the mind/brain, while remaining neutral about the domain of theorisation. On my view, then, theories of CONCEPT should always be understood as internal to a broad explanatory project concerned with explaining the mind/brain.[69] And this is true regardless of whether such theories facilitate the investigation and explanation of, say, how we categorise, how we compare different scientific theories, how our emotions influence behaviour, or even the complexities of our subjective lives.

The upshot is that all that matters is that we acknowledge that the different theories of CONCEPT—e.g. working hypotheses—are internal to an overarching explanatory project to explain and understand the mind/brain. No distinction between a "philosophical" and "scientific" explanatory project needs to be presupposed here. Instead, we can recognise only that different theories of CONCEPT bring with them a commitment to investigating and explaining the mind/brain

---

68 When I use the term "manifest," I am referring to something like Sellar's "manifest image," which he defines as "the framework in terms of which man came to be aware of himself as man-in-the-world" (Sellars, 1963, p. 6).

69 One could think of this general explanatory project in terms of Quine's broad notion of "science" as "not a substitute for common sense but an extension of it" (Quine, 1957, p. 14).

differently, and, ultimately, that these different practices of investigation and explanation are the relevant units of comparison if we want to determine the best theory of CONCEPT.

6.7 Beyond the Meta-Explanatory Challenge

Having now set out my account of theories of CONCEPT as working hypotheses and explained what it means for a theory of CONCEPT to be internal to cognitive science, we are well-positioned to make progress. The reason for this is straightforward: because when theorising about CONCEPT is taken to be an inextricable part of our attempt to investigate and explain the mind/brain any ambiguities about how or what cognitive science explains must be taken into account *when* theorising about CONCEPT. In other words, when theorisation about CONCEPT is taken to be internal to cognitive science it cannot consistently be taken to be at a remove from cognitive science as well.

Recall that the "meta-explanatory challenge"—and, again, the "explanatory challenge to the standard view"—arise when we try to appeal to cognitive science to validate theorisation about CONCEPT. For example, theories about what concepts *are*—e.g. the standard view of concepts—or theories about what kinds of conceptual objects cognitive science is in the business of explaining—e.g. unified, disparate, or single representational kinds. But when theories of CONCEPT are understood as working hypotheses and, as a result, theorisation about CONCEPT is taken to give rise to a number of different approaches to doing cognitive science, such "challenges" have no force. This follows because no-one who takes up my view will also be unequivocally committed to any of the "new" or standard view theories of CONCEPT. Instead, my view permits a range of different theories of CONCEPT—for instance, (a)-(d) above—and places the burden on a future comparison of the kinds of cognitive science they inspire.

The upshot is that both the "explanatory challenge to the standard view" and the "meta-explanatory challenge" should be viewed as irrelevant for assessing theories of CONCEPT, because the first premise of both arguments is concerned with theories of CONCEPT as theories of a single kind of representation and with "new" theories of CONCEPT respectively. And even if such theories could be read as working hypotheses about CONCEPT in their own right, they do not exhaust the possible working hypotheses about CONCEPT. For example, no standard view or "new" theory of CONCEPT introduces the working hypotheses that concepts are states of a dynamically evolving and non-representational system that spans the brain, body, and (sociocultural) environment. But such a theory of CONCEPT—

which might be said to inspire dynamicist or "anti-cognitivist" cognitive science—probably would be defended by, e.g., Hutto and Myin (2013) or Chemero (2009).

Thus, the "meta-explanatory challenge" is left behind. However, in overcoming the "meta-explanatory challenge" in this way, the empirical arbiter for theories of CONCEPT can no longer be viewed as a single and unified 'cognitive science.' Rather, the empirical arbiter of our evaluations of theories of CONCEPT must be re-conceived as the diverse practices of many different kinds of cognitive science, which can be compared according to, say, their relative explanatory power. As such, my argument does not imply that we cannot appeal to cognitive science to help us decide on the best theory of CONCEPT. But my argument does imply that when we do successfully appeal to cognitive science we are not appealing to a homogeneous body of explanatory practices, but to the relative success or failure of many different kinds of cognitive science, each inspired by their own theory of CONCEPT.

7 Why Appeals to Cognitive Science Fail

In chapters two and three, I argued that the results of cognitive science do not clearly support any standard view theory of CONCEPT; e.g. imagism, prototype theory, or exemplar theory. But I also argued that the results of cognitive science may not support any of the "new" theories of CONCEPT—e.g. eliminativist, pluralist, or hybrid theories—, which were developed to remedy the shortcoming of standard view theories of CONCEPT. In chapters four and five, I argued that this concern was real, because of, firstly, our uncertainty about what counts as a genuine explanation in cognitive science and, secondly, our uncertainty about which explanations will be taken by different "new" theories of CONCEPT to be genuinely explanatory. This led to a troubling possibility: that we are without an empirical arbiter for deciding between theories of CONCEPT and, hence, that mere intuition will play the decisive role.

In the last chapter, however, I have shown that this conclusion was premature, because it rested on a flawed conception of what theorisation about CONCEPT entails. Namely, a conception of theorisation about CONCEPT as somehow *external* to cognitive science. My argument there was that we should reject this view and think of theorisation about CONCEPT as *internal* to cognitive science. That is, as inextricably bound up with the activity of doing cognitive science and, even, as (partly) constitutive of that activity. When this view is taken up, the concern about our lacking an empirical arbiter between theories of CONCEPT is assuaged, because different theories of CONCEPT are conceived of as working hypotheses that are constitutive of different kinds of cognitive science, which can be compared according to, say, explanatory power.

If what I have said is right, then the traditional idea of appealing to cognitive science to decide between theories of CONCEPT gets off on the wrong foot, because it assumes that there is theoretical work to be done concerning concepts that is not already part of cognitive science. Such an idea has always been aggressively defended by philosophers that give weight to *a priori*—or armchair—reasoning (Peacocke, 2000; Peacocke, 2005b). But there is no reason to take such views seriously. Any empirically-minded philosopher can always ask:

> how in the end are we to distinguish such claims of "rational insight," "primitive compulsion," inferential practice or folk belief, from merely some deeply held empirical conviction, indeed, from mere dogma?

Even if a lively debate continues about how we can make such a delimitation, this does not imply that the debate itself makes any sense (cf. Bealer, 1999; BonJour,

https://doi.org/9783110708165-007

1998; Devitt, 2002; Horwich, 2005; Rey, 2009, as some examples of defences of rational theorisation).

And this will have repercussions for other debates in (the philosophy of) cognitive science and the philosophy of mind. Consider, for example, debates about *mental content*. If my claims here can be extrapolated to debates about mental content, then it would follow that theoretical work to be done concerning mental content cannot be taken to be "external" to cognitive science. Rather, theorisation about mental content would have to be viewed as "internal" to cognitive science, and, perhaps, as establishing particular working hypotheses—e.g. that cognition is contentful—that expedite different cognitive scientific explanations. Of course, if it could then be showed that such working hypotheses are dispensable, then we would have good reason to abandon such theorisation about mental content. This is exactly the position defended by, e.g., Chomsky (1995, pp. 52–53), who argues that:

> There is no meaningful question about the "content" of the internal representations of a person [...]. No notion like "content", or "representation of", figures within the theory, so there are no answers to be given as to their nature.[70]

Furthermore, consider debates about *nonconceptual content*; that is, debates about whether there are mental states that represent the world even though the bearer of those mental states does not possess the concepts required to specify their content (cf. Stich, 1978; Evans, 1982). Some have argued, for example, that the content of perceptual states is nonconceptual and that it only becomes conceptual when it serves as input to a thinking, concept-applying, and reasoning system (cf. Bermúdez, 2007; Campbell, 2005). But, if my claims here can be extrapolated to debates about nonconceptual content, then then it would follow that theoretical work to be done concerning mental content cannot be taken to be "external" to cognitive science. Rather, theorisation about mental content would have to be viewed as "internal" to cognitive science, and, perhaps, as establishing particular working hypotheses—e.g. that perception is not unified and structured by concepts—that expedite particular cognitive scientific explanations.

This last example reiterates an important implication of my view; namely, that some so-called philosophical debates—e.g. about whether or not nonconceptual content exists—should be eschewed. The reason is because theorisation about, say, nonconceptual content can be understood as a process that establishes working

---

70 It could also be argued that content is a convenient, heuristic feature of explanation that sorts type-identifying structures into kinds according to the role they play in cognitive processing (cf. Egan, 2014, pp. 6–9).

hypotheses that expedite particular kinds of cognitive science, but need not be taken to be true. The idea that positing such things as nonconceptual content is fruitful for some kinds of cognitive science is already well established. Bermúdez and Cahen (2015), for example, note that:

> the basic idea of nonconceptual content provides a promising tool for tackling a range of problems in the philosophy of mind and cognition. Allowing that a creature's representational capacities can outstrip its conceptual capacities makes it possible for philosophers and cognitive scientists to study aspects of cognition and behavior that remain outside the scope of more traditional approaches —from subpersonal computational mechanisms to the psychological states of non-human animals and human infants to the nature of perceptual experience.

But, if what I have said is taken seriously, then we take an even stronger line and argue that theorisation about nonconceptual content is not theorisation whose accuracy can be checked against the results of a single kind of cognitive science. Instead, theorisation about nonconceptual content—like theorisation about CON-CEPT—is (partly) constitutive of particular kinds of cognitive science.

Finally, consider debates about how best we are to theorise about propositional attitudes such as *beliefs*. Some think that having a belief necessarily involves having mental representations with some content (cf. Fodor, 1975; Milikan, 1984; Dretske, 1988; Burge, 2010; Quilty-Dunn and Mandelbaum, 2018); others think that having a belief involves possessing behavioural dispositions pertaining that belief (cf. Braithwaite, 1932; Marcus, 1990; Schwitzgebel, 2002); and others still think that having a belief depends on one observably behaving in such a way that would cause one to attribute beliefs to you in order to explain your behaviour (cf. Dennett, 1987; Davidson, 2001). But, yet again, if my claims here can be extrapolated to debates about how best to theorise about belief, then then it would follow that theoretical work to be done concerning belief would have to be viewed as "internal" to, rather than "external" to, cognitive science.

From this perspective, we are not able to appeal to a single cognitive science to decide between different theories of belief, because theorisation about belief—as that which establishes working hypotheses about belief—would be a component part of some, but not all, cognitive sciences. And this realisation may allow us to make progress in this domain. The idea—in keeping with what I have said about theorisation about CONCEPT—would be to think of theorisation about belief as a process *within* to cognitive science that establishes particular working hypotheses. Then, the task would be to compare the different kinds of cognitive science that are inspired (or not) by different theories—read: working hypotheses—of belief. Therefore, in much the same manner as I have dealt with debates about theorisation about CONCEPT, theorisation about belief could be re-conceived, and debates about theorisation about belief re-oriented, by taking theories of belief to be internal to cognitive science.

This is all work for the future. I am ready to bet, however, that traditional appeals to cognitive science will not help us to resolve any debate in the philosophy of mind about the reality of any aspect of cognition—e.g. nonconceptual content— or about our choice between competing theories of any aspect of cognition—e.g. between representational, dispositional, or interpretational theories of belief. The reason, I contend, is because our assumptions about the reality of such things and about how they are best understood cannot be divorced from the activity of doing a particular cognitive science itself. It is not as though we are doing something extra-cognitive scientific when we engage in theorisation about, say, nonconceptual content or belief—we are constituting a cognitive science with this act of theorisation. Consequently, it is not the case that a single cognitive science can be "appealed to" as an arbiter between our different theories. Once we recognise this point, we can also come to recognise that the answers always lie in cognitive science and that, as a result, the philosophy of cognitive science is philosophy enough.

8 Appendix

8.1 Taylor and Sutton's (2020) frame-based model of Bayesian category learning

The model develop by Taylor and Sutton (2020) is based, like other single system models, on the calculation of $p(w|D, \alpha, \delta)$, which is derived from the joint probability distribution over w, D, α, and δ (elements of the model). They use the same formula (reprinted here with a M label on p to indicate the probability function based on this joint distribution):

$$p_M(w_i|D, \alpha, \delta) \propto p_M(w_i|\alpha) \times p_M(D|w_i, \delta) \tag{4.2}$$

They maintain the small categories preference parameter α, but the similar features preference δ, on their model, sets the preference for how strongly distance from the central node affects the overall similarity score for a set of categories. Definitions of elements of the model are given in Table 8.1. Categories are sets of objects and category schemas are sets of categories. The data input for the model consists of frames, here simplified to objects paired with attribute values and a distance of this value from the central node. Distance from the central node forms the basis for the weighting of attribute values determined by δ.

Tab. 8.1: Definitions for elements of the frame based Bayesian categorisation model.

O	$=$	$\{o_1, \ldots, o_n\}$	A set of observed objects.
C	$=$	$\{c \mid c \neq \varnothing, c \subseteq O\}$	A set of categories.
W	$=$	$\{w \mid w \neq \varnothing, w \subseteq C\}$	A set of sets of categories.
F	$=$	$\{f \mid f \subseteq O\}$	A set of attribute values (i.e. a set of predicates of objects).
ι	$=$	$f : F \rightarrow \mathbb{N}_{>0}$	A function from attribute values to their distance from the central node.
A	$=$	$\{\langle \mathbf{f}, n \rangle \mid \mathbf{f} \in F, n = \iota(\mathbf{f})\}$	A set feature-distance pairs (i.e. a set of distance indexed features).
D	$=$	$\{\langle o, X \rangle \mid o \in O, X \subseteq A\}$	The data: a set of tuples such that for each object, there is a set of feature-distance pairs.
α	$\in$	$[0, 1]$	The small categories preference parameter
δ	$=$	$f : \mathbb{N}_{>0} \rightarrow \mathbb{R}$	The similar features preference parameter. A function from distance measures to real numbers

For simplicity, Taylor and Sutton (2020) assume that for any set of categories, w, no object is in more than one category and every object is in a category. (Sets of

https://doi.org/9783110708165-008

categories completely partition the domain of objects.) In other words, as given in (8.1), for a set of objects, O, for each w, there is a distribution over the categories $c_i \in w$ (the probability function is accordingly labelled O, w, they suppress O in most of the following since they do not consider cases for multiple O sets).

$$\sum_{c_i \in w} p_{O,w}(c_i) = 1 \tag{8.1}$$

The prior probability of a category c relative to a set of categories w is calculated as the number of objects in the category divided by the number of objects so far observed:

$$\text{For each } c \in w, \quad p_{O,w}(c) = \frac{|c|_w}{|O|} \tag{8.2}$$

Other distributions occur at the level of nodes in frames. Each node has a set of possible values (e.g., **red, green** etc., for COLOUR, and **feathers, fur, scales** etc. for COVERING). I say more about such distributions in Section 8.1.2.

8.1.1 The α parameter

The intuitive idea behind the calculation of $p_M(w|\alpha)$ is that w should minimise entropy over the object space (minimize the average amount of information required to identify in which category in w an object belongs). This is given in (8.3). If alpha is set to 1, then the probability is proportional to the inverse log of the entropy of w. If $\alpha = 0$, then, assuming a base-2 logarithm, for all $w \in W$, $p_M(w|\alpha) \propto 2^0$ (i.e. $\propto 1$), thus all $w \in W$ would receive the same prior.[71] In other words, there would be no preferential effect of reducing (or increasing) the number of categories.

$$\text{For all } w \in W: \quad p_M(w|\alpha) \propto 2^{\wedge}\left(\alpha \times \sum_{c_i \in w} (p_w(c_i) \times \log_2(p_w(c_i)))\right) \tag{8.3}$$

As an example of how α operates, consider four objects a, b, c, d and a space of two category sets w_1, w_2. If $w_1 = \{c_1 = a, c_2 = b, c_3 = c, c_4 = d\}$ and $w_2 = \{c_5 = \{a, b, c, d\}\}$, then, for varying vales for α, we get the results in Table 8.2 (values given to 2 decimal places).

8.1.2 The δ parameter

The intuitive idea behind the calculation of $p(D|w_i, \delta)$ is that, with respect to the values for an attribute, each category should minimise entropy (weighted

---

[71] The actual probability is calculated by dividing by the sum of the values given in (8.3) over all $w \in W$.

Tab. 8.2: The effect of α on calculating the prior $p(w|\alpha)$.

	α			
	1	0.5	0.1	0
$p(w_1|\alpha)$	0.20	0	0.47	0.50
$p(w_2|\alpha)$	0.80	0	0.53	0.50

by distance the attribute is from the central node). In other words, minimise the average amount of information it takes to decide which properties an object has if it is in a particular category.

Given that each $d \in D$ is a tuple of an object and a set of attribute value-distance pairs, calculating $p_M(D|w, \delta)$ turns on calculating, for each category c in w, the probability that the objects in c have some particular value for the relevant attribute. Let $|\mathbf{f}_j|_{c_k,w,D}$ be the number of times the attribute value $\mathbf{f}_j$ occurs as a value in category $c_k \in w$ for a data set D. Let $|c_k|_{w,D}$ be the number of objects in $c_k \in w$. $p_{w,D}(\mathbf{f}_j|c_k)$ is, then:

$$p_{w,D}(\mathbf{f}_j|c_k) = \frac{|\mathbf{f}_j|_{c_k,w,D}}{|c_k|_{w,D}} \tag{8.4}$$

namely, for a set of categories w, the total number of times objects in $c_k \in w$ have value $\mathbf{f}_j$, divided by the total number of objects in c_k. This forms a distribution for any set of attribute values that are the mutually exclusive values of some attribute (e.g., a distribution over **feathers** and **fur**, and a distribution over **black** and **brown** in the toy example).

The entropy values for attribute value spaces, given a category, are weighted depending on the distance d the feature is from the central node. This weighting is set by δ, which is a function from d to a real number in the range $[0, 1]$. The weighted entropy value for a category is, then, the sum of the weighted sum of the surprisal values for each attribute value, given a category, also weighted by δ. The weighted entropy value for a set of categories w is the weighted average of the entropy values for each category in w (relative to $p_w(c)$). So, for all $w \in W$:

$$p_M(D|w, \delta) = 2^{\wedge}\left(\sum_{c_k \in w} p_w(c_k) \times \sum_{\langle \mathbf{f}_j, n_j \rangle \in D} \left(p_{w,f,c}(\mathbf{f}_j|c_k) \times \log_2(p_{w,f,c}(\mathbf{f}_j|c_k)) \right. \right.$$

$$\left. \left. \times \delta(n_j) \right) \right) \tag{8.5}$$

Intuitively, $p_M(D|w, \delta)$ is a measure on how well the data is predicted by each w (weighted by δ). This value will be 1 if every piece of data (an object and its attribute values and distances) falls into a totally homogenous category with respect to the objects it contains. This is because the average amount of information to determine the attribute values of members of each category is 0. As categories get more and

Tab. 8.3: The effect of δ on calculating the likelihood $p(D|w, \delta)$ for $\delta(n_j) = n_j^0$, $\delta(n_j) = n_j^{-1}$, and $\delta(n_j) = n_j^{-2}$.

	$\delta(n_j)$		
	n_j^0	n_j^{-1}	n_j^{-2}
$p(D|w_1, \delta)$	1	1	1
$p(D|w_2, \delta)$	0.5	0.71	0.84
$p(D|w_3, \delta)$	0.5	0.5	0.5
$p(D|w_4, \delta)$	0.25	0.35	0.42

more heterogeneous, the value of $p(D|w, \delta)$ will get lower. This is because the average amount on information need to determine the attribute values of members of each category is high.

With four objects a, b, c, d, and also with the four category sets $w_1, w_2, w_3,$ w_4-, if $w_1 = \{c_1 = \{a\}, c_2 = \{b\}, c_3 = \{c\}, c_4 = \{d\}\}$, $w_2 = \{c_5 = \{a, b\}, c_6 = \{b, c\}\},$ $w_3 = \{c_7 = \{a, c\}, c_8 = \{b, d\}\}$, and $w_4 = \{c_9 = \{a, b, c, d\}\}$ we get the impact of altering the δ function as given in Table 8.3 (values given to 2 decimal places). Since w_1 contains only singleton categories, the probability of the data given w_1 is 1 no matter how $\delta(n_j)$ is defined, since for all attribute values and all categories $p_{w_1,f,c}(\mathbf{f}_j|c)$ equals 1 or zero (so the weighted entropy value is 0 and $2^0=1$). The worst performing is w_4, since this contains only one category so heterogeneity for features is high (this is mitigated a little when $\delta(n_j)$ is defined to decrease the homogeneity requirement for attribute values with larger distances from the central node).

One can then make a comparison between w_8 and w_9 (which is important for the toy example). In the case where $\delta(n_j) = n_j^0$ (i.e. where $\delta(n_j)$ is always equal to 1), there is no weighting towards the importance of similarity of values with respect to being close to the central node. This gives us the same result as would be given for a simple unweighted feature list. In other words, given some things that are furry and black, furry and brown, feathered and black, and feathered and brown, the model has no preference towards grouping furry things together and feathered things together over grouping black things together and brown things together.

When $\delta(n_j) = n_j^{-1}$, the result is that entropy is weighted to be halved for values at a distance of two nodes away from the central node. When $\delta(n_j) = n_j^{-2}$, the result is that entropy is weighted to be quartered for values at a distance of two nodes away from the central node. This translates into an increasing preference for no entropy at the inner most nodes and an allowance of higher entropy at further out nodes.

Bibliography

Acheson, D. J. (1990). *Elementary fluid dynamics: Oxford applied mathematics and computing science series*. Oxford: Oxford University Press.

Agazzi, E. (2014). *Scientific objectivity and its contexts*. Springer.

Ahn, W. and M. J. Dennis (2001). "Dissociation between categorization and similarity judgement: Differential effect of causal status on feature weights. In U. Hahn and M. Ramscar (Eds.), Similarity and categorization (pp. 87-107)".

Ahn, W. and N. S. Kim (2000). "The causal status effect in categorization". *Psychology of Learning and Motivation: Advances in Research and Theory* 40, p. 23.

Allen, C. (2013). "The geometry of partial understanding". *American Philosophical Quarterly* 50.3, pp. 249–262.

Allen, S. W. and L. R. Brooks (1991). "Specializing the operation of an explicit rule". *Journal of experimental psychology: General* 120.1, p. 3.

Anderson, J. R. (1991). "The adaptive nature of human categorization". *Psychological review* 98.3, p. 409.

Anderson, J. R. and J. Betz (2001). "A hybrid model of categorization". *Psychonomic Bulletin and Review* 8, pp. 629–647.

Anderson, J. R. et al. (2004). "An integrated theory of the mind." *Psychological review* 111.4, pp. 1036–1060.

Anisfeld, M. (1968). "Disjunctive Concepts?" *The Journal of General Psychology* 78.2, pp. 223–228.

Appley, B. C. and G. Stoutenburg (2017). "Two new objections to explanationism". *Synthese* 194.8, pp. 3069–3084.

Aristotle (1961). *De Anima, Books II and III*. D. W. Hamlyn, trans. Oxford: Oxford University Press.

Armstrong, S. L., L. R. Gleitman, and H. Gleitman (1983). "What some concepts might not be". *Cognition* 13.3, pp. 263–308.

Ayers, M. (1991). *Locke*. London: Routledge.

Baddeley, A. (1992). "Working memory". *Science* 255.5044, pp. 556–559.

Baddeley, A. (1996). "Exploring the central executive". *The Quarterly Journal of Experimental Psychology Section A* 49.1, pp. 5–28.

Baddeley, A. D., R. J. Allen, and G. J. Hitch (2011). "Binding in visual working memory: The role of the episodic buffer". *Neuropsychologia* 49.6, pp. 1393–1400.

Barnes, J. (2014). *Complete works of Aristotle, volume 1: The revised Oxford translation*. Vol. 192. Princeton University Press.

Barnsley, M. F. (1988). *Fractals everywhere*. Academic press.

Barsalou, L. W (1983). "Ad hoc categories". *Memory and cognition* 11.3, pp. 211–227.

Barsalou, L. W. (1987). "The instability of graded structure: Implications for the nature of concepts". *Concepts and conceptual development: Ecological and intellectual factors in categorization* 10139.

Barsalou, L. W (1992). "Frames, concepts, and conceptual fields."

Barsalou, L. W (1993). "Flexibility, structure, and linguistic vagary in concepts: Manifestations of a compositional system of perceptual symbols". *Theories of Memory* 1, pp. 29–31.

Bealer, G. (1999). "A theory of the a priori". *Philosophical perspectives* 13, pp. 29–55.

https://doi.org/10.1515/9783110708165-009

Bechtel, W. (1998). "Representations and cognitive explanations: Assessing the dynamicist's challenge in cognitive science". *Cognitive Science* 22.3, pp. 295–318.

Bechtel, W. (2008). *Mental mechanisms: Philosophical perspectives on cognitive neuroscience.* Taylor & Francis.

Bechtel, W. (2009). "Looking down, around, and up: Mechanistic explanation in psychology". *Philosophical Psychology* 22.5, pp. 543–564.

Bechtel, W. (2011). "Mechanism and biological explanation". *Philosophy of science* 78.4, pp. 533–557.

Bechtel, W. (2013). "From molecules to behavior and the clinic: Integration in chronobiology". *Studies in History and Philosophy of Science Part C: Studies in History and Philosophy of Biological and Biomedical Sciences* 44.4, pp. 493–502.

Bechtel, W. and A. Abrahamsen (2005). "Explanation: A mechanist alternative". *Studies in History and Philosophy of Science Part C: Studies in History and Philosophy of Biological and Biomedical Sciences* 36.2, pp. 421–441.

Bechtel, W. and A. Abrahamsen (2010). "Dynamic mechanistic explanation: Computational modeling of circadian rhythms as an exemplar for cognitive science". *Studies in History and Philosophy of Science Part A* 41.3, pp. 321–333.

Bechtel, W. and R. C. Richardson (1993). *Discovering complexity.*

Bechtel, W. and R. C. Richardson (2010). *Discovering complexity: Decomposition and localization as strategies in scientific research.* Cambridge, MA: MIT Press.

Bechtel, W. and C. Wright (2009). "What is Psychological Explanation?" *Routledge companion to the philosophy of psychology.* Ed. by P. Calvo and J. Symons. Routledge, pp. 113–130.

Beer, R. D. (1995). "Computational and dynamical languages for autonomous agents". *Mind as motion: Explorations in the dynamics of cognition*, pp. 121–147.

Beer, R. D. (2000). "Dynamical approaches to cognitive science". *Trends in cognitive sciences* 4.3, pp. 91–99.

Bennett, M. R. and P. M. Hacker (2008). *History of cognitive neuroscience.* John Wiley & Sons.

Berkeley, G. (1710). *Principles of human knowledge and three dialogues.* Oxford University Press, 2009.

Bermúdez, J. (2007). "What is at stake in the debate on nonconceptual content?" *Philosophical Perspectives* 21, pp. 55–72.

Bermúdez, J. and A. Cahen (2015). *Nonconceptual Mental Content.* In E. N. Zalta (ed.), The Stanford encyclopedia of philosophy (fall 2014 edition).

Bingham, N. H., C. M. Goldie, and J. L. Teugels (1989). *Encyclopedia of mathematics and its applications.*

Bloch-Mullins, C. L. (2017). "Bridging the gap between similarity and causality: An integrated approach to concepts". *The British Journal for the Philosophy of Science*, axw039.

Block, N. (1986). "Advertisement for a Semantics for Psychology". *Midwest studies in philosophy* 10.1, pp. 615–678.

Bloom, P. (1996). "Intention, history, and artifact concepts". *Cognition* 60.1, pp. 1–29.

Bogen, J. (2005). "Regularities and causality; generalizations and causal explanations". *Studies in History and Philosophy of Science Part C: Studies in History and Philosophy of Biological and Biomedical Sciences* 36.2, pp. 397–420.

Bogen, J. (2008). "Causally productive activities". *Studies in History and Philosophy of Science Part A* 39.1, pp. 112–123.

BonJour, L. (1985). *The structure of empirical knowledge.* Cambridge, MA: Harvard University Press.

BonJour, L. (1998). *In defense of pure reason: A rationalist account of a priori justification.* Cambridge University Press.

Bose, S. K. (2015). "The atomic hypothesis". *Current Science* 108.5, pp. 998–1002.

Braithwaite, R. B. (1932). "The nature of believing". *Proceedings of the Aristotelian Society.* Vol. 33, pp. 129–146.

Brandom, R. (2009). *Articulating reasons.* Cambridge, MA: Harvard University Press.

Bressler, S. L. and J. A. Kelso (2001). "Cortical coordination dynamics and cognition". *Trends in cognitive sciences* 5.1, pp. 26–36.

Brewer, W. F. (1999). "Perceptual symbols: The power and limitations of a theory of dynamic imagery and structured frames". *Behavioral and Brain Sciences* 22.4, pp. 611–612.

Brooks, L. R. (1978). "Nonanalytic concept formation and memory for instances". *E. Rosch and B. B. Lloyd (eds.), Cognition and Categorization.* Hillsdale, NJ: Lawrence Erlbaum Associates.

Bruner, J. S., J. Goodnow, and G. Austin (1956). *A study of thinking.* John Wiley and sons.

Burge, T. (2010). *Origins of objectivity.* Oxford University Press.

Campbell, J. (2005). "Information processing, phenomenal consciousness, and Molyneux's question". *Thought, Reference, and Experience*, pp. 195–320.

Carey, S. (1985). *Conceptual change in childhood.* Cambridge: Cambridge University Press.

Carey, S. (2009). *The origin of concepts.* Oxford: Oxford University Press.

Carpenter, G. A. and S. Grossberg (1988). "The ART of adaptive pattern recognition by a self-organizing neural network". *Computer* 21.3, pp. 77–88.

Carruthers, P. (2006). *The architecture of the mind.* Oxford: Oxford University Press.

Carson, R. G. and J. A. Kelso (2004). "Governing coordination: behavioural principles and neural correlates". *Experimental Brain Research* 154.3, pp. 267–274.

Cartwright, N. (1999). *The dappled world: A study of the boundaries of science.* Cambridge: Cambridge University Press.

Casti, J. L. (1992). *Reality rules: Picturing the world in mathematics.* John Wiley & Sons.

Cat, J. (2017). "The Unity of Science". *The Stanford Encyclopedia of Philosophy.* Ed. by Edward N. Zalta. Fall 2017. Metaphysics Research Lab, Stanford University.

Cermak, L. S. and F. I. Craik (1979). *Levels of processing in human memory.* Lawrence Erlbaum.

Chakravartty, A. (2007). *A metaphysics for scientific realism: Knowing the unobservable.* Cambridge: Cambridge University Press.

Chater, N. and M. Oaksford (2008). "The probabilistic mind: Where next". *The probabilistic mind: Prospects for Bayesian cognitive science.* Ed. by N. Chater and M. Oaksford. Oxford: Oxford University Press, pp. 501–514.

Chemero, A. (2009). *Radical embodied cognitive science.* Cambridge, MA: MIT Press.

Chemero, A. and M. Silberstein (2008). "After the philosophy of mind: Replacing scholasticism with science". *Philosophy of science* 75.1, pp. 1–27.

Chomsky, N. (1968). *Language and mind.* Cambridge University Press.

Chomsky, N. (1995). "Language and nature". *Mind* 104.413, pp. 1–62.

Clark, A. (1997). *Being there.* Cambridge, MA: MIT Press.

Clark, A. (2003). *Natural-born cyborgs: Minds, technologies, and the future of human intelligence.*

Clark, A. (2008). *Supersizing the mind: Embodiment, action, and cognitive extension.* Oxford: Oxford University Press.

Clark, A. and D. Chalmers (1998). "The extended mind". *Analysis* 58.1, pp. 7–19.

Close, F. (2004). *Particle physics: A very short introduction.* Vol. 109. Oxford University Press.

Cohen, J. and I. Stewart (1994). "The collapse of chaos: Simple laws in a complex world". *Penguin*.

Conley, Timothy et al. (2015). *Social interactions, mechanisms, and equilibrium: Evidence from a model of study time and academic achievement*. Tech. rep. National Bureau of Economic Research.

Cooper, J. M (eds.) (1997). *Plato: Complete works*. Indianapolis: Hackett.

Cosmides, L. and J. Tooby (1992). "Cognitive adaptations for social exchange". *The adapted mind: Evolutionary psychology and the generation of culture* 163, pp. 163–228.

Craver, C. and W. Bechtel (2006). "Mechanism". *The Philosophy of Science: An Encyclopedia*. Ed. by J. Pfeifer and S. Sahotra. Psychology Press, pp. 469–478.

Craver, C. and J. Tabery (2017). "Mechanisms in science". *The Stanford Encyclopedia of Philosophy*. Ed. by Edward N. Zalta. Spring 2017. Metaphysics Research Lab, Stanford University.

Craver, C. F. (2001). "Role functions, mechanisms, and hierarchy". *Philosophy of science* 68.1, pp. 53–74.

Craver, C. F. (2005). "Beyond reduction: mechanisms, multifield integration and the unity of neuroscience". *Studies in History and Philosophy of Science Part C: Studies in History and Philosophy of Biological and Biomedical Sciences* 36.2, pp. 373–395.

Craver, C. F. (2006). "When mechanistic models explain". *Synthese* 153.3, pp. 355–376.

Craver, C. F. (2007). *Explaining the brain: Mechanisms and the mosaic unity of neuroscience*. Oxford: Oxford University Press.

Craver, C. F. and L. Darden (2001). "Discovering Mechanisms in Neurobiology: The Case of Spatial Memory". *Theory and Method in Neuroscience*. Ed. by P.K. Machamer, R. Grush, and P. McLaughlin. Pittsburgh: University of Pitt Press, pp. 112–137.

Cummins, R. (2000). "How does it work?" versus" what are the laws?": Two conceptions of psychological explanation". *Explanation and cognition*, pp. 117–144.

Dale, R. (2008). "Introduction to the special issue on: pluralism and the future of cognitive science". *Journal of Experimental and Theoretical Artificial Intelligence* 20.3, pp. 153–153.

Dancy, J. (1985). *An introduction to contemporary epistemology*. Vol. 27. Oxford: Blackwell.

Davidson, D. (2001). *Inquiries into truth and interpretation: Philosophical essays*. Vol. 2. Oxford University Press.

Davies, P. S. (2003). *Norms of nature: Naturalism and the nature of functions*. Cambridge, MA:MIT Press.

Dennett, D. C. (1987). *The intentional stance*. Cambridge, MA: MIT Press.

Descartes, R. (1637). *Meditations on first philosophy*. Cambridge University Press, 2013.

Desloge, E. A. (1982). *Classical mechanics*. John Wiley & Sons.

Devitt, M. (1996). *Coming to our senses: A naturalistic program for semantic localism*. Cambridge, Cambridge University Press.

Devitt, M. (2002). "Meaning and use". *Philosophy and Phenomenological Research* 65.1, pp. 106–121.

Dewey, J. (1938). *Logic: The theory of inquiry*.

Dijksterhuis, E. J. (1969). "The origins of classical mechanics from Aristotle to Newton". *Critical Problems in the History of Science*, pp. 163–90.

Douglas, H. (2014). "Pure science and the problem of progress". *Studies in History and Philosophy of Science Part A* 46, pp. 55–63.

Dowe, P. (2000). "Causality and explanation". *The British journal for the philosophy of science* 51.1, pp. 165–174.

Dretske, F. (1981). *Knowledge and the flow of information*. Cambridge, MA: MIT Press.

Dretske, F. (1988). "The explanatory role of content". *Grimm, R. H. and Merrill, D. D. (eds.).*
Contents of thought. University of Arizona Press.

Dretske, F. (1995). "Meaningful perception". *An Invitation to Cognitive Science: Visual Cognition*, pp. 331–352.

Dummett, M. (1993). *The seas of language*. Clarendon Press Oxford.

Dupré, J. (1993). *The disorder of things: Metaphysical foundations of the disunity of science*. Cambridge, MA: Harvard University Press.

Egan, F. (2014). "How to think about mental content". *Philosophical studies* 170.1, pp. 115–135.

Egan, F. and R. J. Matthews (2006). "Doing cognitive neuroscience: A third way". *Synthese* 153.3, pp. 377–391.

Eifermann, R. R. and R. Steinitz (1971). "A comparison of conjunctive and disjunctive concept identification". *The Journal of general psychology* 85.1, pp. 29–37.

Eliasmith, C. and C. H. Anderson (2004). *Neural engineering: Computation, representation, and dynamics in neurobiological systems*. Cambridge, MA: MIT press.

Elman, J. L., E. A. Bates, and M. H. Johnson (1996). *Rethinking innateness: A connectionist perspective on development*. Cambridge, MA: MIT press.

Erickson, M. A. and J. K. Kruschke (1998). "Rules and exemplars in category learning". *Journal of Experimental Psychology* 127, pp. 107–140.

Estes, W. K. (1994). *Classification and cognition*. Oxford University Press.

Evans, G. (1982). *The Varieties of Reference*. Oxford University Press.

Fodor, J. A. (1974). "Special sciences". *Synthese* 28, pp. 97–115.

Fodor, J. A. (1975). *The language of thought*. Vol. 5. Cambridge, MA: Harvard University Press.

Fodor, J. A. (1983). *The modularity of mind*. Cambridge, MA: MIT Press.

Fodor, J. A. (1987). *Psychosemantics: The problem of meaning in the philosophy of mind*. Vol. 2. Cambridge, MA: MIT press.

Fodor, J. A. (1990). *A theory of content and other essays*. Cambridge, MA:MIT press.

Fodor, J. A. (1994). "Concepts: A potboiler". *Cognition* 50, pp. 95–113.

Fodor, J. A. (1998). *Concepts: Where cognitive science went wrong*. New York: Oxford University Press.

Fodor, J. A. (2008). *LOT 2: The language of thought revisited*. Oxford University Press.

Fodor, J. A. and E. Lepore (1996). "The red herring and the pet fish: Why concepts still can't be prototypes". *Cognition* 58, 253–270.

Fodor, J. A. et al. (1980). "Against definitions". *Cognition* 8.3, pp. 263–367.

Frege, G. (1884). *The foundations of arithmetic: A logico-mathematical inquiry into the concept of number*. Second revised edition (1980). Evanston: Northwestern University Pres.

Frege, G. (1893). "On sense and meaning". *M. Black, trans. In P. Geach and M. Black, (eds.), Translations from the Philosophical Writings of Gottlob Frege*. Oxford: Blackwell, 1953.

French, S. (2014). *The structure of the world. Metaphysics and representation*. Oxford: Oxford University Press.

Fuchs, A., V. K. Jirsa, and J. A. Kelso (2000). "Theory of the relation between human brain activity (MEG) and hand movements". *Neuroimage* 11.5, pp. 359–369.

Gaohua, L. and H. Kimura (2009). "A mathematical model of brain glucose homeostasis". *Theoretical Biology and Medical Modelling* 6.1, p. 26.

Geiger, H. (1910). "The scattering of α-particles by matter". *Proceedings of the Royal Society of London. Series A, Containing Papers of a Mathematical and Physical Character* 83.565, pp. 492–504.

Geiger, H. and E. Marsden (1913). "The laws of deflexion of a particles through large angles". *The London, Edinburgh, and Dublin Philosophical Magazine and Journal of Science* 25.148, pp. 604–623.

Gelman, S. A., J. D. Coley, and G. M. Gottfried (1994). "13 Essentialist beliefs in children: The acquisition of concepts and theories". *Mapping the Mind: Domain Specificity in Cognition and Culture*, p. 341.

Gettier, E. L (1963). "Is justified true belief knowledge?" *analysis* 23.6, pp. 121–123.

Giere, R. N. (2004). "How models are used to represent reality". *Philosophy of science* 71.5, pp. 742–752.

Glennan, S. (1996). "Mechanisms and the nature of causation". *Erkenntnis* 44.1, pp. 49–71.

Glennan, S. (2005). "Modeling mechanisms". *Studies in History and Philosophy of Science Part C: Studies in History and Philosophy of Biological and Biomedical Sciences* 36.2, pp. 443–464.

Glennan, S. (2008). "Mechanisms". *The Routledge companion to philosophy of science*. Routledge, pp. 404–412.

Glennan, S. (2009). "Productivity, relevance and natural selection". *Biology & Philosophy* 24.3, pp. 325–339.

Goodman, N. (1976). *Languages of art: An approach to a theory of symbols*. Indianapolis, Ind.: Hackett.

Goodman, N. D. et al. (2008). "A rational analysis of rule-based concept learning". *Cognitive science* 32.1, 108–154.

Gopnik, A., A. N. Meltzoff, and P. Bryant (1997). *Words, thoughts, and theories*. Cambridge, MA: MIT Press.

Gregory, R. (1966). *Eye and Brain*. New York: McGraw-Hill.

Hacking, I. (1983). *Representing and intervening*. Cambridge: Cambridge University Press.

Haken, H., J. S. Kelso, and H. Bunz (1985). "A theoretical model of phase transitions in human hand movements". *Biological cybernetics* 51.5, pp. 347–356.

Hall, M. (2007). "A decision tree-based attribute weighting filter for naive Bayes". *Knowledge-Based Systems* 20.2, pp. 120–126.

Hampton, J. A. (1981). "An investigation of the nature of abstract concepts". *Memory and cognition* 9.2, pp. 149–156.

Hampton, J. A. (1988). "Overextension of conjunctive concepts: Evidence for a unitary model of concept typicality and class inclusion." *Journal of Experimental Psychology: Learning, Memory, and Cognition* 14.1, p. 12.

Hampton, J. A. (1995). "Testing the prototype theory of concepts". *Journal of Memory and Language* 34.5, pp. 686–708.

Hampton, J. A. (2010). "Concept talk cannot be avoided". *Behavioral and Brain Sciences* 33.2-3, pp. 212–213.

Hartmann, S. (1999). "Models and Stories in Hadron Physics". *Models as mediators: Perspectives on natural and social science*. Ed. by M. Morrison and M. Morgan, pp. 52–326.

Heil, J. (2003). "Levels of reality". *Ratio* 16.3, pp. 205–221.

Hempel, C. G. and P. Oppenheim (1948). "Studies in the logic of explanation". *Philosophy of science* 15.2, pp. 135–175.

Hirsch, M. W. (1984). "The dynamical systems approach to differential equations". *Bulletin of the American Mathematical Society* 11.1, pp. 1–64.

Hitchcock, C. and James Woodward (2003). "Explanatory generalizations, part II: Plumbing explanatory depth". *Noûs* 37.2, pp. 181–199.

Holyoak, K. J. and R. G. Morrison (2012). *The Oxford handbook of thinking and reasoning*. Oxford University Press.

Horwich, P. (2005). *Reflections on meaning*. Oxford University Press.

Hume, D. (1739/1978). *A treatise of human nature*. Oxford: Oxford University Press.

Hutchins, E. (1995). *Cognition in the Wild*. Cambridge, MA:MIT press.

Hutto, D. D. and E. Myin (2013). *Radicalizing enactivism: Basic minds without content*. Cambridge, MA: MIT Press.

Hylton, P. and G. Kemp (2019). "Willard Van Orman Quine". *The Stanford Encyclopedia of Philosophy*. Ed. by Edward N. Zalta. Spring 2019. Metaphysics Research Lab, Stanford University.

Issad, T. and C. Malaterre (2015). "Are Dynamic Mechanistic Explanations Still Mechanistic?" *Explanation in Biology*, pp. 265–292.

Jackendoff, R. (1983). *Semantics and cognition*. Cambridge, MA: MIT Press.

Jamalabadi, H. et al. (2012). "A dynamic bio-inspired model of categorization". *International Conference on Neural Information Processing*, pp. 160–167.

Jantzen, K. J., F. L. Steinberg, and J. A. Kelso (2009). "Coordination dynamics of large-scale neural circuitry underlying rhythmic sensorimotor behavior". *Journal of Cognitive Neuroscience* 21.12, pp. 2420–2433.

Jirsa, V. K., A. Fuchs, and J. A. Kelso (1998). "Connecting cortical and behavioral dynamics: bimanual coordination". *Neural Computation* 10.8, pp. 2019–2045.

Jones, G. V (1983). "Identifying basic categories." *Psychological Bulletin* 94.3, p. 423.

Jordi, C. (2012). "Essay Review, S. Kellert, H. Longino and K. waters, eds., Scientific Pluralism". *Philosophy of Science* 79, 317–325.

Kant, I. (1985). *Prolegomena to any future metaphysics that can qualify as a science*. Open Court Publishing, 1985.

Kaplan, D. and C. F. Craver (2011). "The explanatory force of dynamical and mathematical models in neuroscience: A mechanistic perspective". *Philosophy of science* 78.4, pp. 601–627.

Katz, J. J. and J. A. Fodor (1963). "The structure of a semantic theory". *Language* 39, pp. 170–210.

Keas, M. N. (2018). "Systematizing the theoretical virtues". *Synthese* 195.6, pp. 2761–2793.

Keil, F. C. (1979). *Semantics and conceptual development: An Ontological Perspective*. Cambridge, MA:Harvard U Press.

Keil, F. C. (1989). *Concepts, kinds, and cognitive development*. Cambridge, MA: MIT Press.

Keil, F. C. (2010). "Hybrid vigor and conceptual structure". *Behavioral and Brain Sciences* 33.2-3, pp. 215–216.

Keil, F. C. and N. Batterman (1984). "A characteristic-to-defining shift in the development of word meaning". *Journal of verbal learning and verbal behavior* 23.2, pp. 221–236.

Kellert, S. H. (2008). *Borrowed knowledge: Chaos theory and the challenge of learning across disciplines*. University of Chicago Press.

Kellert, S. H., H. E. Longino, and C. K. Waters (2006). *Scientific pluralism*. Vol. 19. University of Minnesota Press.

Kelso, J. and D. Engstrøm (2006). *The complementary nature*. Cambridge, MA: MIT press.

Kelso, J. A. and J. J. Jeka (1992). "Symmetry breaking dynamics of human multilimb coordination." *Journal of Experimental Psychology: Human Perception and Performance* 18.3, p. 645.

Kenny, A. (2010). "Concepts, brains, and behaviour". *Grazer Philosophische Studien* 81.1.

Ketland, J. (2004). "Empirical adequacy and ramsification". *The British Journal for the Philosophy of Science* 55.2, pp. 287–300.

Komatsu, L. K. (1992). "Recent views of conceptual structure". *Psychological Bulletin* 112, pp. 500–526.

Kripke, S. (1972). *Naming and necessity*. Cambridge, MA: Harvard University Press.

Kripke, S. (1977). "Speaker's reference and semantic reference". *Midwest studies in philosophy* 2.1, pp. 255–276.

Kruschke, J. K. (2008). "Bayesian approaches to associative learning: From passive to active learning". *Learning and behavior* 36.3, pp. 210–226.

Kuhn, T. (1962). *The structure of scientific revolutions*. Chicago: University of Chicago Press.

Kunda, Z., D. T. Miller, and T. Claire (1972). "Combining social concepts: The role of causal reasoning". *Cognitive Science* 14.4, pp. 551–577.

Ladyman, J. et al. (2007). *Every thing must go: Metaphysics naturalized*. Oxford University Press.

Lakoff, G. (1987). "Cognitive models and prototype theory". *U. Neisser (ed.), Concepts and conceptual development*. Cambridge: Cambridge University Press, pp. 63–100.

Lakoff, R. (1972). "Language in context". *Language*, pp. 907–927.

Lalumera, E. (2010). "Concepts are a functional kind". *Behavioral and Brain Sciences* 33.2-3, pp. 217–218.

Laurence, S. and E. Margolis (1999). "Concepts and cognitive science". *E. Margolis and S. Laurence (eds.). Concepts: Core readings*. Cambridge, MA: MIT Press, pp. 3–81.

Lewis, D. (1973). *Counterfactuals*. Oxford: Basil Blackwell.

Lewis, J. and J. Brodie (2007). *Unravelling the algae: The past, present, and future of algal systematics*. CRC Press.

Locke, J. (1690). *An essay concerning human understanding. P. H. Nidditch, (ed.)* Oxford: Oxford University Press, 1979.

Löhr, G. (2018). "Concepts and categorization: Do philosophers and psychologists theorize about different things?" *Synthese*, pp. 1–21.

Luenberger, D. G. (1979). *Introduction to dynamic systems: Theory, models, and applications*. Wiley New York.

Lüttge, U. (2006). "Photosynthetic flexibility and ecophysiological plasticity: Questions and lessons from Clusia, the only CAM tree, in the neotropics". *New Phytologist* 171.1, pp. 7–25.

Machamer, P., L. Darden, and C. F. Craver (2000). "Thinking about mechanisms". *Philosophy of Science* 67.1, pp. 1–25.

Machery, E. (2006). "Against hybrid theories of concepts". *Anthropology and Philosophy* 10, pp. 97–125.

Machery, E. (2009). *Doing without concepts*. New York: Oxford University Press.

Machery, E. (2010). "Precis of doing without concepts". *Behavioral and Brain Sciences* 33, 195–244.

Marcus, Ruth Barcan (1990). "Some revisionary proposals about belief and believing". *Philosophy and Phenomenological Research* 50, pp. 133–153.

Margolis, E. (1995). "The significance of the theory analogy in the psychological study of concepts". *Mind & Language* 10.1-2, pp. 45–71.

Margolis, E. (1998). "How to acquire a concept". *Mind & Language* 13.3, pp. 347–369.

Margolis, E. and S. Laurence (1999). "Concepts and cognitive science". *E. Margolis and S. Laurence (eds.), Concepts: Core readings*. Cambridge, MA: MIT Press, pp. 3–81.

Margolis, E. and S. Laurence (2014). *Concepts*. In E. N. Zalta (ed.), The Stanford encyclopedia of philosophy (fall 2014 edition).

Markman, A. B. and E. Dietrich (2000). "Extending the classical view of representation". *Trends in cognitive sciences* 4.12, pp. 470–475.

Marraffa, M. and A. Paternoster (2013). "Functions, levels, and mechanisms: Explanation in cognitive science and its problems". *Theory & Psychology* 23.1, pp. 22–45.

McClelland, J. L. (2009). "The place of modeling in cognitive science". *Topics in Cognitive Science* 1.1, pp. 11–38.

McClelland, J. L. and D. E. Rumelhart (1981). "An interactive activation model of context effects in letter perception: Part 1 An account of basic findings". *Psychological review* 88, pp. 375–407.

McClelland, J. L. et al. (2010). "Letting structure emerge: connectionist and dynamical systems approaches to cognition". *Trends in cognitive sciences* 14.8, pp. 348–356.

Mead, G. H. (1899). "The working hypothesis in social reform". *American Journal of Sociology* 5.3, pp. 367–371.

Medin, D. L. and S. (eds.) Atran (1999). *Folkbiology*. Cambridge, MA.: MIT Press.

Medin, D. L. and A. Ortony (1989). "Psychological essentialism". *Similarity and Analogical Reasoning* 179, p. 195.

Medin, D. L. and M. M. Schaffer (1978). "Context theory of classification learning". *Psychological Review* 85.3, p. 207.

Medin, D. L. and P. J. Schwanenflugel (1981). "Linear separability in classification learning." *Journal of Experimental Psychology: Human Learning and Memory* 7.5, pp. 355–368.

Medin, D. L. and E. J. Shoben (1988). "Context and structure in conceptual combination". *Cognitive Psychology* 20.2, pp. 158–190.

Michaelson, E. and M. Reimer (2017). *Reference*. In E. N. Zalta (Ed.), The Stanford Encyclopedia of Philosophy (Spring 2019 Edition).

Milikan, R. (1984). *Language, thought, and other biological categories*. Cambridge, MA: MIT Press.

Miłkowski, M. (2013). *Explaining the computational mind*. Cambridge, MA: MIT Press.

Miłkowski, M. (2016). "Unification strategies in cognitive science". *Studies in Logic, Grammar and Rhetoric* 48.1, pp. 13–33.

Miller, G. A. (1956). "The magical number seven, plus or minus two: Some limits on our capacity for processing information." *Psychological review* 63.2, p. 81.

Muller, F. A. (2011). "Reflections on the revolution at Stanford". *Synthese* 183.1, pp. 87–114.

Murphy, G. L. (2002). *The big book of concepts*. Cambridge, MA: MIT Press.

Murphy, G. L. and D. L. Medin (1985). "The role of theories in conceptual coherence". *Psychological Review* 92.3, p. 289.

Nathan, M. J., W. Kintsch, and E. Young (1992). "A theory of algebra-word-problem comprehension and its implications for the design of learning environments". *Cognition and instruction* 9.4, pp. 329–389.

Neisser, U. (2014). *Cognitive psychology: Classic edition*. Psychology Press.

Newell, A. (1990). *Unified theories of cognition*. Cambridge, MA: Harvard University Press.

Newton, I. (1999). *The Principia: Mathematical principles of natural philosophy: A New Translation*. tr. I. B. Cohen and Anne Whitman. University of California Press.

Nosofsky, R. M. (1986). "Attention, similarity, and the identification-categorization relationship". *Journal of Experimental Psychology: General* 115.1, p. 39.

Nosofsky, R. M. (1988). "Exemplar-based accounts of relations between classification, recognition, and typicality". *Journal of Experimental Psychology: Learning, Memory, and Cognition* 14, pp. 700–708.

Nosofsky, R. M. (1992). "Similarity scaling and cognitive process models". *Annual Review of Psychology* 43.1, pp. 25–53.

Nosofsky, R. M., E. M. Pothos, and A. J. Wills (2011). "The generalized context model: An exemplar model of classification". *Formal approaches in categorization*, pp. 18–39.

Oppenheim, P. and H. Putnam (1958). "Unity of science as a working hypothesis". *Minnesota Studies in the Philosophy of Science* 2, 3–36.

Osherson, D. and E. Smith (1981). "On the adequacy of prototype theory as a theory of concepts". *Cognition* 9, pp. 35–58.

Ott, E. (1993). *Chaos in dynamical systems*. Cambridge university press.

Oullier, O. et al. (2005). "Spontaneous interpersonal synchronization". *European workshop on movement sciences: Mechanics-physiology-psychology*, pp. 34–35.

Palade, G. E. (1952). "The fine structure of mitochondria". *The Anatomical Record* 114.3, pp. 427–451.

Papineau, D. (1987). "Reality and representation". *Noûs* 26.3, pp. 379–389.

Peacocke, C. (1992). *A study of concepts*. Cambridge, MA: MIT Press.

Peacocke, C. (2000). "Explaining the a priori: The programme of moderate rationalism". *New essays on the a priori*, pp. 255–285.

Peacocke, C. (2005a). "Rationale and Maxims in the Study of Concepts". *Noûs* 39.1, pp. 167–178.

Peacocke, C. (2005b). "The a priori". *The Oxford handbook of contemporary philosophy*, pp. 739–763.

Peirce, C. S. (1958). *Collected papers of Charles Sanders Peirce*. Vol. 7. Cambridge, MA: Harvard University Press.

Petersen, W. (2015). "Representation of Concepts as Frames". *Meaning, Frames, and Conceptual Representation*. Ed. by T. Gamerschlag et al. Düsseldorf: Düsseldorf University Press, pp. 39–63.

Piccinini, G. and C. F. Craver (2011). "Integrating psychology and neuroscience: Functional analyses as mechanism sketches". *Synthese* 183.3, pp. 283–311.

Piccinini, G. and S. Scott (2006). "Splitting concepts". *Philosophy of Science* 73.4, pp. 390–409.

Pitt, D. (2018). "Mental Representation". *The Stanford Encyclopedia of Philosophy*. Ed. by Edward N. Zalta. Winter 2018. Metaphysics Research Lab, Stanford University.

Poland, J. (1994). "Physicalism, the Philosophical Foundations".

Posner, M. I. and S. W. Keele (1968). "On the genesis of abstract ideas." *Journal of Experimental Psychology* 77.3.1, p. 353.

Poston, T. (2016). "Explanationist plasticity and the problem of the criterion". *Philosophical Papers* 40.3, pp. 395–419.

Potter, M. (1993). *Set theory and its philosophy: A critical introduction*. Oxford: Clarendon Press.

Price, H. H. (1953). *Thinking and Experience*. London: Hutchinson's Universal Library.

Prinz, J. J. (2002). *Furnishing the Mind: Concepts and Their Perceptual Basis*. MIT Press.

Psillos, S. (2005). "Scientific realism and metaphysics". *Ratio* 18.4, pp. 385–404.

Quilty-Dunn, J. and E. Mandelbaum (2018). "Against dispositionalism: Belief in cognitive science". *Philosophical Studies* 175.9, pp. 2353–2372.

Quine, W. V. (1953). "Mr. Strawson on logical theory". *Mind* 62.248, pp. 433–451.

Quine, W. V. (1957). "The scope and language of science". *The British Journal for the philosophy of Science* 8.29, pp. 1–17.

Quine, W. V. (1964). "On simple theories of a complex world". *Form and strategy in science.* Springer, pp. 47–50.

Quine, W. V. (1974). *The roots of reference.* Lasalle, Ill: Open Court.

Quine, W. V. (1981). *Theories and things.* Cambridge, MA: Harvard University Press.

Ramsey, F. P (1931). "Theories". *The Foundations of Mathematics*, pp. 212–236.

Reed, S. K (1972). "Pattern recognition and categorization". *Cognitive psychology* 3.3, pp. 382–407.

Rehder, B. (2003a). "A causal-model theory of conceptual representation and categorization". *Journal of Experimental psychology: Learning, Memory, and Cognition* 29, pp. 1141–1159.

Rehder, B. (2003b). "A causal-model theory of conceptual representation and categorization". *Journal of experimental psychology: Learning, memory, and cognition* 29, pp. 1141–1159.

Rehder, B. (2003a). "Categorization as causal reasoning". *Cognitive Science* 27.5, pp. 709–748.

Rescher, N. (1993). *Pluralism: Against the Demand for Consensus.* Oxford University Press.

Rescher, N. (1996). *Process metaphysics: An introduction to process philosophy.* New York, USA: SUNY Press.

Rey, G. (1983). "Concepts and stereotypes". *Cognition* 15, pp. 237–262.

Rey, G. (1985). "Concepts and conceptions: A reply to Smith, Medin, and Rips." *Cognition* 19.

Rey, G. (1997). *Contemporary philosophy of mind: A contentiously classical approach.* Wiley-Blackwell.

Rey, G. (2009). "Review of Edouard Machery, Doing Without Concepts". *Notre Dame Philosophical Reviews* (Online journal. Epub: 2009.07.15.) Available at https://ndpr.nd.edu/news/doing-without-concepts/.

Rey, G. (2010). "Concepts versus conceptions (again)". *Behavioral and Brain Sciences* 33.2-3, pp. 221–222.

Rips, L. J. (1995). "The current status of research on concept combination". *Mind and Language* 10.1-2, pp. 72–104.

Rogers, T. T. and J. L. McClelland (2004). *Semantic cognition: A parallel distributed processing approach.* Cambridge, MA: MIT press.

Rosch, E. (1975). "Cognitive representations of semantic categories." *Journal of experimental psychology: General* 104.3, p. 192.

Rosch, E. and C. B. Mervis (1975). "Family resemblances: Studies in the internal structure of categories". *Cognitive psychology* 7.4, pp. 573–605.

Rosch, E. et al. (1976). "Basic objects in natural categories". *Cognitive psychology* 8.3, pp. 382–439.

Rosch, E. H. (1973). "Natural categories". *Cognitive psychology* 4.3, pp. 328–350.

Rumelhart, D. E., G. E. Hinton, and R. J. Williams (1986). "Learning representations by back-propagating errors". *nature* 323.6088, p. 533.

Ruphy, S. (2016). *Scientific pluralism reconsidered.* Pittsburgh: Pittsburgh University Press.

Russell, B. (1921). *Analysis of mind.* New York: MacMillan.

Rutherford, E. (1914). "The structure of the atom". *The London, Edinburgh, and Dublin Philosophical Magazine and Journal of Science* 27.159, pp. 488–498.

Salmon, W. C. (1984). *Scientific explanation and the causal structure of the world.* Princeton, USA: Princeton University Press.

Sanborn, A. N., T. L. Griffiths, and D. J. Navarro (2006). "A more rational model of categorization". *Proceedings of the 28th annual conference of the Cognitive Science Society*,
pp. 726–731.

Schofield, A. (1973). "Yes! We have no Disjunctive Concepts—Or have we?" *The Journal of
General Psychology* 89.1, pp. 11–14.

Schoner, G. and J. A. Kelso (1988). "Dynamic pattern generation in behavioral and neural
systems". *Science* 239.4847, pp. 1513–1520.

Schwitzgebel, E. (2002). "A phenomenal, dispositional account of belief". *Noûs* 36.2, pp. 249–
275.

Sellars, W. (1963). "Philosophy and the scientific image of man". *Science, perception and
reality* 2, pp. 35–78.

Shafto, P. et al. (2011). "A probabilistic model of cross-categorization". *Cognition* 120.1, pp. 1–
25.

Shepard, R. N. (1964). "Attention and the metric structure of the stimulus space". *Journal of
mathematical psychology* 1.1, pp. 54–87.

Shepherd, G. M. (1988). *Neurobiology*. Oxford: Oxford University Press.

Simon, H. A. (1996). *The sciences of the artificial*. Cambridge, MA: MIT press.

Skinner, B. F. (1974). *About Behaviourism*. New York: Vintage.

Sloman, S. (2005). *Causal models: How people think about the world and its alternatives*.
Oxford University Press.

Smith, E. E. and D. L. Medin (1981). *Categories and concepts*. Cambridge, MA: Harvard University Press.

Smith, E. E., E. J. Shoben, and L. J. Rips (1974). "Structure and process in semantic memory: A
featural model for semantic decisions." *Psychological review* 81.3, pp. 214–241.

Smith, E. E. et al. (1988). "Combining concepts: A selective modification model". *Cognitive
Science* 12, 485–527.

Smits, A. J. (2000). *A physical introduction to fluid mechanics*. Wiley.

Sober, E. (1994). *From a biological point of view: Essays in evolutionary philosophy*. Cambridge:
Cambridge University Press.

Sober, E. (2015). *Ockham's razors*. Cambridge: Cambridge University Press.

Soja, N. N., S. Carey, and E. S. Spelke (1991). "Ontological categories guide young children's
inductions of word meaning: Object terms and substance terms". *Cognition* 38.2, pp. 179–
211.

Standing, L. (1973). "Learning 10000 pictures". *Quarterly Journal of Experimental Psychology*
25.2, pp. 207–222.

Sterelny, K. (1990). "Animals and individualism". *P. P. Hanson (ed.), Information, language,
and cognition*. Vancouver: University of British Columbia Press.

Stewart, I. (2003). "Mathematics: Conjuring with conjectures". *Nature* 423.6936, pp. 124–127.

Stich, S. P (1978). "Beliefs and subdoxastic states". *Philosophy of Science* 45.4, pp. 499–518.

Stich, S. P. (1983). *From folk psychology to cognitive science: The case against belief*. Cambridge, MA: MIT Press.

Stoutenburg, G. (2015). "Best explanationism and justification for beliefs about the future".
Episteme 12.4, pp. 429–437.

Strevens, M. (2008). *Depth: An account of scientific explanation*. Cambridge, MA: Harvard
University Press.

Suppes, P. (2002). *Representation and invariance of scientific structures*. CSLI publications
Stanford.

Taylor, S. D. (2019a). "Concepts as a working hypothesis".

Taylor, S. D. (2019b). "Two kinds of explanatory integration in cognitive science". *Synthese*. DOI: 10.1007/s11229-019-02357-9.

Taylor, S. D. and P. R. Sutton (2020). "A frame-theoretic model of Bayesian category learning". *Concepts, frames and cascades in semantics, cognition and ontology*. Ed. by S. Löbner et al. Dordrecht: Springer.

Taylor, S. D. and G. Vosgerau (2019). "The explanatory role of concepts". *Erkenntnis*, pp. 1–26. DOI: 10.1007/s10670-019-00143-0.

Tenenbaum, J. B. (1999). "Bayesian modeling of human concept learning". *M. S. Kearns, S. A. Solla, and D. A. Cohn (eds.), Advances in neural information processing systems 11*. Cambridge, MA: MIT Press, 59–65.

Thagard, P. (2002). *Coherence in thought and action*. Cambridge, MA: MIT press.

Thagard, P. (2005). *Mind: Introduction to cognitive science*. Cambridge, MA: MIT press.

Thagard, P. (2007). "Coherence, truth, and the development of scientific knowledge". *Philosophy of science* 74.1, pp. 28–47.

Thagard, P. (2014). *Cognitive Science*. In E. N. Zalta (ed.), The Stanford encyclopedia of philosophy (fall 2014 edition).

Thagard, P. (2018). *Conceptual revolutions*. Princeton, USA: Princeton University Press.

Thurston, W. P. (1979). *The geometry and topology of three-manifolds*. Princeton, NJ: Princeton University Press.

Tversky, A. (1977). "Features of similarity." *Psychological review* 84.4, pp. 327–352.

Tversky, B. and K. Hemenway (1984). "Objects, parts, and categories." *Journal of experimental psychology: General* 113.2, pp. 169–193.

Van Fraassen, B. C. (1980). *The scientific image*. Oxford: Oxford University Press.

Van Gelder, T. (1993). "Is cognition categorization". *Psychology of Learning and Motivation* 29, pp. 469–494.

Van Gelder, T. (1995). "What might cognition be, if not computation?" *The Journal of Philosophy* 92.7, pp. 345–381.

Van Gelder, T. (1998). "The dynamical hypothesis in cognitive science". *Behavioral and brain sciences* 21.5, pp. 615–628.

Vicente, A. and F. Martínez Manrique (2014). "The big concepts paper: A defence of hybridism". *The British Journal for the Philosophy of Science* 67.1, pp. 59–88.

Vincenti, W. G. (1990). *What engineers know and how they know it*. Baltimore, MD: Johns Hopkins University Press.

Warren, W. (1995). "Self-motion: Visual perception and visual control". *Perception of space and motion*. Elsevier, pp. 263–325.

Wason, P. C. (1968). "Reasoning about a rule". *Quarterly journal of experimental psychology* 20.3, pp. 273–281.

Wason, P. C. and D. Shapiro (1971). "Natural and contrived experience in a reasoning problem". *The Quarterly Journal of Experimental Psychology* 23.1, pp. 63–71.

Watson, J. D. (1963). "Involvement of RNA in the Synthesis of Proteins: The ordered interaction of three classes of RNA controls the assembly of amino acids into proteins". *Science* 140.3562, pp. 17–26.

Weiskopf, D. A. (2009). "The plurality of concepts". *Synthese* 169, pp. 145–173.

Weiskopf, D. A. (forthcoming). "The explanatory autonomy of cognitive models". *Integrating Psychology and Neuroscience: Prospects and Problems*. Oxford University Press, pp. 21–74.

Werning, M., W. Hinzen, and E. Machery (2012). *The Oxford handbook of compositionality*. Oxford Handbooks in Linguistic.

Wimsatt, W. C. (1997). "Aggregativity: Reductive heuristics for finding emergence". *Philosophy of science* 64, S372–S384.

Wittgenstein, L. (1953). *Philosophical investigations*. G.E.M. Anscombe and R. Rhees (eds.), G.E.M. Anscombe (trans.), Oxford: Blackwell.

Woodward, J. F. (2017). "Scientific Explanation". *The Stanford Encyclopedia of Philosophy*. Ed. by Edward N. Zalta. Fall 2017. Metaphysics Research Lab, Stanford University.

Wu, J. et al. (2014). "Dual instance and attribute weighting for naive Bayes classification". *Neural Networks (IJCNN), 2014 International Joint Conference*, pp. 1675–1679.

Yang, S., Y. Lu, and S. Li (2013). "An overview on vehicle dynamics". *International Journal of Dynamics and Control* 1.4, pp. 385–395.

Zalta, E. N. (2001). "Fregean senses, modes of presentation, and concepts". *Philosophical Perspectives* 15, pp. 335–359.

Zamecnik, P. C. (1953). "Incorporation of radioactivity from DL-leucine-1-C14 into proteins of rat liver homogenate". *Federation Proceedings*. Vol. 12, p. 295.

Zilles, K. and K. Amunts (2009). "Receptor mapping: Architecture of the human cerebral cortex". *Current Opinion in Neurology* 22.4, pp. 331–339.